THE
NATION
KEEPERS

Canadian Business Perspectives

Edited by
ISAIAH A. LITVAK
McMaster University

Foreword by
LESTER B. PEARSON
Prime Minister of Canada

McGRAW-HILL

| NEW YORK | TORONTO | LONDON | SYDNEY |
| JOHANNESBURG | | | MEXICO |

THE NATION KEEPERS

Library of Congress Catalog Card Number 67-18806

1234567890 JD67 6543210987

94834

Printed and bound in Canada

CONTENTS

The Setting

ISAIAH LITVAK
RAYMOND A. YOUNG

Government and Business

A. A. CUMMING

T. C. DOUGLAS

v

The Economy is People

Directions for Destiny

PREFACE

A centennial should be an occasion for a celebration. However, it is more likely that the Canadian centennial will prove to be a time for national deliberation and evaluation. For Canada has still not answered, to the satisfaction of all her people, the vital national questions of identity and destiny. This indecision is a result of complex economic and social factors, rooted in our history, whose political implications persist to the present day.

One of Canada's major problems has been the lack of a distinct national image. This is partly attributable to the divisive effects of unusually cohesive ethnic sub-cultures, coupled with a very purposeful provincialism and a partly relative condition resulting from the strong declaration of national identity generated by our southern neighbour. Nonetheless, despite this background of diversity and conflict, particularly in the realm of English-Canadian and French-Canadian relations, there is in Canada today an emerging sense of nationalism. This nationalism is perhaps traceable to the growing realization by Canadians of the degree of American influence on their economy. Thus Canadian nationalistic tendencies are not so much the product of a shared heritage as the fear of losing a common birthright—independence. To illustrate that this concern exists at the highest levels, it need only be noted that all major Canadian political parties have incorporated into their party platforms a plank on Canadian-U.S. economic relations.

If the Canadian people are not sensitive to the dynamics of their environment, they will forfeit the opportunity to fashion Canada's political and economic future. If Canadians do not exercise their franchise and elect their choice for the future, circumstances will mould it for them. And judging by the speed of integrative events in the nations of the world, the current generation of Canadians may be the last to be able to make this choice.

History has shown that for a nation to retain its vitality and maintain its progress it must foster a continuing dialogue among its citizens. Furthermore, only when this dialogue is communicated to its citizenry can a nation hope to profit, via the democratic mandate, from such discussion and debate.

I believe it fitting that such a dialogue be provided for the Canadian populace in their centennial year. To this end I have solicited the participation of a number of respected Canadians in presenting a diversity of views on a variety of significant Canadian questions from a "business perspective"—a theme deliberately chosen by the editor.

Education is a worthy objective of all members of society, no more so of businessmen than of others. Like all other segments of our society, businessmen must be continually stimulated, informed and enlightened. It is the purpose of this book in some measure to achieve those ends.

Ideally, Canadian management should make its decisions against the background of a total understanding of the Canadian environment, and with an awareness of the trends and currents of change in that environment. However, pressures of month-to-month problems often restrict management's view to a narrow perspective on a top priority problem basis.

Some of the larger companies, who both recognize the long-term costs of such management tunnel-vision and can afford to supply management with a more integrated perspective of the total environment, are doing so by means of top management seminars and colloquiums. Despite the good intentions of such enlargement programs they often suffer from an industry myopia and national ethnocentricity. On the other hand, the greater portion of Canadian management do not have the resources to support even such a comprehensive evaluation of their own industrial setting. Furthermore, many of these Canadian businessmen lack an awareness of the inherent danger of such an ignorance.

The chief aim of this book is to supply an integrated perspective of the business environment, a perspective which is either wholly or partly lacking among the majority of Canadian businessmen.

This objective will be realized through an intensive examination of those components of the social, economic and political dimensions which are having, and will continue to have in the foreseeable future, the most profound effect on Canadian business. The examiners consist of leading Canadian public figures from business, government, labour, and education, who by virtue of birth or association represent the major geographical, political and socio-cultural elements of the Canadian nation.

However, while this book hopefully will contribute to the comprehension of significant factors in the Canadian environment, the implications of these factors will vary with the particular business. In addition, this book will provide more questions than answers. This is precisely what makes "business education a continuing proposition."

• • •

The editor would like to acknowledge at this point the cooperation of the authors for making a valuable donation of their time and energy to the accomplishment of the book's objective, and for having agreed to contribute all proceeds from the sale of the book to the establishment of a post-graduate scholarship in business. I believe it is a fitting tribute to their dedication and public-spiritedness that the Prime Minister of Canada, Lester B. Pearson, has consented to write the foreword to the book.

Of the individuals whose help and encouragement I must acknowledge, I wish to record a very special gratitude for the constant support and encouragement I received from Raymond A. Young. Among my colleagues at McMaster University who have been helpful in many ways throughout the preparation of the book, I should like particularly to thank G. S. French, A. F. Isbester, P. J. George, J. E. L. Graham, and C. J. Maule. Useful advice was also received from G. Dean and B. E. Mallen.

FOREWORD

by Lester B. Pearson

It is one of the recurrent dreams of political leaders, as I am sure it is of business and labour leaders, that a way should be discovered to be always right in every judgment and decision. Unfortunately, as we all know so well, this is not possible.

We know more today than ever before about the management of our country's economic and political affairs. But we still know very little, and there remains much to do before we will even be able to consider that we are making the best of the knowledge we have.

As I understand it, the chief aim of this book is to provide an integrated perspective of the business environment for Canadian businessmen. I trust that politicians will be welcome to benefit from such a worthy effort at extending our economic knowledge, too.

It has become one of the truisms of our time that all of our decisions need to be made against objective facts. The trouble is that we have uncovered such vast mountains of new facts about our universe and all aspects of our existence that it has become increasingly difficult to know what the latest facts are.

We cannot let this new complexity discourage us, however, for we will never be able to return to simpler times. Nor should we wish to. We must go on in our endeavours to assimilate our new knowledge and then to apply it toward making our prosperity secure.

As the Economic Council of Canada has pointed out, we are living today in an age of rising expectations. The people of Canada have come to expect much from their economy, which means much from their governments and much from their business community. I am pleased to support the purpose of this book because I believe one of the essential ingredients for our continued progress and growth is information, a wider and better knowledge of what we must do to live successfully with our prosperity.

As the Economic Council has said in its latest report:

> To meet this challenge it is essential to broaden and deepen knowledge and understanding about how our economic system works, and about how it can be made to work better in the future.

If the series of articles and essays in this book contributes to this essential broadening and deepening of our economic knowledge, as I am sure they will, this project will serve as another useful instrument for the maintenance and growth of our prosperity.

The Setting

Isaiah A. Litvak, Raymond A. Young

DYNAMICS OF THE CANADIAN ENVIRONMENT

Isaiah A. Litvak
   Isaiah A. Litvak was born in Shanghai, China. He received a Bachelor of Commerce degree from McGill University and Master of Science and Doctor of Philosophy degrees from Columbia University. Dr. Litvak has written extensively in the areas of marketing and international business, contributing articles to leading North American journals, and has also authored a booklet, Trading with the Communists, *for the Canadian Institute of International Affairs, and edited* Marketing: Canada, *a book of readings published by McGraw-Hill. In addition to his duties as Professor in the McMaster University School of Business, Dr. Litvak has been engaged as a consultant by the federal government and several provincial governments, as well as management consultant to certain Canadian and foreign companies.*

Raymond A. Young
   Raymond A. Young is Research Associate with General Foods, Limited. His business career includes experience with

*a leading consumer paper products manufacturer and one of
Canada's largest consumer research agencies. Mr. Young, who has
written a number of articles in Canadian business journals,
holds an Honours degree in Commerce and a Master of Business
Administration degree, both from McMaster University.
He is a member of the American Marketing Association's
Toronto chapter, and is chairman of that organization's
Census Advisory Committee.*

Businessmen have been told for some time that events external to
their immediate environment of firm or industry will ultimately
result in the expansion of that environment. Two principal examples of such external forces are the trends towards political and
economic internationalism, and the increasingly more direct influence being exercised by non-business institutions on the business
community. However, these facts require more than simple ac-
knowledgement. Rather, they make immediate demands upon
businessmen, first to forecast the effects on their activities, and
second to begin to fashion and implement appropriate strategies of
action.

Admittedly the heightening pressures of competition and the
accelerating sophistication of business technology are almost ir-
resistible forces combining to impose an inward or micro-func-
tional view on businessmen. And unfortunately, the time devoted
to these daily imperatives necessarily increases at the expense of
consideration of the less visible but ultimately more consequential
influences.

Therefore, it is the intent of this article to provide the reader
with an integrated perspective of the total Canadian environment.
This over-view will consider the pertinent historical factors which
have shaped the nation, as well as the contemporary realities—
political, social, and economic.

Political Perspective

Fundamental to Canada's history has been the "tug-o'-war"
between two similar but divergent political ideals—classical federalism and legislative union. As Professor James A. Corry has
explained:

Classical federalism saw the national and state governments

in the system as independent entities, each going its own way in the enjoyment of its own powers under the check of a watchful electorate with a minimum of either association or collision. Because the electorates would limit narrowly the actual use made by governments of their extensive legislative powers under the constitution, the governments would not run foul of one another as long as each minded its own business. If some forgot themselves and encroached on the domains of the others, the courts would remind governments of their place. . . . Both unity and genuine diversity would flourish.[1]

The following excerpt from a speech by the Hon. John Alexander Macdonald (Attorney General West) to the Legislative Assembly on February 6, 1865, illuminates the chief characteristics of a legislative union.

. . . as regards the comparative advantages of a Legislative and a Federal union, I have never hesitated to state my own opinions. I have again and again stated in the House, that, if practicable, I thought a Legislative union would be preferable. I have always contended that if we could agree to have one government and one parliament, legislating for the whole of these peoples, it would be the best, the cheapest, the most vigorous, and the strongest system of government we could adopt . . . (However) . . . if you only consider the innumerable subjects of legislation peculiar to new countries, and that every one of those five colonies had particular laws of its own, to which its people have been accustomed and are attached, you will see the difficulty of effecting and working a Legislative union, and bringing about an assimilation of the local as well as general laws of the whole of the provinces.[2]

As pointed out by P. B. Waite in his book, *The Life and Times of Confederation, 1864-1867*, "What was sought by the Quebec Conference (1864) and later by the Colonial Office was a mean between the federation of the United States and the legislative union of Great Britain."[3] The essence of the problem was that of "establishing bodies politic which shall be more than municipal corporations but less than confederate states—bodies possessing such large powers and above all such valuable sources of revenue as shall render them content to be subject to the central authority in matters of general concern."[4]

The general public viewed the new central government in

Ottawa as the amalgamation of all the colonial legislatures into a single entity, with some new powers added. This new body politic would control the primary sources of revenue and would perform the chief functions of a responsible colonial government. The confusion that everyone recognized concerned the proper role to be assigned to local (provincial) governments. In this dilemma the American states' governments could not be used as models because they were sovereign. "Most British-Americans did not consider that sovereignty was an attribute of the local governments. In French Canada there were people and newspapers who did think so, but the basic dichotomy at the heart of the federal principle eluded most commentators."[5]

The study of Canadian opinion at the time of Confederation illuminates a number of important elements in this confusion. First there was no clear and common understanding of the principle of federalism and particularly of the subtle differences between federal and legislative union. In fact to many these terms were interchangeable. Both the substance and the flavour of the controversy have been admirably captured by P. B. Waite:

> Canadians and Acadians alike will infuse as little of the federal principle into their union . . . as will suffice to meet the absolute necessities of the case. Thus the Montreal Gazette on August 24 (1864). The Globe, October 15, was not dissimilar: Federation is, in a large degree, but an extension of our political system, and is sustained by precisely the same reasoning as are municipal institutions. This last was too much for the Montreal True Witness, and on October 28, it read both papers a lesson in political theory. Federation was not a quantity. It was not analogous to municipal institutions. It differed from a legislative union 'not in degree but in kind.' There was a 'formal and essential difference' between legislative and federal union.
>
> This was a lesson that few British North American newspapers and politicians learned, and their ignorance was indisputably part of their conception of Confederation. With some significant exceptions, they did not believe that federation meant the fundamental recognition of the sovereignty of both central and local governments. They would have regarded with suspicion a principle that would establish such governments in a way that would make each co-ordinate and independent! If that was the federal principle, they did not

want it. Most, however, never fully understood the principle that they were opposing.[6]

A second factor contributing to the confusion was that the American posture at the time was threatening, and indeed acted as a catalyst in the direction of a strong central authority. A third reason reported by P. B. Waite was that:

> The antipathy and fear of the United States felt by many was joined to a lively appreciation of the lessons to be learnt from the collapse of its constitution. British North Americans had witnessed 'the rise and fall of the Great Republic.' Most were agreed about that, as they were about the lessons to be learnt from it. No understanding of Confederation is possible unless it be recognized that its founders, many of its supporters, and as many of its opponents, were all animated by a powerful antipathy to the whole federal principle.[7]

Finally and most important was the basic difference in the objectives sought by the representatives of the various provinces in Confederation.

> In Nova Scotia and in English Canada there is revealed, again and again, the desire for legislative union. Even after Confederation, the Attorney General of Nova Scotia . . . summed up in a sentence the popular prejudice against federation: 'whatever renders a legislative union impossible must make a federal union fatal . . .' . At the same time the newspapers show how essential federal union was to French Canadians, Prince Edward Islanders, and some New Brunswickers.[8]

There were many grandiose speeches and affirmations proclaiming the glory of Confederation, but the practical motives were of a different hue. The French Canadians feared Canada West (Ontario) and looked to the Maritime provinces to help curb the grasping ambitions of Canada West which threatened to overshadow them. To Canada West, Confederation represented triumph over the French Canadians.

There was also a variety of individual expectations. John A. Macdonald clearly favoured a strong central power. Charles Tupper and Alexander Tilloch Galt preferred legislative union. George Brown pursued the objective or representation by population, while George Etienne Cartier and Etienne Taché were confident that French Canadian privileges could be better defended by

French Canadian ministers in a central government than by local legislature.

While, as we have seen, the roots of discord are found in the history of differing motives and interpretations, their tendrils permeate the contemporary scene. Because of the original compromised nature of the "federal-provincial" agreement, all Canadian governments to the present day have been forced into a political programme founded on a principle which might best be described as "rotational bribery"/ Under this system the federal government placates one province of the country only to be faced by the insistent demands of another, which it in turn placates. Such appeasement may take the form of either economic benefits to those provinces which require them and/or concessions in the area of political autonomy to those provinces which are so motivated.⏋ *Due to Confed. 1867?*

To relate the implications of federalist decentralization even more closely to the businessmen's immediate concern, one need only consider the attempts of certain provincial governments to disregard economic realities in an attempt to endow the provincial political boundaries with an obviously spurious economic integrity. As Professor Brewis observes in a recent article entitled *Area Economic Development: Pursuit of a Policy*:

> Some provincial governments . . . award contracts that favour suppliers within their own boundaries—paying such suppliers up to 12 per cent or more than the price quoted by outside competitors—a policy constituting, in effect, an internal tariff.[9]

While such a policy would be welcomed by manufacturers already located within the particular province, from a broader business viewpoint, any policy which influences a given manufacturer to select plant locations in response to political rather than purely economic considerations constitutes an unjust reduction of his return on investment. And from a national viewpoint, such policies result only in greater inefficiencies of resource allocation and tend to contribute to higher than necessary consumer prices.

SOCIAL PERSPECTIVE

Any discussion of the important social factors in Canada must be founded on an understanding of the composition of the Canadian society. It is useful to consider the Canadian society as consisting of what might be called the "old" Canadians and the "new" Canadians. The strongest argument in favour of this view is chronology. The establishment of an entente between the two founding races, and the subsequent multi-racial immigration represent two distinct stages in the evolution of Canadian society.

The history of Canada is rooted in the conflict between French and British imperialism in the "New World". The Canadian entente between these two founding races was only possible within a political framework which was founded on the assurance that the two sets of cultural traditions would not be merged, but would be distinctly preserved and given a parallel existence in the national polity. Thus Confederation did not create two nations but rather a single nation, founded on the then unique principle of guaranteed diversity of culture. It had the dual purpose of politically uniting two diverse cultures while preserving the cultural freedom of the minority.

Lurking beneath our current major social problem of English-French relations is the inescapable fact that "it has always seemed to the French Canadians better to husband and protect the French soul in North America under the British flag, however limited and confined it must therefore be, than to be melted down into an American button, and lose identity forever."[10] The guarantee offered by Confederation provided that French Canadians should not be disadvantaged in this national polity because of their language, religion or other cultural traditions. However, Confederation could not, and in fact did not, make any guarantees pertaining to the commercial, educational or other local consequences of parochialism. Confederation could make no such guarantees concerning local consequences, because in answer to French-Canadian demands it had incorporated enough of the Federalist principle to define "local" (provincial) decisions as without its domain.

Yet it is precisely the consequences of these local decisions, rather than any national disadvantage, which underlie current French Canadian dissatisfactions. For one example, the current feeling of exclusion on the part of French Canadians from the commercial power structure in Québec seems largely attributable to the mutually sustaining (both in intent and in result) combination of a classical educational system and a rural-religious viewpoint. The rationale of these decisions, as explained by Professor Parenteau, was that "industrialization was resented by the elite of French Canada. They regarded it as pernicious, since they were convinced that only rural life could assure the survival of the ethnic group and safeguard the traditional moral values on which French Candians prided themselves."[11] While the authors are not concerned with laying blame, we are vitally interested in ferreting out the root causes of present conditions.

The latest but by no means the only manifestation of ultimate French dissatisfaction with the "pseudo-Federal solution" is the *Separatiste* movement. Even in their preamble to the Preliminary Report of the Royal Commission on Bilingualism and Biculturalism, Messrs. A. Davidson Dunton and Andre Laurendeau (Co-Chairmen) and their associates report . . .

> . . . What the Commissioners have discovered . . . (is) . . . that Canada, without being fully conscious of the fact, is passing through the greatest crisis in its history . . . [further] . . . The source of the crisis lies in the Province of Quebec; that fact could be established without an extensive inquiry . . . [and finally] . . . it would appear from what is happening that the state of affairs established in 1867 and never since seriously challenged is now for the first time being rejected by the French Canadians of Quebec.[12]

While we agree with these observations, we take strong exception to the terms of reference of the Commission, which we feel contain the potential to render a disservice to Canada. The pertinent phrases are included in the following excerpt:

> . . . to inquire into and report upon the existing state of bilingualism and biculturalism in Canada and to recommend what steps should be taken to develop the Canadian Confederation on the basis of an equal partnership between the two founding races, taking into account the contribution made by the other ethnic groups to the cultural enrichment of Canada and the measures that should be taken to safeguard that contribution. . . .[13]

As we have shown, the concept of "equal partnership" is invalid. What was guaranteed was bicultural co-existence. "Bilingualism and biculturalism in Canada" was only an objective in the sphere of national politics. Beyond this, as Professor Donald Creighton has recently pointed out, "no special concessions to the French language had ever been considered, or even suggested, in Canada West [the future Ontario] or in Nova Scotia, Newfoundland or in Prince Edward Island . . . [and] . . . the idea of a bicultural compact, implicit in the B.N.A. Act, explicit in the original constitutions of Manitoba and the North West Territories, is a myth."[14] In brief, the concepts of bilingualism and biculturalism have no relevance within any provincial framework except that of Québec. Finally, if there exists in Québec any problem with regard to bilingualism and biculturalism, that problem will require a provincial solution because Confederation expressly precludes a Federal solution.

Nevertheless, the existence of such a problem in Québec is a fact. One need only attend to the perhaps shrill but undoubtedly sincere expression of this problem and of the *Separatiste's* solution. One prominent spokesman for the cause of separatism, Dr. Marcel Chaput declares:

> In the name of French reason, I ask you where is the illusion? In the achievement of one great bilingual Canada where at best we can run a close second, or in the formation of a sovereign, French Québec in which we would be able to be the sole masters? In the name of French valor, I ask you which is defeatism? The stubborn battle for crumbs, trinkets and trifles, or the enlightened march toward the free country our ancestors wanted? The French-Canadians, like any proud people are ready to fight as much as necessary to ensure their liberation and to fulfill the most legitimate and natural of aspirations—to build a nation of their own.[15]

In rebuttal, we submit the following indictment of the "legitimacy" of this aspiration by Miss Gwethalyn Graham, a journalist and author, who has twice won the Governor-General's Award:

> In addition to their [separatists] failure to answer the detailed and closely reasoned objections of the economists and their essentially defeatist all-or-nothing attitude toward sovereignty, have they yet even tried to show us how an independent Québec will produce a better artist or scientist or engineer? Even if none of these grounds for being anti-separatist existed, there would still remain one crucial fact which ought to be enough to damn the movement outright: **it is fundamentally racist.** The separatist thesis rests on an ethnic foundation and, whatever its present political orientation, there is

a danger that it will veer further and further to the Right, because racist political parties usually do, until they are captured by ultra-nationalists and turn into overt facism. I cannot see the separatist position evolving into anything else because the separatists themselves have made it abundantly clear that they put ethnic before economic and social values. One has only to read a little history to hear the echoes from the twenties when Hitler and Mussolini were still sounding like innocent nationalists concerned only with the advancement of their own people.[16]

While the separatist position illustrated may not encompass all motivations for separatism, and while we recognize that separatism is not confined within the borders of Québec, the authors submit that the probable consequences of separatism are intolerable, however defended.

It must be remembered of course, above all else, that the separatists represent but one faction of French Canadian thought albeit a vociferous one. Therefore, in fairness to French-speaking Canadians, we feel compelled to adjust the balance. This we hasten to do by acknowledging our agreement with the following introductory remarks to *A Canadian Manifesto* by a group of prominent young Canadian intellectuals who also reside in Québec.*

> We are a group of citizens strongly opposed to the present state of affairs in Canada generally, and in our province in particular. We condemn the indifference of the public and private sectors of our society in the face of many pressing problems. We declare our disagreement with most of the panaceas at present in vogue among our politicians.
>
> Canada, today, is a country in search of a purpose. Emphasis on regional interest and the absence of leadership from the central government risk the utter disintegration of the Federal State.
>
> In the Province of Québec, the "Quiet Revolution"—while it has a number of achievements to its credit—has nonetheless been limited to a mere waving of symbols in many sectors, and, in others, has come to a complete halt, already exhausted. The reform movement appears to be on the verge of becoming compromised, of deviating badly. Emotional

---

*The group includes Albert Breton, Raymond Breton, Claude Bruneau, Yvon Gauthier, Marc Lalonde, Maurice Pinard, and Pierre-Elliot Trudeau.

cries often drown out the voice of reason, and racial appeals take the place of objective analysis of reality.

In the present context of Canadian politics, it is necessary above all else to reaffirm the importance of the individual, without regard to ethnic, geographic or religious accidents. The cornerstone of the social and political order must be the attributes men hold in common, not those that differentiate them. An order of priorities in political and social matters that is founded upon the individual as an individual, is totally incompatible with an order of priorities based upon race, religion or nationality.

This then, is a manifesto. It is an affirmation of faith in man, and it is on the basis of human criteria that we demand policies better adapted to our world and our times. This is our only motivation. Of "appeals to pride and dignity," we care for none other.[17]

While it is true that Canadians of British origin represent the plurality in the Canadian population (44 per cent), it is equally true that, to foreigners, the French fact is the most obvious characteristic distinguishing Canada from both Britain and the United States. However, as foreign observers in Canada soon discover, the pervasive Canadian character can be best described as British North American.

British influence permeates all aspects of Canadian life. It is manifest in such institutions as Parliament, which is traditionally opened by the Queen's representative in Canada (the Governor-General) and is the focal point of Canadian symbolism, exemplified in the national anthem and, until recently, in the Canadian flag. Certain Canadian regiments also trace their history to British predecessors, and the prevalence of the prefix "Royal" attached to such Canadian institutions as the mounted police, military colleges, and in fact the national military services, all reflect British origins. Finally, with the exception of Québec, the pervasiveness of the English language and the Protestant ethic reinforce the implicit association that is made explicit by Canada's membership in the Commonwealth.

The sensitive observer can also detect subtler British influences on Canada's national character, particularly as compared to the American stereotype. The Canadian personality exhibits a greater degree of British reserve and conservatism, a lesser degree of American emotionalism and opportunism, all founded on an underlying hierarchical social stratification. In short, the British influence in Canada has tended to exalt social orderliness while accepting the inequality of opportunity and lesser social mobility which stability implies. One need not even visit the traditional bastions of the "Empire" such as Toronto, Victoria, or Halifax, to attribute these traits to the Canadian characer.

Although English Canadians do not harbour the same fears concerning the preservation of their culture and traditions as do the French Canadians, it is only because the fact of their plurality eliminates such concerns. However, this should not imply that pockets of British parochialism are any scarcer than their French Canadian counterparts, nor any more desireable.

While it might have been adequate in the not-too-distant past, and would certainly have been tempting, to truncate the discussion of the Canadian society at this point, all Canadians must certainly realize that the founding duet has become a trio. Table 1 indicates that in 1961 one out of every four Canadians was of stock other than British or French. In fact, as the Honourable Walter Gordon recently pointed out, "If the 'all other' category is extended to include the Scots, the Irish, and the Welsh, we would have three groups of nearly equal size."[18]

Table I
ETHNIC COMPOSITION, CANADA: 1901-1961
Ethnic Origin

Year	British Isles Number (000)	Per cent	French Number	Per cent	Other Number (000)	Per cent	Total (000)
1901	3,063	57.0	1,649	30.7	659	12.3	5,371
1911	3,999	55.5	2,062	28.6	1,146	15.9	7,207
1921	4,869	55.4	2,453	27.9	1,466	16.7	8,788
1931	5,381	51.9	2,928	28.2	2,068	19.9	10,377
1941	5,716	49.7	3,483	30.3	2,308	20.0	11,507
1951	6,710	47.9	4,319	30.8	2,981	21.3	14,009
1961	7,997	43.8	5,540	30.4	4,486	25.8	18,238

Source: Dominion Bureau of Statistics, 1961 *Census*, Bulletin 1. 2-5, Table 34, p. 34-1.

In addition to recognizing the aggregate composition of Canada, it is interesting to note the regional dispersion of the population by ethnic origin. As can be seen from Table 2, Canadians of British origin are only in the majority in the Maritime provinces, Ontario, British Columbia, and the Yukon. The French, of course, only form the majority in Québec. Manitoba, Saskatchewan, Alberta, and the Northwest Territories have majorities composed of the "all other" group.

While the net effect of immigration to the United States has been described as a "melting pot", ethnic and language differences with some assistance from geography have tended to divide Canada into a mosaic of sub-cultures. And because there have been no major unifying events in Canada, as contrasted with the United States, the various sub-cultures have not been synthesized into a unified whole but to this day retain their separate identities within the political Dominion.

Further, the lack of a national identity to supply a focal point for the various ethnic groups bestows an inordinate amount of significance on the facts of geography. This is manifested, for example, by British Columbians who feel they have more in common with their U. S. neighbours to the south than with fellow-Canadians who are separated by the Rockies. Similarly, many Prairie residents feel a greater kinship towards fellow southern agrarians than to eastern industrialists. In fact, with the possible exception of Québec, many Canadians are oriented along a north-south axis.

When you add to these facts the strivings of French Canadians to preserve a cultural identity of their own within a provincial framework, and also English Ontario's strong familial ties to Britain and the Commonwealth, thoughtful Canadians cannot help but wonder whether their Dominion is more than a mere geographical union.

ECONOMIC PERSPECTIVE

If purely economic considerations had prevailed in North America in the nineteenth century, Canada probably would not have been founded. Rather, the settlements north of the 49th parallel would have succumbed to the economic polarization of the regions of the United States. But Canada was created to satisfy political objectives, not economic. In fact, these objectives are explicit in refer-

Table II
DISTRIBUTION OF THE POPULATION BY ETHNIC ORIGIN
Canada and Provinces, 1961

Province or Territory	Total Population	British Number	%	French Number	%	Other Number Ethnic Origin	%
Canada	18,238,247	7,996,699	43.84	5,540,346	30.37	4,701,232	25.75
Newfoundland	457,853	428,899	93.67	17,171	3.75	11,783	2.57
Prince Edward Island	104,629	83,501	79.80	17,418	16.64	3,710	3.57
Nova Scotia	737,007	525,448	71.29	87,883	11.92	123,676	16.78
New Brunswick	597,936	329,940	55.17	232,127	38.82	35,869	5.99
Québec	5,259,211	567,057	10.78	4,241,354	80.64	450,800	8.52
Ontario	6,236,092	3,711,536	59.51	647,941	10.39	1,876,615	30.09
Manitoba	921,686	396,445	43.01	83,936	9.10	441,305	47.88
Saskatchewan	925,181	373,482	40.36	59,824	6.46	491,875	53.16
Alberta	1,331,944	601,755	45.17	83,319	6.25	646,870	48.56
British Columbia	1,629,082	966,881	59.35	66,970	4.11	595,231	36.53
Yukon	14,628	6,946	47.48	991	6.77	6,691	45.74
Northwest Territories	22,998	4,779	20.78	1,412	6.13	16,807	73.08

Source: 1961 Census of Canada; Catalogue 92-561, Vol. 1, Part 3; "Population: Language by Ethnic Groups".

ences by the founding fathers to maintaining sovereignty, withstanding American absorption, and preserving cultural integrity. Yet the realization by the founding fathers of the economic realities is implicit in the economic policies which they implemented to preserve their nation.

As Professor Donald Creighton pointed out in his study prepared for The Royal Commission on Dominion-Provincial Relations:

> The creation of a national economy was the economic counterpart of the establishment of a new political nationality . . . the central economic ambition of the Fathers of Confederation was to increase the production, to hasten the expansion and to promote the prosperity of the British North American provinces by the establishment of a new national economy . . . It was believed that the resources and industries of British North America were diversified and complementary: it was argued that the integration of these various elements would provide the requisite basis of a stable economic life.[19]

In order to achieve this necessary economic independence in the shadow of American expansionism, post-Confederation policy incorporated three principal ingredients. The first major task was to establish a lateral identity for the nation to combat the latent north-south polarity. Translating this prerequisite into economic terms meant but one thing—an east-west railroad. Only such an instrument could span the vast geography of the new nation and make viable the economic integration envisaged by the founding fathers. That the railroad accomplished this objective is generally acknowledged, and moreover as Professor F. H. Underhill has observed, it was "an exploit to which we look back now as the most magnificent expression in our history of our national faith in ourselves."[20]

The second major ingredient of Canada's economic policy was to obtain the human resources necessary both to build the economy and to populate the empty expanses between the far flung settlements, lest this vacuum imply a weakness and an opportunity to American expansionists. While the immigration policy was partially successful to this end, it is legitimate today to raise the question of whether Canada was a reservoir or merely a channel for immigrants. The latter situation is suggested by the fact that while 6,815,000 immigrants entered Canada between 1901-1961,

4,484,000 people emigrated from Canada. In short, for every three people who immigrated to Canada during this period, two other Canadian residents migrated from Canada. Thus, during the first sixty years of his century, Canada benefited from the residency of only one in three of its immigrants. Table 3 documents the various dynamics of population change between 1901-1961.

Table III

COMPONENTS OF POPULATION GROWTH: 1901-1961

(thousands)

Period	Births	Deaths	Natural Increase	Immigration	Net Migration	Net Increase
1901-1911	1,931	811	1,120	1,759	716	1,836
1911-1921	2,338	988	1,350	1,612	231	1,581
1921-1931	2,415	1,055	1,360	1,203	229	1,589
1931-1941	2,294	1,072	1,222	150	—92	1,130
1941-1951[a]	3,186	1,214	1,972	548	169	2,141
1951-1961[b]	4,478	1,327	3,151	1,543	1,078	4,229

Dominion Bureau of Statistics, Canadian Vital Statistics Trends, 1921-1954, Reference Paper No. 70, Ottawa, Queen's Printer, 1956, pp. 7-9; and Department of Citizenship and Immigration, 1962 Immigration Statistics, Ottawa, Queen's Printer, 1963, p. 7.
[a]Not including Newfoundland.
[b]Including Newfoundland.

To the extent that the predominant direction of this drainage was towards the United States, it is reasonable to assume that these people represented the more skilled immigrants, attracted by the relatively higher incomes which their skills would command in the United States market. It is also probable that the lack of a Canadian national identity to magnetize the newcomers, coupled with the relatively less penetrable social hierarchy in Canada, contributed greatly to the erosion of this channel.

The third major ingredient of Canada's economic policy was a system of protective tariffs designed to shield Canada's embryonic industrial structure from foreign competition. Introduced in 1879 by Sir John A. Macdonald, the tariff policy shared with the railroad and immigration policies the purpose of enabling the Canadian economy to withstand the pressures of American expansionism.

While the "infant industry" argument was a legitimate concern in Sir John A. Macdonald's time, its persistence to the present day as a major mainstay of Canadian protectionist thought would seem to imply that the infant would perish if this protectionist breast were removed from its mouth.

The intent of the tariff policy was to encourage domestic entrepreneurs, with the backing of British capital, to assist in the delivery of a Canadian industrial complex and to protect it during the vulnerable, formative stages of its development. In 1900, upon the twenty-first birthday of this policy, the rich "British uncle" had in fact contributed eighty-five per cent of all foreign capital invested in Canada. While this would have been encouraging to the original protectionist mid-wives, three generations of their descendants have observed this percentage dwindle to a mere 14.3 per cent in 1961. This trend does not represent any lessening of enthusiasm on the part of the "British uncle", but rather it chronicles the increasing involvement in response to economic opportunities of the self-appointed American godfather. By 1961, as can be seen from Table 4, 76.2 per cent of all foreign capital invested in Canada was owned in the United States.

The explanation for this development was simply that while the national tariff policy helped to discourage the United States from exporting manufactured goods to Canada as intended, it subsequently encouraged American entrepreneurs to export capital to this northern market. Judging by the consequences of this influx of American capital, certain economic analysts have observed that the tariff policy "designed to increase the economic strength of Canada and to help secure her from the steady threat of American expansionism . . . inaugurated in 1879 has been the most conspicuous (but least generally recognized) misdirection of national endeavour in Canada's history."[21]

Appraising The Consequences of Economic Nationalism

To this point we have endeavoured to explain that Canada was a politically motivated rather than an economic creation. We have also described the instruments of national policy which were implemented in the attempt to sustain this creation. It remains only to evaluate the consequences of this economic nationalism.

That Canada remains today an independent, sovereign nation

Table IV
FOREIGN CAPITAL INVESTED IN CANADA
selected year ends 1900-59

Year	Owned in United Kingdom		Owned in United States		Owned elsewhere outside Canada		Total non-resident investment
	$ million	Per cent	$ million	Per cent	$ million	Per cent	$ million
1900	1050*	85	168	14	14	1	1232
1914	2778†	72	881	23	178	5	3837
1918	2729	60	1630	36	177	4	4536
1926	2637	44	3196	53	170	3	6003
1930	2766	36	4660	61	188	3	7614
1939	2476	36	4151	60	286	4	6913
1945	1750	25	4990	70	352	5	7092
1948	1610	22	5567	74	332	4	7509
1954	2181	17	9692	77	704	6	12,577
1955	2356	17.5	10,275	76.3	842	6.2	13,473
1956	2668	17.1	11,789	75.7	1112	7.1	15,569
1957	2917	16.7	13,264	76.0	1283	7.3	17,464
1958	3088	16.2	14,436	76.0	1481	7.8	19,005
1959	3199	15.4	15,811	75.9	1823	8.8	20,833
1960	3359	15.1	16,718	75.3	2137	9.6	22,214
1961	3385	14.3	17,966	76.2	2219	9.5	23,570

SOURCES: Irving Brecher and S. S. Reisman, Canada-United States Relations, Table 16, p. 88. DBS, The Canadian Balance of International Payments 1960 and International Investment Position, Table II, pp. 68-9. Roy A. Matthews, "Canada's Balance of Payments", The Conference Board Record, Vol. 1, No. 4, p. 30.

*Estimated by Dr. Jacob Viner, Canada's Balance of International Indebtedness, 1900-1913 (Cambridge, Mass., 1924).

†Estimated by Professor F. A. Knox from Excursus appearing in H. Marshall, F. L. Southard, Jr., and K. W. Taylor, Canadian-American Industry (New Haven, 1936).

is a fact. However, it has preserved this political status at a definite economic cost. The magnitude of this cost is simply the difference between Canada's standard of living and that of the United States. For it is reasonable to assume that had Canada relinquished her sovereignty and followed the pull of economic forces

Table IV

FOREIGN CAPITAL INVESTED IN CANADA
selected year ends 1900-59

Year	Owned in United Kingdom		Owned in United States		Owned elsewhere outside Canada		Total non-resident investment
	$ million	%	$ million	%	$ million	%	$ million
1900	1050*	85	168	14	14	1	1232
1914	2778†	72	881	23	178	5	3837
1918	2729	60	1630	36	177	4	4536
1926	2637	44	3196	53	170	3	6003
1930	2766	36	4660	61	188	3	7614
1939	2476	36	4151	60	286	4	6913
1945	1750	25	4990	70	352	5	7092
1948	1610	22	5567	74	332	4	7509
1954	2181	17	9692	77	704	6	12,577
1955	2356	17.5	10,275	76.3	842	6.2	13,473
1956	2668	17.1	11,789	75.7	1112	7.1	15,569
1957	2917	16.7	13,264	76.0	1283	7.3	17,464
1958	3088	16.2	14,436	76.0	1481	7.8	19,005
1959	3199	15.4	15,811	75.9	1823	8.8	20,833
1960	3359	15.1	16,718	75.3	2137	9.6	22,214
1961	3385	14.3	17,966	76.2	2219	9.5	23,570

SOURCES: Irving Brecher and S. S. Reisman, Canada-United States Relations, Table 16, p. 88. DBS, The Canadian Balance of International Payments 1960 and International Investment Position, Table II, pp. 68-9. Roy A. Matthews, "Canada's Balance of Payments", The Conference Board Record, Vol. 1, No. 4, p. 30.

*Estimated by Dr. Jacob Viner, Canada's Balance of International Indebtedness, 1900-1913 (Cambridge, Mass., 1924).

†Estimated by Professor F. A. Knox from Excursus appearing in H. Marshall, F. L. Southard, Jr., and K. W. Taylor, Canadian-American Industry (New Haven, 1936).

into a union with the United States, Canada would today share the American standard of living.

In broader terms, the total cash cost of the Canadian tariff is represented by the one billion dollars which Canadian consumers pay annually to subsidize Canada's inefficient manufacturing industry, particularly the secondary sector. While the most visible component of this cost is the duty paid by Canadians on imported goods, the more significant component is represented by the difference between the cost of a good in Canada and the cost of the equivalent imported good. Professor J. H. Young in his study of Canadian Commercial Policy for the Gordon Commission estimated that the annual cash cost of this latter component "amounts to $0.6 billion to $0.75 billion or about 3.5% to 4.5% of the gross private expenditure net of indirect taxes. The inclusion of government expenditure and retail distribution would raise the estimate considerably, and it is likely that a comprehensive estimate of this kind made for 1956 would be of the order of $1 billion".[22] And as Professor H. G. Johnson has observed:

> One billion dollars per year is a lot of money, even in Canada. Considered as a tax imposed on the Canadian public, it may be compared with the explicit taxes. It amounts to over 80% of the amount of individual income tax collected (for 1956) and to about 22½% of the budgetary revenue of the Government of Canada (for the same year); in other words, the taxation levied on the public through the tariff is nearly one quarter as much as is levied through all other federal taxes. Do the benefits conferred on the public by protection justify the level of taxation? I find it impossible to believe that they do.[23]

Not only has the tariff had this immediate cost, but it is also responsible for encouraging American firms particularly to export capital into Canada as an alternative to exporting finished goods. This prospect was made even more attractive by the adoption of Imperial Preferences in the 1930's which gave firms with plants in Canada the added incentive of preferential entry to other Commonwealth markets. The result of these developments has been to create in Canada an industrial structure which is a miniature replica of the American. While this structure is suitable in the American setting, it is inappropriate for Canada. A little reflection on this question will indicate that the industrial structure required to service a consumer population of 200 million is bound to be uneconomic when its market is reduced to ten per cent of that number.

However, while Canada has been paying these economic costs of political sovereignty, the interplay of economic forces has resulted in a continuing trend towards economic interdependence with the United States.

To many American businessmen Canada is either a supplier, a customer, an investor, or an investment. While a statistical analysis of these four relationships from the American viewpoint may be significant, from the Canadian perspective these same relationships are critical, and in fact underlie much of the Canadian national concern. Exhibit I illustrates these relationships and their relative statistical significance to the United States and Canada.

EXHIBIT I

U.S. VIEWPOINT	CANADIAN VIEWPOINT
Canada As A Supplier	*U.S. As A Supplier*
22% of all imports come from Canada	68% of all imports come from the U.S.
Canada As A Market	*U.S. As A Market*
20% of all exports go to Canada	55% of all exports go to the U.S.
Canada As An Investment	*U.S. As An Investment*
32% of all foreign direct investment is in Canada	65% of all foreign direct investment is in the U.S.
Canada As An Investor	*U.S. As An Investor*
24% of all foreign direct investment in the U.S. is Canadian	82% of foreign direct investment in Canada is American

At the risk of an unpalatable pun we wish to emphasize the fact that Americans have a significant stake in Canada. Their investment and participation in Canada is greater than in any other single foreign country. Most leading U.S. companies have subsidiaries in Canada with the result, noted earlier, that many Canadian markets are miniature replicas of American markets. For example, the "American Big Three" car manufacturers are also the "Canadian Big Three". However, American investment in Canada has not only been very significant, it has also been extremely selective. In an attempt to maximize return on investment, it has been concentrated in growth industries.

As the Honourable Walter L. Gordon noted in his recent book, *A Choice for Canada*, ". . . the latest figures available, which were for 1961 show that non-residents controlled 69 per cent of the value of investments in petroleum and natural gas, 59 per cent in mining and smelting, and 59 per cent in maufacturing".[24] It has become fashionable among economic nationalists in Canada to deplore non-resident ownership of much of our resources and means of production. Their objections are based on the political consequences which may ultimately ensue from the perpetuation or extension of this condition. These consequences whose probability we must acknowledge but cannot quantify, range from the imposition of restrictions by U.S. parent companies, and indirectly by their government on Canadian economic policies, to ultimate economic integration with the U.S. and consequent political absorption.

While American domination of the Canadian economy, and the growth sectors in particular, places definite constraints upon the freedom of action of Canadian policy makers, it must be recognized that American capital has not only supported but is to a large extent responsible for the economic growth that Canada has enjoyed. Let not our present concern discredit this contribution nor dissuade future participation by American investors.

. . .

Having now applied the last broad brush-strokes to our political, social and economic landscape of Canada, we invite the reader to attend to the following discussions of specific aspects of this environment by a number of distinguished Canadians.

FOOTNOTES

Source: Dominion Bureau of Statistics and U.S. Department of Commerce (a, 1963; b, 1962)

[1]James A. Corry, "Constitutional Trends and Federalism," in Paul Fox (ed.), *Politics: Canada* (Toronto: McGraw-Hill, 1962), p. 26.

[2]P. B. Waite (ed.), *The Confederation Debates in the Province of Canada 1865* (Toronto: McClelland and Stewart Limited, 1963), pp. 40-41.

[3]P. B. Waite, *The Life and Times of Confederation 1864-1867* (Toronto: University of Toronto Press, 1962), pp. 325-326.

[4]*Ibid.*, cited from a minute reporting an interview with a member of the Vancouver Island legislature, 1866.

[5]*Ibid.*, p. 327.

[6]*Ibid.*, p. 114.

[7]*Ibid.*, p. 33.

[8]*Ibid.*, pp. 324-325.

[9]Thomas N. Brewis, "Area Economic Development: Pursuit of a Policy," in John J. Deutsch, *et al.* (eds.), *The Canadian Economy* (Toronto, the Macmillan Company, 1965), p. 436.

[10]George W. Wilson, *et al.*, *Canada: An Appraisal of its Needs and Resources* (Toronto: University of Toronto Press, 1965), p. xxiv.

[11]Roland Parenteau, "The Impact of Industrialization in Quebec," in I. A. Litvak and B. E. Mallen (eds.), *Marketing: Canada* (Toronto, McGraw-Hill, 1964), p. 97.

[12]*A Preliminary Report of the Royal Commission on Bilingualism and Biculturalism* (Ottawa: Queen's Printer, 1963), p. 13.

[13]*Ibid.*, p. 151.

[14]D. G. Creighton, "The Myth of Biculturalism," *Saturday Night*, Vol. 81, No. 9 (September, 1966), pp. 37-38.

[15]Marcel Chaput, "Why I Am A Separatist," in Richard Laskin (ed.), *Social Problems: A Canadian Profile* (Toronto: McGraw-Hill, 1964), pp. 53-54.

[16]Gwethalyn Graham, Dear Enemies" (co-author, Solange Chaput Rolland), in Richard Laskin (ed.), *op cit.*, p. 79

[17]Albert Breton, Raymond Breton, Claude Bruneau, Yvon Gauthier, Marc Lalonde, Maurice Pinard and Pierre-Elliott Trudeau, "An Appeal For Realism In Politics," *The Canadian Forum*, Vol. XLIV, No. 520 (May, 1964), p. 29.

[18]Walter L. Gordon, *A Choice For Canada* (Toronto: McClelland & Stewart Ltd., 1966), p. xii.

[19]D. G. Creighton, "British North America At Confederation", in John J. Deutsch, *et al.* (eds.), *The Canadian Economy* (Toronto: The MacMillan Co., 1965), pp. 449-450.

[20]F. H. Underhill, *In Search of Canadian Liberalism* (Toronto: 1960), p. 99.

[21]George W. Wilson, *et al.*, *op. cit.* p. xxxi.

[22]J. H. Young, *Canadian Commercial Policy* (Ottawa: Queen's Printer, 1957), p. 73.

[23]H. G. Johnson, *The Canadian Quandary* (Toronto: McGraw-Hill, 1963), p. 109.

[24]Walter L. Gordon, *op. cit.*, p. 80

Government
and Business

A. A. Cumming

ARE WE **LEGISLATING** PRIVATE ENTERPRISE OUT OF CANADIAN BUSINESS?

Alison A. Cumming

A. A. Cumming was born in Truro, Nova Scotia, and graduated from Dalhousie University with a Bachelor of Science degree in chemistry. In 1934 he joined the National Carbon Company, and in 1955 he was named Vice-President of the parent Company, Union Carbide Canada Limited. In 1956 he became its President, and in 1965 Chairman of the Board.

Private enterprise means different things to different people, and certainly over the years several interpretations have been made of it.

Basically it indicates the ability in a free democratic society to commence a legitimate business in competition with existing concerns, and to operate the business, if possible, at a profit.

The business may consist of any manner of enterprise. It can be an extractive industry, such as a mine or a lumber operation; it can be a factory, making anything from nails to pots and pans; it can be a haberdashery or a book store, buying products at wholesale prices and marking them up to competitive retail prices. It can be a service, such as a gas station, a laundry or a parking lot.

By common consent or accepted usage, however, the term private enterprise has more generally applied to the manufacturing field than to any other. It is in this segment of modern society that the expression has been most used, either by management—to distinguish the operation from state-owned or government-controlled enterprises—or by the opponents of the system, who subscribe to either socialism in the extreme or, in lessening degree, to a certain measure of public ownership of the means of production.

The proponents of the system as it exists in the mid-Twentieth Century say that it has provided an expansion of the economy in terms of higher wages, achieved through free, collective bargaining; more jobs, despite the theoretical challenge to an expanding work force from technological improvement and innovation; more leisure, arising from increasing plant efficiency and a shrinking work week; and a higher standard of living, achieved by greater productivity, higher rates of pay and the consumer's broad freedom of choice of goods produced under this system.

The opponents of private enterprise have varying shades of dislike for it, ranging from the old-line Communist conception of "from each according to his abilities, to each according to his needs", through to the moderate who argues only that public utilities should not be the preserve of the entrepreneur.

The articulate enemy of the system argues that, at worst, it is piratical, battering down weaker competitors by a variety of tactics aimed at increasing the practitioner's share of the existing market, and that at best it is a haven of privilege dominated by the "boss" image, clubbing with individuals in the same line of endeavour to mount a rear-guard action against rising wages, improved working conditions and broadening social welfare.

The foeman of private enterprise who is an active demagogue charges price-fixing and market rigging; the opponent who is less vindictive argues simply that the "haves" must accept responsibility for the "have nots" and that taxation must be employed to redistribute income to an even greater degree than it is now.

The private enterprise system has never been without an army of assailants.

". . . The very rise of capitalism," wrote Dr. William H. Peterson, a leading New York economist, a few years ago, "with its almost immediate improvement in job opportunities and wages from the Industrial Revolution on, was matched by a rise of an anti-capitalist mentality epitomized in demands for socialism, communism, syndicalism, massive interventionism, and other forms of collectivism.

> Historians, essayists, philosophers, and even some businessmen heaped scorn upon the capitalist. Thomas Carlyle, the British historian, for example, flayed England's captains of industry and characterized classical free enterprise economics as the "dismal science". Robert Owen, a successful English businessman, succumbed to the socialist spell and socialist societies. St. Simon, a leading French socialist, intellectually fathered such utopians as Auguste Compte and Charles Fourier.
>
> Marx and Engels launched their **Communist Manifesto,** a savage attack on the bourgeoisie whose profit motive they said was "veiled by religious and political illusions" and was nothing but "naked, shameless, direct, brutal exploitation".
>
> Besides the communism of Marx and Engels, the last 100 years has spawned the socialism and planning of the German Historical school, the British Fabians, the American Institutionalists and Technocrats, the French Syndicalists, and the Italian, German, Spanish and Argentinian Fascists. A remarkable century—remarkable that business survived at all.

No one in Canada's hundredth birthday year would deny that freedom of enterprise, as practised by many nineteenth century capitalists of the "robber baron" variety, was oppressive in the extreme, and not in the interests of society as a whole.

Some of these early entrepreneurs treated labour as a commodity to be bought when they needed it, in the same way they bought materials. They traded on uncertainty and job insecurity which, in the last analysis, was as much responsible for the emergence of strong trade unionism as was the desire to secure a larger share of the fruits of production.

But times have changed radically since Karl Marx declaimed some 120 years ago that the spectre of communism was haunting Europe. Today organized labour plays a role every bit as important in the national society as that of management and government. The wages of blue collar workers have been rising faster in recent years than the salaries of the white collar class, and the gap between the incomes of the craftsman and the senior office employee is narrowing rapidly.

Obviously, an expanding world economy and the onslaught of the machine have been chiefly responsible for improving living levels in the free enterprise society under which we operate. The benefits of this business method, which have reached their present peak after a bare century of existence, are more spectacular if one delves a bit more deeply into the lot of mankind as it was before the system evolved. Even a superficial comparison between an historical yesterday and the mid-sixties proves the material benefits that have accrued to the broad mass of the general population from the enterprise method of business.

Reflect for a moment on the life lived by the average man on this continent as Canada approached Confederation in 1867. Paved streets, proper drainage, water supply, street lighting—such basic services as these hardly existed, even in the largest of cities. Except for the pioneer who went west, it was a rare man who, in the course of this whole life, ever ventured more than a few miles from his birthplace, for the simple reason that travel was impossibly costly in terms of both time and money. Who now remembers that in those years before the coming of the railroads it took at the very least three full months to get from Halifax to Vancouver?

Vast numbers of people existed in ill-ventilated, badly lighted shacks. The death rate was high because of the lack of basic services and, in the case of children, because of the inability of parents to provide them adequately with the means of staying alive. Medicine and decent health care, good housing and a proper education were the prerogative of the rich.

For the most part, and certainly outside the big cities, this was still the age of the self-employed man—the craftsman, the blacksmith, the small farmer, the rugged individualist. Within the cities, a man counted himself lucky to have a job in one of the infant manufacturing industries, where the 12-hour day was the norm and $5 a week a good wage.

This was not the life of medieval times, but life as lived by our great grandparents. In the context of history, this was just yesterday.

What has happened since yesterday? Essentially of course, the

changes have resulted from modern industrialization, with application of the mass production techniques of men like Samuel Colt,
Eli Whitney, and Henry Ford and his $5 daily wage, to the engi-
neering and distributive geniuses who have brought television and
frozen orange juice within reach of almost everyone in this generation.

In short, what has happened is that private enterprise, representing the combined efforts of inventors, men of capital, entrepreneurs, skilled labour, professional management, has confound-
ed the unhappy Marx by all but eliminating the glaring and
age-old gap between the "haves" and the "have nots."

In the course of these few decades, invention and research
have spawned the means to a whole new way of life—an im-
measurably richer life, not for the few but for the great mass of
the people. The locomotive, the harnessing of electricity, the telephone, the automobile, radio and movies, plastics and other synthetic materials, electronics and miracle drugs, computers and jet
aircraft—merely to enumerate these things is to realize the
enormity of the change that has taken place since the birth of the
industrial era. And, of course, what must not be forgotten is that
this is an accelerating process; the luxuries of yesterday are tending ever more rapidly to become the commonplaces of today.
Witness television, an electronic wonder some twenty years ago,
an accepted piece of household equipment today.

The progressive advent of all these things has been accom-
panied by a revolution in social attitudes. The public conscience,
as expressed in legislation involving such items as workmen's com-
pensation, minimum working conditions, progressive taxation and
redistribution of wealth, not to mention the rising power of labour
unions and the impact of two World Wars; all these have played
an important part in reshaping society as it exists today.

But the most powerful factor of all was the realization by
business, and more specifically by the manufacturing industry,
that it is vastly cheaper and more efficient to produce for the many
rather than for the few.

Production in quantity naturally presupposes the ability of the
millions to buy and consume what is produced. Thus it is that, for
business itself, highest possible levels of employment and highest
possible wages consistent with rising productivity have become the
paramount requirements. This is the logic of mass production.

Consequently, what we now see is not merely a lesser gap than ever before between the incomes of the well-to-do and the not so well-to-do, but just as significantly, an equality of affluence in terms of what we eat, what we wear, how we live and, to a certain extent, what we do. The wives of men earning $6,000, $12,000 and $25,000 a year all shop in the same supermarket, wear much the same kind of clothes, buy and eat much the same kind of foods, live in much the same way.

In effect, therefore, the enterprise system—a dynamic, evolving and democratic method of doing business—has gone far towards the creation of a classless society through a dramatic upward levelling of the living standards of all who have been exposed to it. In so doing it has enlarged the dimensions of freedom of the average man and woman on this continent far beyond anything imaginable a century, or even half a century ago.

The creation of this cornucopia of plenty has, of course, given rise to problems of its own. There are still Canadians who, by modern standards, could hardly be classed as affluent; perfect harmony between management and labour is still but a vague dream. In fact the conflict between management and labour is still very much alive—in the enterprise society it probably never could be eliminated completely—but intelligent management is interested in the ambitions of labour.

These ambitions are a powerful force to harness to production, while improved production, in turn, means better profits, better wages and reasonable labour-management harmony. Even partial employer-employee harmony in the enterprise society redounds to the benefit of not only the members of the productive team but to all segments of the society, including the government which, whatever the tax structure, garners more in good times than in periods of business depression.

The current corporate tax level makes government an equal partner with industrial management in the profitable operation of an enterprise, for it takes half the profits regardless of the fact that it assumes none of the risks. In the bargain, it is responsible for legislation which can be construed in some instances as constrictive and, in the case of the more aggressive entrepreneur, actually hamstringing.

This brings us to the question: Are we legislating private enterprise out of Canadian business?

An examination of the challenges, legislative trends, and governmental decisions over a period of years certainly throws some light on the question. One of the main gauntlets at the feet of the enterprise system was that hurled in 1848 in Karl Marx's Manifesto, a document which became far better known after Lenin's communists achieved power in Russia at the time of the collapse of the Czarist regime in 1917.

The Manifesto urged the violent overthrow of capitalism and the securing of power in order to centralize all instruments of production in the hands of the state. Ten specific steps to achieve the elimination of "the conditions of bourgeois production" were spelled out. Interestingly enough some of them have actually been brought into existence without bloodshed by democratic governments, and have been accepted with varying degrees of cheerfulness by the general populace.

The one step adopted almost universally has been the heavy progressive or graduated income tax, familiar to all working Canadians but, strangely enough, a comparatively new impost in the history of our country. Until 1916, the Government of Canada relied almost exclusively for its revenue on customs and excise taxes. In that year, a Business Profits War Tax was enacted which provided for a tax of 25 per cent on the profits of an incorporated business to the extent that such profits exceeded seven per cent of the capital employed in the business. This tax was extended by annual revisions to the end of 1920 and was also increased in rate.

In July, 1917, the Minister of Finance took the unprecedented step of imposing a four per cent tax on corporate profits (to be paid if greater than the Business Profits War Tax) in addition to levying a tax on personal incomes. In the following year, the corporate rate of the war profits tax was raised to six per cent.

The end of the First World War did not halt the upward trend in corporation taxation. In 1919, the corporation income tax was raised to ten per cent. In the following year, the basic tax structure was completed by the introduction of the general sales tax. The only departure from the trend towards increasing corporation taxes was the reduction of the corporate rate in 1926 from ten per cent to nine per cent.

In 1930, with the pressure for increased revenues to balance their budgets, the provinces for the first time established corporation profits taxes, starting with rates ranging from one to four per cent. Originally, these were only enacted in the provinces of British Columbia, Alberta, Saskatchewan, Manitoba, Ontario and Quebec. In 1932 and 1935, there were further tax increases, with the Federal Government now taxing corporation profits at 15 per cent.

To sum up, in the ten years from 1929 to 1939, the federal corporation income taxes had almost doubled. Moreover, by the end of this decade, all of the then nine provinces were taxing corporation incomes at rates varying from one to ten per cent.

During the Second World War, the taxes paid by corporations were greatly increased by the establishment of an excess profits tax. These imposts, which before the war rarely yielded more than $50 million annually, in 1944 brought in revenue of $740 million from the combination of corporation and excess profits taxes.

With the end of the war, the excess profits tax was gradually reduced and ultimately eliminated in 1947, when the corporation income tax was established at a flat rate of 30 per cent, 10 per cent less than the minimum rate payable during the war. For 1949-1950, the corporation tax was changed to a two-bracket levy of ten per cent on the first $10,000, and 33 per cent on the excess. In 1952, the corporation rates, now including an old age security tax of two per cent, were raised to 22 per cent on the first $10,000, and 52 per cent on the excess.

Though minor revisions have taken place during the subsequent years, the basic structure has remained constant. At the present time, corporation income tax rates are 18 per cent on the first $35,000 of taxable income, and 47 per cent on the excess over the $35,000. In addition, corporations are required to pay an old age security tax of three per cent on their total taxable income. Adding these two taxes together, the federal rates are 21 per cent on the first $35,000 of the taxable income, and 50 per cent on the remainder.

Taking into account the federal tax abatement to the provinces, the combined federal and provincial rates (including the old age security tax) are, in the industrial provinces of Ontario and Quebec, 23 per cent on the first $35,000 of taxable income, and 52 per cent on the excess. In Manitoba and Saskatchewan, they are 22 per cent and 51 per cent respectively; in the remaining provinces, they total 21 per cent and 50 per cent.

Thus it will be seen that in the past 40 years the federal and provincial governments have become substantial partners in Canadian industry, sharing largely in the earnings of successful companies.

In the field of municipal taxation, the situation has not greatly changed over the past 50 years, except that the tax rates and assessment on all properties have mounted with the increased needs of municipalities. There has been, however, a movement to tax corporations and other business firms at higher rates than residential and farm owners. For instance, in the Province of Ontario, by a system of grants, the actual rate of tax paid by homeowners and farmers is each year considerably lower than that paid by industrial and commercial owners. Thus corporations and other businesses, in addition to paying a business tax in relation to occupied property, pay ordinary property taxes at a higher mill rate than do other property owners.

In addition to the payment of federal and provincial taxes, corporations face many problems and difficulties arising from tax laws and regulations. In the first place, extra burdens and difficulties arise because the Provinces of Ontario and Quebec have not accepted the offer of the Federal Government to collect their corporation taxes, but have their own laws and collection machinery. Thus companies must file separate returns and make payments to such provincial governments and, for this purpose, must allocate their profits among the particular provinces according to prescribed and by no means simple formulas.

Moreover, with the passage of years, tax legislation has tended to become increasingly complicated so that more and more companies find it necessary or advantageous to employ skilled tax experts. For instance, complicated rules have developed regarding such matters as the depreciation of industrial property and allowable expenses for tax purposes, as well as the intricate rules applicable to the numerous tax incentives which have been established, modified, and frequently withdrawn in whole or in part, during the past ten years.

A corporation, in addition to paying its own tax, must also collect other taxes and remit the money to the federal and provincial governments. Thus, all corporations are required to withhold from wages and salaries the tax payable by their employees, according to tax tables based on earnings and family status.

Moreover, manufacturing corporations are required to collect a 12 per cent federal sales tax on the goods they sell, and this tax also must be remitted to the Crown. In some cases, provincial retail sales taxes are involved and must be collected. The collection and remission of all these taxes places a heavy reponsibility on the employer and necessitates the employment of additional staff to carry out these duties.

And then there is the matter of the combines laws and their effect on modern Canadian business. Canadian combines legislation, which is now contained in the Combines Investigation Act, was originally enacted in 1889, ostensibly to preserve competition in manufactured goods and other products. Generally speaking, the legislation applies only to the production and distribution of articles that may be the subject of trade or commerce and, with a few exceptions, does not apply to services.

One important effect of the legislation is that it discourages desirable co-operation between manufacturers. While the legislation stipulates that certain acts of a co-operative nature are not illegal, and specifies others which are per se unlawful, it has the effect of discouraging legitimate co-operation for the improvement of business practices and resultant benefit to the economy.

Similarly, a manufacturer who wishes to expand by buying the business of a competitor must take into account the provisions of the Combines Act dealing with mergers. These provisions are difficult to interpret and for this reason there is often considerable doubt as to whether a proposed merger may contravene the law.

In addition, the combines legislation contains provisions regarding trade practices relating to the distribution of goods. These provisions are directed against price discrimination, predatory pricing, discriminatory promotional allowances, misleading price advertising, and resale price maintenance. While this legislation was designed to eliminate practices which are unfair to the competitors of a preferred purchaser or to the general public, the legislation has often caused uncertainty as to what practices of companies in the distribution of their goods are permitted.

Manufacturers and other distributors of goods must constantly review their distribution practices in the light of the trade practices provisions of the Combines Investigation Act.

Private enterprise has been legislated almost completely out of one industry—hydro-electric power—over a period of some 60 years. When, in the early years of the Twentieth Century, it became evident that the development of hydro-electric power would become a key industry in Canada, more especially in the central provinces of Ontario and Quebec, a strong movement arose in favour of keeping the water powers of the country in the public domain instead of allowing their development by private corporations. This "public ownership" movement gained especial strength in Ontario and finally led to the establishment of the Hydro-Electric Power Commission. The publicly-owned hydro-electric undertaking of Ontario, known in the province as the "Hydro", is an organization of a large number of partner-municipalities, co-ordinated into groups or systems for securing common action with respect to power supplied.

It had its beginning in 1903 when, as a result of public agitation to ensure the provision of adequate supplies of electric power for distribution throughout the province at low cost, seven municipalities united under statutory authority in appointing an investigating commission to deal with power problems.

This commission, known as the Ontario Power Commission, completed its work in 1906, and by special act in the same year the Ontario Government created the present Hydro-Electric Power Commission of Ontario. The operations of this undertaking have grown rapidly and today some 90 per cent of the electrical power consumed in the province is supplied by the Commission.

Subsequently Manitoba, Nova Scotia, New Brunswick, and Saskatchewan established Hydro-Electric Commissions on the model of the Ontario system. In Quebec and British Columbia, on the other hand, the development of hydro-electric power was left in the hands of private corporations until comparatively recent times.

British Columbia was the first of these two big provinces to "nationalize" power. On Tuesday, August 1, 1961, the Social Credit government of Premier W. A. C. Bennett took over control of the B.C. Electric Co. Ltd. as well as the reports, plans and studies of the Peace River Power Development Co., which was formed by the interests of Swedish financier Axel Wenner-Gren.

Three days later, after the third and final reading of the take-over bill, the government sent a cheque for nearly $111 million to the Company to compensate shareholders.

The dissatisfied shareholders pressed for a better settlement and, in 1962, the government increased its payment to $171.8 million. Subsequent legal action resulted in a provincial Supreme Court decision that the expropriation of the power company was not only beyond the authority of the Legislature, but that the government's expropriation price was about $20 million lower than its value to the original owners.

Finally, in September, 1963, a little more than two years after the take-over of the utility, an out-of-court agreement was reached on a price of a little more than $197 million.

Unlike the long battle experienced on Canada's west coast following expropriation, Quebec's decision to take over ownership of several private power companies and assign them to the province's Quebec Hydro was accepted by the shareholders, albeit grudgingly. In fact the directors of the largest of the private companies involved, Shawinigan Water and Power, advised shareholders that, although the government's per share offer was inadequate, the alternative to accepting it might produce a more unsatisfactory net result.

An example of legislative exclusion of private enterprise in the field of transportation was the creation in 1937 of Trans-Canada Air Lines as a government monopoly of the transcontinental air services in Canada. In 1936 the Canadian Government exhorted the owners of private airlines to organize a transcontinental airline, but difficulties in raising capital in the depression years were apparently too great for the private concerns without direct assistance from the government.

Consequently, the government approached the two Canadian transcontinental railways and the largest airline operator, Canadian Airways. It was proposed that the airports and communications system would be provided by the government and that the new airline would operate on a non-profit basis with the government indemnifying it against losses. Each of the three participants would appoint two directors to the new company's board, with the government naming three directors because of its preparedness to underwrite any losses.

The government's offer proved unacceptable to both the Canadian Pacific Railway and Canadian Airways because they saw no difference between directors representing the CNR and those representing the government. In their view five of the nine directors would be government appointees, with the CNR and government combined contributing only a third of the capital.

Result was the incorporation of Trans-Canada Air Lines as a subsidiary of Canadian National Railways in April, 1937. Exclusive rights to transcontinental and international air services were vested in the government's airline. Furthermore, a subsequent government order directed that any company engaged in other forms of transportation must divest itself of any airline affiliate within one year after the war.

While the Government later rescinded its divestment order insofar as TCA and Canadian Pacific Air Lines were concerned, and allowed CPA limited domestic service and the right to participate to a certain extent in international air carriage, the dominant and quasi-monopolistic position of Trans-Canada Air Lines, now known as Air Canada, has been maintained.

There also exists in Canada today considerable legislation at the federal, provincial, and municipal levels which gives government agencies and farmers the power to take measures for controlling the marketing of farm products. In the case of tobacco there is even a system of production control, and in the instance of alcoholic beverages the sale to the general public is controlled by provincial and territorial government liquor control authorities.

It is not the intention of the author to challenge, or even examine critically, the reason for the introduction of these various acts of legislation. They do not constitute anything like a complete list and they are recorded in only the briefest of form to indicate that legislation exists which maintains control of certain aspects of business even though, by and large, Canadian legislators at all three levels of government subscribe to the principles of private, competitive enterprise.

Clearly, the old debate about private enterprise versus state control has lost much of its point and no longer quite fits today's situation. Ours is now a mixed economy with both a private and a public sector in which, while private enterprise activities predominate, government intervention, supervision and control are playing an ever greater role.

Professor David W. Slater, in the summer 1966 issue of *The Canadian Banker*, notes that the Department of Industry and the emerging Department of Manpower are indicators of machinery and programs for more active intervention by the Federal Government in economic development.

"Considerations in Canadian commercial policy, issues of foreign ownership and control, regulations of international capital flows, poverty programs, regional development interests and policies, national policies in scientific and medical research and the pursuit of national educational interests—all provide new impetus to the government to use its power for national plans of social and economic development," comments the Queen's University professor in his capacity as editor of the journal of The Canadian Bankers' Association.

Yet—and this is important—Canada's stand in economic planning, despite the evidence of recent activity, is still both experimental and cautious. Presumably, the thinking of the federal legislators continues to be influenced by the knowledge that, come what may, the contribution of the producer will still be essential to the soundness of our economy and our society. But the producer, with his responsibility for converting national resources into national wealth, will only be enabled to give of his best if he knows that there is both respect and encouragement for private enterprise within the society in which he operates.

How can private enterprise be encouraged? The answer lies in a national fiscal policy that will facilitate the attainment of Canada's basic economic objectives. The establishment of such a policy was suggested in the first annual review of the Economic Council of Canada.

"We therefore urge that such policy be developed with a view to encouraging progress towards these objectives in two important ways," wrote the authors of the review. "First, it must be designed to promote adequate growth of total demand in the economy as a basis for attaining high employment and high output. Second, it must be vitally concerned with the impact of the tax system on the competitive position of Canadian producers. This implies, among other things, the need for removing, or avoiding the use of, particular fiscal measures which handicap the competitive production and marketing capabilities of Canadian suppliers, especially in relation to those of their chief competitors in the United States."

The last sentence of the quoted paragraph certainly fitted the government's 11 per cent sales tax on production machinery and equipment, a piece of legislation which most definitely was punishing to the producer and which raised the hackles of the business community to such an extent that the government decided to abandon it in stages.

Worthwhile cuts in corporation income taxes are also implicit in any fiscal policy designed to encourage enterprise and, to substantiate this argument, the following quotation from an address by the late President Kennedy takes on added weight:

"The single most important fiscal weapon available to strengthen the national economy is the federal tax policy. The right kind of tax cut at the right time is the most effective measure that this government could take to spur our economy forward. For the facts of the matter are that our present tax system is a drag on economical recovery and economic growth, biting heavily into the purchasing power of every taxpayer and every consumer. . . ."

And again: "Our tax rates, in short, are so high as to weaken the very essence of the progress of a free society, the incentive for additional return for additional effort. . . ."

President Kennedy was referring to the situation in the United States, but his comments are equally valid when applied to Canada.

It has been said that our society's increasing complexity will inevitably result in more government direction and participation in business affairs, but this does not necessarily mean that the more complex the society, the more the automatic need for government control. The increasing complexity of the national economy, however, presents a stiffer and stiffer challenge to Canadian businessmen. To combat the threat of more and more socialistic legislation, the entrepreneur must prove on a continuing basis that private enterprise is best for Canada as a nation and all Canadians as individuals.

One of the most articulate of the champions of free enterprise, Clarence Randall, a man who found time not only to run a great steel company in the United States but to write convincingly of the vitality and meaningfulness of the enterprise system, had this to say in *Freedom's Faith*, one of his books on this subject:

"Free enterprise exists not to serve the individual, but to serve society. It encourages each man to advance his own interests, but only so long as what he does also advances the welfare of the community. The test of whether a businessman fully understands and believes in the system is that of whether he displays at all times an awareness of his social responsibility. Each decision that he takes for his company and each policy that he establishes must meet that test, or he jeopardizes our way of life and invites reprisal from an angry public through some form of collective intervention in his affairs."

John A. Fuller, who was chairman and chief executive officer of the Shawinigan Water and Power Company before it was taken over by the Quebec Government, warned in a public address before the Canadian Manufacturers' Association in 1962 that businessmen must evidence a greater degree of missionary zeal on behalf of the free enterprise way of life. He was, however, far from pessimistic about the future of the system despite the dangers surrounding it.

". . . . the present is a time of challenge for the competitive free enterprise system and it will face even greater challenges in the future," he said. "It is too dynamic a thing and has too large a potential for even greater benefit to mankind to lose by default. Indeed, by its very nature, it should produce within itself those responses of courage, initiative, realism and action that are required for its survival."

Such an approach would indicate that, although private enterprise faces a constant threat, the defence against it being legislated out of Canadian business lies squarely in the lap of the entrepreneurs themselves. They have to present constant proof that, despite its obvious advantages, the enterprise system is also the best way to keep Canada on the road to even greater prosperity than she enjoys today.

Summing up, it must be said that the current healthy condition of private industry as a whole in Canada, nourished as it has been over recent years by massive injections of new investment capital, both native and foreign, hardly supports the proposition that private enterprise is being legislated out of Canadian business.

Against this must be set the implications of government's growing role in the economy and of legislative developments in Quebec and British Columbia within the past half dozen years which have had the effect of making the production of one vital and basic commodity, namely hydro-electric power, a near public monopoly in Canada today. If this can happen so easily and with so small an outcry in the case of one industry, can it not happen again in others?

At the federal level, the vagaries of national policy have always been an imponderable with which the entrepreneur has had to reckon. The recent Canada-U.S. Auto Agreement serves as a reminder that changing national policies, while they may offer new opportunities for some, can signal the beginning of the end for others. In short, in today's world, they are more than ever a potential occupational hazard to be taken into account by even the most prosperous of companies.

BIBLIOGRAPHY AND MATERIAL SOURCES

Dr. William H. Peterson, Associate Professor of Economics, Graduate School of Business Administration, New York University, in 1962 address to CMA's Annual General Meeting at Montreal.

The Manifesto of the Communist Party, by Karl Marx and Frederick Engels.

Hydro—Canada Year Book, 1939 and subsequent years to 1965. (N.B. The ten per cent of Ontario electricity not supplied by Hydro is generated by industries and by urban municipalities such as Gananoque, Fort Erie, and Sault Ste. Marie.)

Shawinigan Water & Power and B.C. Electric "take-overs", material assembled from various sources, chiefly Canadian Press and other newspaper reports, carefully checked for accuracy.

Government legislation to control marketing of Farm Products: Canada Year Book 1966 and 1963-64.

Humphrey B. Style, president of the Canadian Manufacturers' Association, 1965-66, address on "Canadian Industry and the National Economy" before the National Defence College, Kingston ,Ontario, October 12, 1965.

Clarence Randall, Chairman of the Board, Inland Steel Co., United States of America, and author of several books on private enterprise (*Freedom's Faith, A Creed for Free Enterprise*).

John A. Fuller, Chairman and Chief Executive Officer, Shawinigan Water and Power Company, Montreal, quoted from address "Whither Private Enterprise?" at CMA Annual General Meeting, Montreal, 1962.

Economics of Canada Transportation, by A. W. Currie.

First Annual Report of Trans-Canada Air Lines, 1937

Taxation in Canada (Third Edition) by J. Harvey Perry, published by University of Toronto Press.

The National Finances 1965-66, published by the Canadian Tax Foundation, Toronto.

Combines Investigation Act, R.S.C. 1952, as amended, The Queen's Printer, Ottawa.

The Canadian Banker, Summer, 1966, Journal of the Canadian Bankers' Association.

Economic Council of Canada—First Annual Review, December, 1964, The Queen's Printer, Ottawa.

T. C.
Douglas

THE GOVERNMENT AND THE ECONOMY

T. C. Douglas, M.P.

*T. C. Douglas was born at Falkirk, Scotland, in 1904, and came
to Canada with his family in 1911. He attended school in
Winnipeg, and received degrees from Brandon College and
McMaster University. Mr. Douglas was first elected to the House
of Commons in 1935 as a C.C.F. Member of Parliament, and
from 1944 to 1961 served as Premier of Saskatchewan. Since
1961 he has been Federal Leader of the New Democratic Party,
and since 1962 Member of Parliament for the constituency of
Burnaby-Coquitlam, B.C.*

In my view there is a clear and positive case today documenting
the need for an expanded government role in the overall direction
of the Canadian economy. The case rests upon the evidence of the
long sweep in our social evolution, upon the contemporary experience and evident failure of our economy to measure up to its
potentials, and upon the political and social goals which we set for
ourselves as a Canadian people. Contrary to what is often as-
serted, the expansion of government need not at all imply a

growth of restriction, an erosion of freedom, or a loss of initiative and enterprise. Rather, the people of this country, acting through democratically-elected governments, can broaden our freedom and opportunity, assure higher standards of living for ourselves, and impart a new dimension to national growth. But to do so we must have governments prepared to accept an enlarging role, inspired to meet new challenges and organized to carry out creative new responsibilities.

As we move into the second century of Confederation, it is well to remind ourselves that the role of the state has always loomed large in our history. The economic historians have documented the story. The creation of Canada as a nation and a national economy in 1867 was first and foremost a deliberate political act. In our formative decades a framework of deliberate government policies—western land settlement and resource development, all-Canadian east-west rail and water transportation, and the protective tariff to aid the establishment of industry in the central provinces—all gave shape, dynamism and direction to the national economy.

Subsequently, the sweeping impact of two major world wars, of the Great Depression of the 1930's, of the revolution in economic thinking, and of the growth of urbanization and industry, inevitably propelled our governments into a greatly expanded economic and social role. The responsibility and potential capacity of government to act in many new fields came to the fore. Perhaps the most fundamental was the need to combat the waste of unemployment. But the provision of broader economic and social services, the regulation and control of monopoly, and the securing of a more equitable distribution of income were all increasingly recognized as important tasks of government. By the end of World War II the concept of the "mixed economy", in which government accepted responsibility, in theory at least, for full employment, stable income, and a broadening range of services, was well established. Perhaps only an unreconstructed minority, resentful of the continuing evolution in economic thought and social practice, remained to mourn the demise of the superstitions of classical "laissez-faire".

*   *   *

The experience of the past two decades and the prospect before us now bring new evidence of the need for more dynamic and creative government leadership in economic affairs. Not only has there been a failure to fulfil well-established responsibilities, but even more a dismal inertia in facing up to the major new issues of the rapidly changing world. Throughout much of the past two decades—as shown in the 1962 report of the Royal Commission on Banking and Finance, the annual reviews of the Economic Council of Canada, and numerous other studies—the actual performance of the Canadian economy has lagged seriously behind its real capacity and potential. Recurrent heavy unemployment, a slow rate of growth in per capita income and productivity, successive spurts of inflationary price increases, periodic international imbalance, a mushrooming of foreign ownership and control of Canadian industry, and considerable regional economic distress— all these economic failures have been documented and measured, leaving no room for complacency even in a relatively affluent Canada. In part, some of these adverse developments have stemmed from external forces over which we have little control. But much of the responsibility can be traced to weak policies by the government, and ultimately to its reluctance to intervene in the economy with the necessary vigour, imagination and long-range common sense.

It is instructive to note at least a few of the broad dimensions of some of these problems, because they emphasize the urgent importance of enlarged government policies and programmes to grapple with them. In their first two reviews the Economic Council has provided a basis for estimating roughly the extent of the total national loss in goods and services suffered by the people of Canada because of the failure of our economy to produce up to its potential capacity. The shortfall of performance below potential is shown in Chart 1, which also makes clear the waste incurred because of excessive unemployment. Over the nine years from 1957 to 1965, losses of output valued in constant 1957 prices aggregated over $21 billion—about $1200 for every man, woman and child in the country. In annual terms this represented an average of close to $2.4 billion, equivalent to the average annual investment in total non-residential construction over the same period.

As Chart I shows, the largest part of the loss in output can be attributed to severe unemployment, which ran well above the rate of 3 per cent of the labour force set out by the Council as a realistically attainable goal. At the same time, gains in production per employed person in Canada have also lagged well behind potential levels. Here the Council has shown that between 1953 and 1963 the increase in gross national product per capita was one of the lowest among industrially advanced countries (Chart 2). Over that period, they commented, "the Canadian economy appears to have experienced one of the slowest rates of growth of any industrially advanced country of the world, both in terms of average productivity and average living standards."

Even with some improvement achieved in the business upswing between 1960 and 1965, the Organization for Economic Cooperation and Development has reported that the increase in output per employed person in Canada over this recent period, averaging 2.6 per cent annually, was *below* that of any of its member countries except Britain, which averaged 2.5 per cent. Japan had a record of 8.3 per cent increase in output per worker, the United States 2.9 per cent, and the average for all OECD countries was 3.7 per cent.

Despite this lagging productivity performance, the overall rate of growth in the economy since 1961 has been strong. This has been largely due, of course, to the rise in total employment, stemming from both a rapid increase in the number of workers in the labour force and from a reduction of unemployment below the extreme 7 per cent levels of five years ago. But this growth and improvement has brought a new set of problems—or rather, revived an old set—which present government policies and normal market forces have never been able to solve. The most serious, of course, is the recent rapid rise in the general price level and the cost of living. For the fourth time in the past two decades we are going through a serious inflationary spiral of prices. Apart altogether from the unjust burdens this process inflicts upon millions of Canadians in the lower-income brackets, and especially upon those with low fixed incomes such as pensioners, these periodic price outbursts have always adversely affected both economic efficiency and sustained, long-run economic growth.

It has long been accepted that in a mixed economy the alert and vigorous use of fiscal and monetary policies to maintain economic stability is a basic government responsibility. But both historical experience and contemporary evidence have shown that a simple-minded reliance upon these tools alone—even when very broadly interpreted—is completely inadequate to meet the economic challenges of full employment, rapid growth, reasonable price stability and international balance in a world of accelerating change. Rather, we must also have a wide array of supplementary and selective government policies and programmes. They must be organized, moreover, not just for emergency intervention in times of crisis, but they must be planned on a comprehensive and continually evolving basis.

This kind of economic planning involves, first, arrival at a consensus upon broad economic goals, then the elaboration and reconciliation of specific operational targets to be achieved in moving toward these goals, and finally a readiness to plan and implement the still more detailed policies and action programmes which will carry the economy forward on target. In all of this government must obviously play a key leadership role. This is not the place to try to set out just what the government should do, but some of the broad and more pressing requirements of the contemporary economic situation—supplementary to basic fiscal and monetary policy—might be briefly mentioned.

It is clear, for example, that maintaining a rapid growth in employment, given the accelerating pace of labour-saving technology and automation, has become a very complex process. An indispensable adjunct to normal market forces is an array of labour market services embracing adequate information and forecasting of employment change, aids for geographic and occupational mobility on the part of workers, long-range manpower training and retraining, and effective adjustment programmes to meet technological and economic shifts in employment. The improvement in productivity advance calls for expanded investment in many forms of human capital and human skills, a great extension in public social capital, particularly in meeting the mushrooming needs of our cities, and a rapid expansion of industrial construction, machinery and equipment. A far greater effort in research and development, in the application of new technology, and in basic scientific investigation must be launched. We need to explore methods for increasing specialization in Canadian industry, for expanding foreign trade on a truly multi-lateral basis, and for effecting a sweeping rationalization of our industrial structure to make our economy more fully competitive in the international league. An important lift to growth in real production and consumption should be sought, on one hand, by the expansion of long-standing public services and the introduction of new public programmes. On the other hand, there is a pressing urgency to provide adequate consumer protection and information and to curtail wasteful production processes and inflated selling costs. These latter add nothing to the real level of output, and in fact impose a burden upon our economy equal in cost to many of our basic social services.

In all of these economic areas there is urgent need and wide scope for extending the role of government. But little will be gained if this extension takes place only on a makeshift, haphazard basis, with response to this pressure and that, usually at the last moment. The obvious result of the traditional sticking-plaster approach to the problems of a complex, integrated economic system has been confusion, inconsistency and conflict in public policy. Rather, as I have stressed, the expansion of the government's role must proceed in a planned, co-ordinated way, with a firm but flexible integration and consistency among strategic economic goals, specific operational targets, and applied action programmes.

In this planned approach it is essential to adopt new vigour, imagination, and a willingness to experiment and innovate in the whole range of traditional techniques of government intervention; for example, in fiscal, monetary and commercial policies, in the use of legislation and statutory regulation, in new forms of grants, subsidies and incentives to private enterprise, and in the broad revenue and spending powers of all levels of government. In the same way, if government is to effectively carry out its larger and more complex responsibilities in the period ahead, it must also be prepared to intervene directly in the economy. This includes recognizing the need for an expanded role for government enterprise whenever it is appropriate to the circumstances, the need for new vehicles to mobilize private savings for industrial investment, the possibilities for a productive partnership with private industry, and the long-range importance of direct participation in research and development.

*   *   *

Thus while the longer-term evolution of modern economic organization and the need for greatly improved economic performance point to an expanding role for government in the Canadian economy, there are equally compelling social and political objectives moving us in the same direction. These later objectives depend in part upon the successful achievement of faster and more stable economic growth. But they may also, in themselves, involve removing important causes of waste and inefficiency in the use of human and material resources. In this way they powerfully reinforce longer-run progress toward higher levels of output. At the same time there may well be situations where the goal of maximum economic performances comes into conflict with social and political objectives. Here again the important problem of measuring economic costs against broad social benefits, and of resolving conflict the best way, can usually only be met by responsible government action.

One of the most important issues concerns the pressing need for greater social equality of all Canadians and a more equitable distribution of income. Statistical data on the distribution of income by size show that between the early 1930's and the end of World War II we made some progress in narrowing the gap between the very rich and the very poor. But from 1951 onward, although average incomes have risen appreciably, the proportions of the total going to each income class have barely changed. Thus in 1951 the lowest 20 per cent of non-farm families and single individuals received only 4.0 per cent of all income payments. By 1963 this figure had crept up to only 4.5 per cent. In contrast, in the latter year the most affluent 20 per cent of non-farm families and single individuals received 42.5 per cent of total income payments.

The data from the Dominion Bureau of Statistics also show that 18 per cent of all non-farm families and single individuals struggle along on less than $2,000 each year, and 29 per cent on less than $3,000. Incomes among farm families, of course, average considerably less than those in the non-farm sector, so that these figures understate the real extent of comparative poverty in our country. It is little wonder that in recent years we have come to an increasing awareness and concern about the severity of this problem, and about the shockingly large numbers of Candians—including employed workers and income earners, as well as those retired from or not participating in the labour market and other specially-disadvantaged groups—whose needs and potential contributions are so poorly dealt with in our economic and social system. The scope for increased government action clearly embraces substantial improvement in minimum wage levels, more adequate income-support measures, and special programmes directed on a long-range basis toward rescuing many potentially productive workers from the trap of self-perpetuating poverty.

There is a second issue of fundamental importance to our identity as Canadians and to our continued existence as a nation. This is the need to bring about balanced development among the major distinct regions which comprise our country so that each may participate in and contribute more fully to national growth. Here again the Economic Council has reported upon the great differences in average levels of income among the ten provinces and five broad regions. These differences have persisted over a long period of time, with marked disparities in rates of economic development among the regions. While parts of the country enjoy a high and rising level of prosperity, other parts have experienced severe losses of population, stagnancy and a pronounced relative decline. The result inevitably has been a feeling of disunity and even of disenchantment in the experiment of Canadian nationhood.

This does not mean, of course, that the "natural" economic advantages of some regions over others can be ignored. But government intervention with vigorous regional development policies and programmes, planned in a comprehensive way to search out and fully utilize the resources and assets of the lagging areas of the country, could go far toward redressing the persistent state of imbalance. Planned development, moreover, far from imposing a burden upon our economy, may well turn the tide in underdeveloped regions and thus make a net positive contribution both to greater interregional income equality and overall Canadian growth.

This leads me to a further problem of very great importance— how to deal with the significant extension of foreign ownership and control in the Canadian economy and all that it implies in terms of the loss of national economic vigour and political independence. This is an extremely complex, vital issue. Highly relevant information is hard to come by—largely because of the timidity of our government—and in any case the interpretation and evaluation of the effects of the growing external control of our domestic industry is extremely difficult. It is a field, moreover, where purely economic criteria alone cannot provide a guide to policy, since political and social values rightly play a large, if not easily measured, role. Thus there is deep disagreement between those who appear to believe that increasing foreign control has had a net beneficial effect upon Canada and those who are concerned that so-called continental integration tends to reduce our country to the status of an economic and political satellite of the United States. But for better or for worse, it will undoubtedly be intervention on the part of government, or lack of such intervention, which will be decisively important in charting our future course.

There is little dispute concerning the widespread extent of the foreign takeover of many of our most important manufacturing and resource development industries—principally by American capital. While it is no doubt true that such capital has played an important part in Canadian economic development, it is equally true that foreign direct investment to secure ownership or control will have serious effects upon the longer-run health of our economy.

In the first place, the growth of such investment, mainly from the United States, means a high, growing and never ending service of this capital in the form of dividends, or a further pyramiding of foreign control through the leverage of retained earnings.

Second, foreign direct investment has had a significant effect upon the structure and performance of our manufacturing industry. Foreign investment has occurred through the establishment of subsidiaries and branch plants of large international companies. Our economy is vitally influenced by the policies of these companies toward their branch plants in the fields of exports and imports, sales and purchases between units of each company, allocation of capital funds, and research and development. Accumulating evidence—such as that compiled by Mr. Eric Kierans, for example, or that presented before U.S. Congressional hearings—indicates that for a great many international corporations the role of a foreign subsidiary is principally to increase the market for the parent corporation and in various ways to augment the earnings accruing at the centre, even at the cost of growth and profitability by the subsidiary concern. Moreover, the resulting "branch plant economy" which has been built up in Canada leads to a structure of industry in which there are a large number of relatively small scale units of production, each maintained by a giant American firm, and among which competition is likely to be only nominal. This branch plant industry is fostered in part by tariff protection, but by its very nature it tends to be high in cost and lacking in competitive capabilities. Moreover, it is likely to be sorely deficient in research and development, in initiative and aggressiveness, in adaptability and response to new opportunities.

An attempt to contain, if not actually reduce, the extent of foreign control does not at all imply either restrictive measures upon the inflow of foreign capital or a further retreat behind tariff walls. Rather, we must first seek to direct as much of this capital inflow as possible into the form of loan rather than equity investment. This is the pattern successfully followed, for example, by most of the provincial and municipal governments and by our publicly-owned utilities. It is clear that significant further strides in this direction could be taken by publicly owned companies and development corporations—initially financed as to equity by domestic savings—in many industrial fields. Government action, moreover, can do much—even if only by way of more active tax enforcement—to require fuller disclosure of relations between subsidiaries and parent companies and to assure that these relations are really carried on in a way appropriate to Canada's domestic economic interests. Finally, all the techniques and programmes aimed at effecting a more productive and internationally competitive Canadian economy—the increase and channelling of domestic savings into equity investment, greater stability and planning of capital investment, the negotiation of tariff reductions on a multilateral basis, increased encouragement and direct public participation in research and development, increased aid for education and training, and programmes to foster greater specialization and rationalization of industry with adequate safeguards for domestic consumers—all of these measures, actively pursued under government leadership, will make for a stronger, more independent Canadian economy.

The more our economic independence grows, the less we should be exposed to possible instability in the American economy. Even more, our capacity to fulfil our political obligations on the international scene will be enhanced. This is essentially the strategic role of a fairly affluent and independent middle power, closely attached to the advanced nations of Europe and America, steadily extending relations with the Communist world, and looked up to and relatively trusted by most developing countries.

Our relationship with the developing countries also provides an important imperative for expanded government economic action and policy. This is a matter, first, of a moral or social obligation in the shrinking world of today where the needs of economic development are so large and pressing. Increasingly, whatever happens in seemingly far-away places must weigh upon our conscience as world citizens. But it is also true that whatever assistance we extend to the developing nations—either direct aid or special efforts to expand trade relations favourable to them—will redound to our long-range interests and advantage. In many ways we have lost and continue to lose opportunities for making a distinct Canadian contribution through our traditional connections in the Commonwealth, through our unique position and potentially unique role vis-à-vis Latin America, and through our undoubted acceptance and prestige among many of the newly-independent nations. To overcome this default of the past and the growing challenge of the future we stand in great need of the kind of bold government leadership which will advance our domestic economic growth, our social goals, and our political identity and maturity.

CHART 1
ACTUAL OUTPUT AND EMPLOYMENT AS PERCENTAGE OF POTENTIAL OUTPUT AND EMPLOYMENT

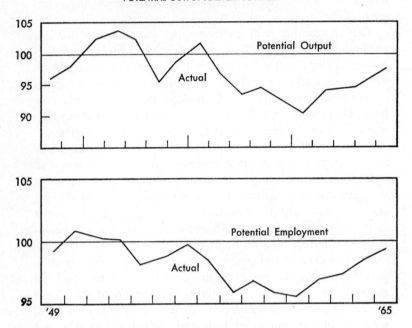

Note: Potential civilian employment defined as 97 per cent of the civilian labour force.
Source: Economic Council of Canada, 2nd Annual Review.

CHART 2
INDEX NUMBERS OF REAL OUTPUT
1953 - 100

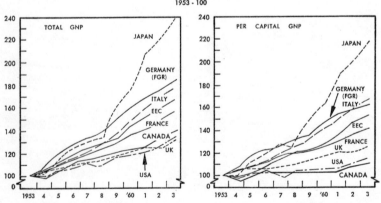

Source: Economic Council of Canada and Organization for Economic Co-operation and Development.

Gérard
Filion

A LEGITIMATE ROLE FOR GOVERNMENT
IN BUSINESS

Gérard Filion
   Gérard Filion was born at L' Isle-Verte, Quebec, in 1909.
He holds a Bachelor of Arts degree from Laval University
and a Master of Commerce degree from L'Ecole des Hautes
Etudes Commerciales in Montréal. Mr. Filion has been known
chiefly as the publisher and editorial writer of the French-
language newspaper, Le Devoir, *from 1947 to 1963, and as*
Vice-Chairman of the Canada Council from 1963 to 1964. He is
the present Vice-President of the General Investment Corporation
of Québec, and President of Marine Industries Limited.

The active participation of government in the business world is a
fact which may be deplored, but which first of all must be con-
ceded. Only in Québec, a province that can hardly be accused of
either out-and-out or even disguised socialism, does the government own about ten commercial enterprises, more or less flourishing, ranging from the production and distribution of electrical
energy to the construction of bridges and roads, and including a

mining development company, a sugar refinery, and the trade in alcoholic beverages. The activities of the federal government are even more diverse, as the abundance of corporations designated by "department", by "mandatory", and by "ownership" prove.

Before passing judgement on this phenomenon, perhaps it would be advisable to ask oneself why governments have been led to "invade" the field of economic activity. To begin with, it seems evident to me that, with the exception of certain cases which I will discuss later, these incursions have not followed any methodical plan of subversion perfected at length by some anonymous technocrat. Indeed oftentimes the government has intervened to save enterprises on the edge of bankruptcy that are judged essential to the general welfare; for example, railways and public transportation. In these cases it is simply a matter of salvaging crucial services whose disappearance would have grave consequences for the national economy. It is true that such actions have at times proved very profitable to certain private concerns who have helped themselves to public funds in order to replenish their own finances; however, this consideration has not the slightest relevance here.

A second series of interventions took place, during wartime especially, when it became necessary to create at great expense certain industries that private enterprise either would not or could not touch. This type of intervention produced the Polymer Corporation, Air Canada, Eldorado Mining, Atomic Energy of Canada, as well as various munitions plants. Once launched and making a profit, several have asked the reason for this act of unofficial "socialism" and demanded status as private industries. It was for this reason that the aluminum industries created by the American government during the last war were subsequently sold at competitive prices to certain large corporations. Similarly, Comsat was handed over to American private enterprise. At present several voices are openly demanding why the public funds invested in these industries were sold so cheaply to private interests, who used them to their own advantage rather than to the continuing benefit of the nation as a whole.

A third group of enterprises was created under pressure of strictly ideological considerations. The spectre of alcoholism, aided by an enormous and abusive propaganda program, has led governments to monopolize the sale of spirits, although no serious empirical study has proven this measure effective. The worst critics of alcoholic beverages go so far as to maintain that the government must assume partial responsibility for the ravages of excessive drinking, since it has the sole right to sell alcohol—a business which, it may be added, is very lucrative. What is more important, most of the governments of the western world reserve the right to own and exploit certain natural resources, especially electricity and coal. In this case it is a question of specific sectors whose potential is such that state control is essential for harmonious and autonomous economic development.

All in all, the impression is scarcely of a coherent and well-ordered policy, either in theory or in practice. On the contrary, it has been a matter of large-scale improvisations and decisions made with an eye to expediency, often without sufficient consideration of either consequences or implications. Here we are in the middle of the great comfortable tradition of Anglo-Saxon empiricism, which disregards problems so long as the discomfort they cause doesn't become intolerable. Even then the least painful remedy is sought, and one continues on his merry way, confident that each headache will have its time-tested-and-approved aspirin.

However, we must ask ourselves if these makeshift policies are still relevant today. Whether or not one accepts the theories of Professor McLuhan, which place us in the middle of a new revolution—the "communications" revolution—the fact remains that we now have at our disposal the analytical instruments which are the means of leaving the improvisation stage behind forever. First of all, on the macroeconomic level, it is becoming increasingly possible to describe what is real by means of a large number of highly sophisticated equations, and to solve these equations by feeding them to electronic brains of enormous capacity and extraordinary ability. Adam Smith's "invisible hand", which was, in fact, a simple confession of ignorance, is now revealing its fingers, tendons, and muscles. It is but one short, bold step to utilize these means to attain ends that we, not chance, have chosen.

While economics and econometrics have been flourishing, managerial techniques have been developing at a parallel rate. Thus from macroeconomics we can move on to consider industry and the very flexible and efficient process whereby its decisions are made and acted upon. In other words, just as we can control vast economic systems, so can we direct large commercial em-

pires; in both cases it is possible to introduce a practical rationalism and working effectiveness, and to utilize those precise instruments discussed above to attain fixed goals with a better-than-
average chance of success.

In a world that is becoming more and more rational in terms
of instruments whose calibration is known, it is absurd and even
dangerous to remain at the rudimentary stage of improvisation
and to make hasty action a habit. It is of the utmost necessity that
intervention on the part of public administration in the world of
business be subject to rationalization, justification, and efficacy.

First of all, let us consider rationalization. The super-abun-
dance of the so-called "crown" corporations with their various
charters must be examined coldly from two points of reference. In
the first place, one must determine which corporations are obsolete and then eliminate them; this is a fairly easy task and one
which is unlikely to lead to any major difficulties. The second
consideration calls for a much greater creative and imaginative
effort, requiring a redefination in the design and methods of interventions already made in order to assure their maximum efficacy.

At this point we run up against the thorny problem of whether
these interventions themselves are justified. I have already emphasized that most have been made as immediate circumstances
have warranted and often as a last resort. Is there a justification
that goes deeper? I believe there is.

It would be an easy mistake to make—as the numbers who
have already made it prove—to try to show that effective planning is not possible unless the private sector of industry is large
enough to be able to check and balance an economy which, in the
mass, is not state-controlled. For example, control of the banks
enables private enterprise to manage credit and to extend it to
those industries that will adhere to the terms of the credit plan;
this type of rationing is more effective than any number of ex-
hortations. In the same way, industries that have been national-
ized fit beautifully into the designs of the planners and can make
things difficult for those who refuse to conform; if, for example,
the state-owned iron industry refuses to raise its prices, and if it
enjoys a certain amount of preference, private enterprise will be
forced to follow suit in order not to jeopardise its long-term
profits.

However, it seems to me that this type of reasoning is worthless in practice. Whatever one's politico-economic ideology, massive nationalization, or even selective nationalization of important industrial sectors in Canada, is at most a very long-range prospect. Although an illustration of this type of planning could have a certain theoretical value, it would lead to useless speculation and contribute nothing to our present discussion. But the absence of these imposing perspectives should not imply that our discussion is mere idle chatter. In fact it is easy to show that there is a need for state intervention at two levels which, although less spectacular perhaps, are both crucial and urgent.

The first level is of a basically economic nature; it concerns balanced development. It is an established fact that any economy that has passed what Rostows calls "the kick-off stage", and that has reached the stage of mass economy, must be organized according to certain set exigencies. The crucial element in these constraints is harmony. Harmony must exist, first, between the different sectors of the economy; it must exist, too, among the different regions of the country.

Compatibility between sectors requires a balance among primary industries, secondary and tertiary industries, and what are known today as quarternary industries (education, research, development). Of course, one could always rely on the forces of nature or of competition to attain this desired balance. However, the efficacy of such an approach is not guaranteed, and, in any case, it would probably require an unduly long period of time. Therefore, any acceleration in the pace of the natural process must presuppose unusually large outlays, which, on a short-term basis, would have little profit value for what one might call the nation's industrial sub-structure. For example, it is currently admitted that industrial research is necessary if the economy is to progress. In the United States several large private firms specializing in this area (e.g. A. D. Little, Battle Memorial Institute) have achieved a large measure of success. It is imperative that similar organizations be set up in Canada if we do not wish to become mere vassals of the dynamic American technology. However, because of the weakness and the very structure of our industry, this sort of enterprise does not attract private capital; hence, it becomes necessary for government intervention through the creation of such organizations as the Ontario Research Foundation, the Saskatchewan Research Council, or the future Québec

Research Council. Moreover, the history of the Ontario Research Foundation is highly informative; far from being a financial burden to the government, this organization is beginning to earn at tractive profits after several years of operation. However, these examples are only isolated cases and it is to be deplored that our administrations do not make a systematic attempt to identify the elements lacking in our economic framework and to create them if necessary.

In addition, there are certain changes in structure that must be made if our industry is to remain strong and durable in the face of international markets and foreign commercial giants. If basic reorganization of certain industries becomes essential, the government should not wash its hands of the task. At present, the creation of organizations such as the General Society of Financing in Québec appears to be not only feasible but urgent. A similar case can be made for a speed-up in the development of primary resources: if there is not sufficient private capital for the job, I do not see why more companies such as SOQUEM (Société québecoise d'exploitation miniére) should not be considered, with the purpose of working side by side with established interests rather than against them.

Moreover, experience has shown that overall prosperity in a country does not mean that regional disparities in income, education, and employment will disappear. As a result, the government of every country has found it necessary to supplement its macroeconomic policies with regional development schemes, whose aim it is to build up areas that are either backward or lagging in their development. In fact, this problem is so complex that the solution, theoretical or practical, has completely eluded the investigators and officials. Even though continued competition may eventually assure the appearance of a certain amount of intersectorial harmony at the centre of a growing economy, a similar approach will not aid the development of outlying areas. The fact that these areas are not near established trade arteries makes them economically and socially depressed; what is more, far from improving with time their situation only deteriorates further with each passing year. The elimination or even the reduction of these regional disparities will not be brought about unless public authority intervenes with a very large allocation of capital, then sees to it that its investmest achieves maximum effect.

All the various regional development programs are inspired by a philosophy which, under the appearance of intervention, is basically non-interventionist. The programmers are content to offer certain tax concessions or cash subsidies to industries that want to set themselves up in these areas, and don't concern themselves particularly with the coherence of such actions or with the type of industry that has been established. In this way the state plays a purely passive part: rather than acting, it reacts, limiting its role to an occasional alteration in an isolated aspect of the problems that attend the development of a new industry. Thus even at the beginning it is debatable whether or not the new industries created in this way will continue to check the depression of the poor areas.

Our editorial writers and commentators, economic as well as political, emit occasional rumblings over the intolerable influence of foreign investment on our economy. This is indeed a very serious and delicate problem, as a whole graveyard of defunct political careers, as well as recent events, conclusively prove. Various solutions have been put forward, and some have even begun to be acted upon. At any rate, it seems certain that this situation cannot be solved, either on a long- or short-term basis, by the forces of the market alone. Here again the government must be expected to intervene in one way or another, perhaps acting jointly with private enterprise. The Canada Development Corporation served as the first trial balloon, but it now appears to have burst.

From the three-fold point of view of industrial reorganization, regional development, and economic independence, government intervention in the industrial and commercial sectors is not only inevitable but necessary. But what form should this intervention take? At the present time the government's rather nebulous plan of action is determined by past decisions coupled with current needs, and the net effect is both sporadic and disorganized. In the view of classical liberalism this is the only acceptable strategy; in the view of contemporary economic liberalism, which aims at maximum effectiveness and return, a different attitude and approach are necessary.

In this way we arrive full circle at the demands of rationalism mentioned above, which imply, if not reorganization, at least co-ordination of government initiative. The methods of co-ordination can be rather informal at first, uniting the directors of various government-controlled enterprises in work committees to ensure that their policies converge in the direction of maximum economic development. As a second step it would be necessary to assure that their plans for investment and development are in keeping with one another; if the state cannot blueprint the economic decisions of its own companies, one may suspect a priori that it is incapable of setting forth a larger plan for the economy as a whole.

Eventually, perhaps at some fairly distant date, the creation of a department of government participation to oversee all the various forms of government investment will become a necessity. Foreign countries have already taken the lead in this regard; for example, in Italy there is the IRI, in Mexico la Nacional Finanziera. At the present time it is becoming possible to invite the public at large to participate in the progress of these bodies by issuing common stock. Thus more than 80% of the monetary needs of the enterprises controlled by the Italian IRI are assured through standard financial channels. In this way the government can increase the impact of its investments and set up interdependent industrial organizations that will progress steadily in an ideal climate of co-operation. Viewed in this way, concrete planning becomes possible, and the economic future of the country is no longer at the mercy of irrational or purely extrinsic forces.

David
Lewis

HOW MUCH WELFARE DOES SOCIAL RESPONSIBILITY DEMAND?

David Lewis, M.P.

David Lewis, Q.C., is Member of Parliament for the constituency of York South in Metropolitan Toronto, and Deputy Leader of the New Democratic Party. Mr. Lewis came to Canada from Poland in 1921 at the age of twelve. He received his early education in Montréal, and later attended Oxford University as a Rhodes Scholar. During his long political career he has served as National Secretary, Vice-Chairman, Chairman, and President of the C.C.F. Party, was a leading member of the National Committee which founded the New Democratic Party in 1961, and has served as Vice-President since.

Canadians don't often realize that only three decades ago social security in Canada was almost nonexistent. At the federal level there was a niggardly old age pension at seventy with a means test, and pensions and allowances for war veterans. This was about all. There was no unemployment insurance, no universal pension, no contributory pension, no family allowances, no hospital insurance, no medicare. At the provincial and municipal levels there was not much more, except that these governments had the direct responsibility for welfare to indigents and for primary and secondary education.

The change in our laws has been dramatic in the last generation. So has the change in our attitudes. Not so long ago government pensions were condemned as humiliating to a person's self-respect. To be hungry, cold and destitute was somehow considered more dignified than to eat and be warm on a government pension. The old man whose feet were frozen because his shoes were worn through could say proudly, "but the holes in my shoes are mine own". And anyone who didn't see the virtue in this was a spendthrift and a parasite.

These old attitudes derived from the early mores of a work-oriented society and the exclusiveness of private charity. A dumb, submissive creature who worked hard and did what he was told was considered far superior to the sensitive person who rebelled against being treated like a workhorse. One was a useful, hard-working member of society; the other, even if he sang, painted, or wrote poetry, was an irresponsible wastrel. And helping the poor was a private matter. It was a privilege reserved to those who had a surplus to share, more or less generously, who recognized it as a duty which gave satisfaction in the present world and might help gain a more pleasant place in the next.

It took a couple of centuries of industrial unrest and social agitation before this attitude changed radically. In Britain and in Canada the decisive break came during the Second World War and the affluence which followed it. In part, the notion that we have a collective responsibility for the environment which produces want, ignorance, emotional disturbance and the helpless anger of frustration is now widely accepted, but the battle is not yet altogether won.

We still think too exclusively of transfer payments, of providing the needy with income, the ill with hospital and medical insurance. This is, of course, basic and important. But twenty-five years ago Sir William Beveridge warned us against accepting social security as the only aim. It is worth recalling his statement:

> The Plan for Social Security is put forward as part of a general programme of social policy. It is one part only of

an attack upon five giant evils; upon the physical Want with which it is directly concerned, upon Disease which often causes that Want and brings many other troubles in its train, upon Ignorance which no democracy can afford among its citizens, upon the Squalor which arises mainly through haphazard distribution of industry and population, and upon the Idleness which destroys wealth and corrupts men, whether they are well fed or not, when they are idle. In seeking security not merely against physical want, but against all these evils in all their forms, and in showing that security can be combined with freedom and enterprise and respon- sibility of the individual for his own life, the British com- munity and those who in other lands have inherited the British tradition have a vital service to render to human progress.

Certainly income or transfer payments by governments have grown enormously both absolutely and relatively. This can be illustrated in many different ways. The following table, for ex- ample, shows the total of such payments by the three levels of government as a percentage of Gross National Product. Although the proportion naturally depends not only on the increases in transfer payments but also on the rate of growth in the economy, the sharp upward curve is unmistakable. And no doubt the pay- ments will continue to increase substantially in the next few years as a result of the gradual reduction to sixty-five of the age limit for old age pensions, the introduction this year of supple- mentary income to pensioners, and the increase in welfare pay- ments by provinces and municipalities.

It is surely clear that this is not the end of the road in the broad areas of social security. For the sad fact of our abundant economy is that we have widespread poverty even among those who work as well as those who are too young, too ill or too old. Numerous studies disclose that in Canada, as in the United States, one in four of our people lives on an income below the poverty line. The studies also show that in most cases the poverty is handed down from generation to generation in the same family. The attitude and atmosphere created by such inherited poverty does incalculable harm to the personality of young and old alike. The heartbreaking demoralization of a quarter of our people is a challenge which we ignore at our peril.

TABLE I
GOVERNMENT TRANSFER PAYMENTS AS A
PERCENTAGE OF GROSS NATIONAL PRODUCT
ALL THREE LEVELS OF GOVERNMENT
CANADA—1926—1965

Year	Percentage of G.N.P.	Year	Percentage of G.N.P.	Year	Percentage of G.N.P.
1926	1.4	1941	2.3	1956	5.8
1927	1.4	1942	2.1	1957	6.5
1928	1.4	1943	1.9	1958	8.0
1929	1.5	1944	2.2	1959	7.9
1930	2.0	1945	4.8	1960	8.6
1931	3.0	1946	9.3	1961	9.2
1932	4.2	1947	6.4	1962	9.2
1933	5.2	1948	5.7	1963	8.7
1934	5.5	1949	5.8	1964	8.7
1935	5.1	1950	5.7	1965	8.7
1936	4.8	1951	4.9		
1937	4.5	1952	5.7		
1938	4.3	1953	5.8		
1939	4.1	1954	6.6		
1940	3.1	1955	6.4		

Source: D.B.S. National Accounts

There is a problem here not only of income but of sociological and psychological dimensions. And it will not disappear; it will not steal away. It requires an imaginative application of our concept of social welfare. We have reached a point in social development when we must begin to think seriously of the feasibility of a minimum income to provide opportunity for decency and of a long-term educational and social program to eradicate ignorance and squalor. This will involve more than transfer payments; it will involve the participation of educators and social psychologists and it will also involve, in my opinion, basic questions of investment, of allocation of funds, of regional development and of distribution of income generally.

The traditional limits to the notion of welfare are inadequate for the second half of the twentieth century. Help to the young in the form of family allowances is meaningless without the means of obtaining an education that will fit them for modern life and work. An old age pension, even a generous one, cannot enrich the life of a retired Canadian if studies in geriatrics do not produce solutions to his emotional need to continue to be of use to himself and to society. Nor will his feeling of abandonment be eased if he is condemned to live in a little room and nurse his illness in solitude. Housing and health care are as important to him as a cash cheque. The same is true for the widow and the orphan, the unemployed and the unemployable.

Thus when dealing with welfare we are, or should be, concerned with expenditures in related fields. The same significant rise in government costs emerges when we look, for example, at expenditures on education and on health services, as shown in the following two tables:

TABLE II
EXPENDITURE ON FORMAL EDUCATION, VOCATIONAL TRAINING AND OTHER EDUCATIONAL ACTIVITIES ALL LEVELS OF GOVERNMENT PLUS NON-GOVERNMENTAL 1954—1962

Year	Education Expenditure ($000,000)	Education Expenditure as % of G.N.P.
1954	729	2.9
1955	827	3.0
1956	929	3.0
1957	1,110	3.5
1958	1,264	3.8
1959	1,459	4.2
1960	1,657	4.6
1961	1,913	5.1
1962	2,324	5.8

Source: D.B.S., Survey of Education Finance

Finally, the growth of government involvement is graphically illustrated when one traces the curve of total non-military expenditures by all levels of government, as is done in the following table. In looking at the increases in overall expenditures we must, of course, remember that additions to the federal and provincial civil service and to the cost of equipment and supplies are in significant part related to increases in social welfare and social services. The payments to beneficiaries of programs are not the total cost of such programs; there is also the substantial cost of added staff and overhead.

TABLE III
NET GENERAL EXPENDITURE ON HEALTH SERVICES
ALL GOVERNMENTS IN CANADA, BY LEVEL OF
GOVERNMENT
1947—1962
(millions of dollars)

Year	Federal	Provincial	Municipal	Total	% of Govt. Non-Military expenditure
1947	57	87	27	171	5.4
1948	60	114	31	205	6.1
1949	69	156	38	263	7.1
1950	72	172	43	287	7.3
1951	82	190	51	323	7.5
1952	88	210	53	351	6.9
1953	94	229	54	377	7.0
1954	100	257	67	424	7.3
1955	103	271	69	443	7.0
1956	112	288	74	474	6.7
1957	118	332	85	535	6.8
1958	186	363	80	629	6.8
1959	280	470	72	822	7.9
1960	330	554	69	953	8.4
1961	429	621	72	1,122	9.0
1962	470	719	77	1,266	9.3

Source: Royal Commission on Health Services;
D.B.S. National Accounts.

These and similar facts have begun to reawaken old doubts about our social direction. We again hear statements railing against too much government, alleging loss of personal initiative and questioning how much more we can afford. The arguments are more sophisticated than they were thirty years ago, the objections more muted, but there is a reaction evident in certain circles against rapidly growing government expenditures.

Table IV is, of course, not limited to expenditures on what are commonly called welfare services. It includes government costs for schools and universities, hospitals and public health, roads and sewage, parks and ice rinks, police and fire protection, public buildings and public housing (what there *is* of it), urban renewal and slum clearance (what there is of *it*), homes for the aged

TABLE IV
GOVERNMENT NON-MILITARY EXPENDITURE AS A PERCENTAGE OF GROSS NATIONAL PRODUCT CANADA 1926—1965

(Includes both transfer payments and payments for goods and services for all levels of government; excludes inter-governmental transfers)

Year	Percentage of G.N.P.	Year	Percentage of G.N.P.	Year	Percentage of G.N.P.
1926	16.0	1941	14.9	1956	23.1
1927	15.7	1942	13.5	1957	24.7
1928	15.1	1943	14.4	1958	28.3
1929	16.4	1944	15.6	1959	29.7
1930	19.7	1945	19.5	1960	31.4
1931	25.6	1946	26.2	1961	33.3
1932	29.4	1947	24.2	1962	33.5
1933	28.5	1948	22.1	1963	33.3
1934	27.6	1949	22.7	1964	33.1
1935	26.5	1950	21.8	1965	33.6
1936	25.0	1951	20.3		
1937	23.7	1952	21.3		
1938	24.8	1953	21.5		
1939	21.6	1954	23.4		
1940	18.0	1955	23.3		

Source: D.B.S. National Accounts

and care of the sick, centres for disturbed and homes for retarded children, grants for research and for culture, and numerous other activities indispensable to our collective life.

Included also are large sums to help promote or maintain economic activity. There are expenditures for the Agricultural Rehabilitation and Development Act, subsidies for coal and subventions for transportation, help for designated areas and assistance for regional development, expenditures for vocational training, for assistance to farmers and to business.

If one compares Table I and Table IV above, one finds that the huge sums needed to build the infra-structure of modern living and to help in the production process are almost three times as large as the cost of pensions, family allowances, mother's allowance and other transfer payments. If one added defence expenditures into the equation, the proportion spent on transfer payments would, of course, be much smaller still.

It is obvious that there are still gaps in our welfare arrangements and even more in our social services. It is true that at last we have the major framework of a social security system. But in the years ahead we will have to consider seriously the question of a guaranteed minimum income for Canadian families and individuals. Obviously this idea presents many difficulties of administration and even more obstinate problems of economic and social policies. It will require a great deal of study which should be started without delay.

However, the notion is one which commends itself to one's sense of social responsibility. Because of its origins and topsy-like development the present welfare pattern is uneven and arbitrary. Categorical payments are related to political considerations rather than to a scientific study of need. There is certainly no equality of treatment among provinces and municipalities. The whole system would be more humane and would look less like charity if there were a recognized minimum income for dignity and decency to which every family and every individual without dependents would be entitled. This is the only way to ensure that poverty will cease to be handed down from generation to generation, that the financial cause of human degradation will disappear.

This alone, as indicated elsewhere in this essay, will not solve the problem of poverty, particularly when it has been for decades characteristic of an underdeveloped area or region or community. The whole environment will need changing and the people will have to be persuaded that they have the capacity as well as the right to become self-reliant.

This underlines the gaps in our social services: the lack of basic amenities in too many areas, the inequalities in the quality of as well as in the opportunities for education, the continuing presence of degrading accommodation and of social neglect of every sort.

Poverty is no longer the lot of the majority, as it was a hundred years ago, but it is still far too wide-spread for an affluent society, were it governed by reason and compassion. In these circumstances, no one can be complacent about our level of social welfare or social equality. The limits of imperative collective involvement are still without reach. Indeed, they are constantly expanding as technical inventiveness grows, as material wealth increases and, particularly, as our understanding of human behaviour and relationships deepens.

What, then, is the shouting about? To spend about one-third of all production on the total of those things which alone make community life possible and personal life worthwhile is surely not too much. And, in any case, how does one measure these things? Surely it is not even thinkable that we should live without schools or sewers or water or roads or police or fire protection or any of the other services which we take for granted. They are all services and facilities which must be provided collectively because no one in the community can provide them for himself.

Furthermore, as J. K. Galbraith has brilliantly and whimsically pointed out, the richer we become in the possession and use of material goods the more we require by way of collective action to enable us to enjoy our goods and to become even richer. The very advances in the process of production and of living require new expenditures to make life bearable.

The more automobiles we drive, the more roads and parking lots we need. The faster and bigger the airplanes we use, the larger the airports we must collectively build. As our technology develops, more and more of our people flood our cities and cause housing and school problems and traffic congestion of immense proportions. These problems cannot be solved by individual enterprise in accordance with the rules of the market place; they must be tackled by governments through large public outlays.

There was a time, not so long ago, when education was sought for its own sake, when the search for knowledge and inquiry into the universe were exciting goals in themselves. For many this is still true. But the era of automation has given what is called a "practical" dimension to education. Jobs are increasingly more scarce for those without or with little education. And one occupation will no longer last a lifetime. Most people will have to learn two or three skills, train and retrain every decade or so. Social investment in education is now an economic must.

The industrial society is producing or aggravating other acute problems. Air and water pollution poison the atmosphere in our cities, and not only offend our senses but threaten our health. The pressures of living in the jet age are producing a shocking rate of mental illness and hundreds of thousands of disturbed children for whom there are no treatment centres and no hope. Crime is on the increase and juvenile delinquency haunts homes in every economic class. As we develop new and more abundant means to meet our material needs, we endanger the quality of our lives. A people that awakens to these dangers must be ready to deal with them collectively. No one can do so on his own.

As Professor Galbraith expressed it, "Nearly all of the investment in individuals is in the public domain. And virtually all of it is outside the market system." Yet our traditions cause us to question public investment in people, whether through cash payments or through the provision of health services, educational opportunities, safe roads, clean waters, fresh air, decent homes, green belts, planned cities, slum clearance, recreational facilities or artistic and cultural riches. If governments spend money, it is immediately suspect, even though without it life would be almost as dismal for the well-to-do as for the poor.

An increasing proportion of our economic and social life requires government participation and the use of the public purse. The elimination of poverty in all its aspects is as much an imperative of social welfare as help for special classes of the poor. The training of psychologists, psychiatrists and social workers is as urgent a moral and social need today as are transfer payments to the old and helpless. Beautifying and cleansing our cities and providing opportunities for productive leisure are as vital an expression of human concern in the 1970's as were Poor Laws a hundred years ago. The pressures of modern life lead our young astray more efficiently than Fagan ever did. And, to change authors, the injunctions of Polonius are just as boring and ineffective now as they were in the seventeenth century.

The point of this essay is a plea that we expand our concept of welfare to include all public activity concerned with the individual and his life in a complex and frequently mixed-up society. No doubt there is value in separate categories of government involvement for the sake of different academic disciplines and departmental responsibilities. But in life the boundaries are fictitious and they lead to invidious and meaningless comparisons. They lead also to political arguments and popular resentments which have no relation to reality.

It is time we recognized that our tax contributions to public treasuries are merely a payment for indispensable facilities and services which can only be provided collectively. Although some expenditure seems to benefit a single defined group in the community, there is hardly a category which does not receive some advantage at the expense of the treasury. Even the wealthy tax-paying corporation benefits from public expenditure on research, or from tax abatement for development and exploration, or from some other fiscal incentive. Moreover, the advantages it gains from public expenditures for training its engineers, scientists and other specialist personnel are the foundation of its existence in the scientific age.

Providing the old, the ill and the unemployed with the means to live is, of course, a moral duty, but it is also more than that. In practical power terms it is by far the least expensive way of preventing the disorders, instability and disruption which their neglect would surely produce. And only an extreme, anachronistic doctrinaire would fail to recognize that the relative stability of purchasing power resulting from welfare programs is essential to the stability and growth of the economy as a whole.

In short, social responsibility places no limits on the amount of welfare as a social goal. This is not to say that there will not always be differences of opinion as to what is socially desirable or necessary. Nor is it suggested that the differences in view will ever be free of personal, group or class prejudices. It is certainly not contemplated that the various aspects of welfare can be provided without regard to the state of the economy at a given time or the effects of resulting fiscal and monetary policies. Arguments about priorities and about choices there will always be aplenty.

What is urged is that we abandon the traditional attitudes to government spending, that we cease to regard it as an evil to be contained. We must, of course, make sure that, like all spending, it should be useful and relevant. But modern society cannot function without huge and increasing collective expenditures. The infrastructure for a decent existence cannot be built by individuals and families; it is a function of the nation or the community. Like the rest of life, the infrastructure grows more complex and more costly as technology enriches and complicates our individual and collective existence.

Carl A. Pollock

THE CASE FOR FREE ENTERPRISE

Carl A. Pollock
 Carl Pollock attended the University of Toronto, Faculty of Applied Science, and Oxford University. After completing his studies he returned to Kitchener, Ontario, where he joined Dominion Electrohome Industries Limited, a company founded by his father. At present Mr. Pollock is President and Chairman of the Board of the Company.

The case for free enterprise is so often treated as a subject for academic exercise in analysing economic systems. How the public's needs and wants are to be supplied, without making some much richer and others much poorer, seems to be the burden of all the argument. But this do-good red herring, the emphasis of the analysis is made to point to end results which come about, not because of the system, but because of individual attitudes to private enterprise. Private enterprise is people. Thus, the free enterprise system is on trial for the abuses people make of the system and not for the things which may be wrong with the system itself. Many have, of course, tried private enterprise and found it difficult, so they find the free enterprise system wanting. Yet the countries with the highest standard of living, the greatest measure of social justice, and the maximum amount of personal freedom are those where development and growth have taken place within the framework of democratic free enterprise.

The popular solution is that the lot of those who have not should be improved by those who have. Only those who are required to provide could be unhappy with such an arrangement, but its basic weakness is that it reduces the initiative of both rich and poor. A society and economy flourishes because its private enterprisers have the interest to improve their way of life and the initiative to institute personal actions, both individual and group. The basis of the free enterprise system is, therefore, that the good things of life are available to those who earn them by their efforts. To make the system operate efficiently, all citizens should be working to this objective. Amenities are not anyone's right because they think they have earned them, or because their society can afford to provide them that they are thus entitled to them, or because other people, to promote their own interests, say they ought to be provided. The only right all citizens have is the opportunity to improve their lot, without interfering with the freedom of others to do likewise, and they earn and retain that right by the use they make of the opportunity. We must learn to be satisfied with the abilities we have, but dissatisfied with the use we make of them. The case for free enterprise, therefore, rests on the wisdom of the average citizen.

The history of mankind records the hopes and discouragements, the successes and failures, the benevolence and machinations of life. These gamuts of experience come about because individuals and consortiums of men have planned and acted with the knowledge that, by their private enterprise, they can profit either by benefitting themselves economically or by achieving for themselves vital personal satisfactions. It must be remembered that, economically, freedom of enterprise is a profit-and-loss system. Freedom to profit, however, contains the seeds of discord between men, because the stronger willed always dominates his fellows, some ascendencies being ethical, others expedient. To the extent successful men act in a law-abiding manner and in keeping with public well-being, they win public approval. These men make the system work well, but there will undoubtedly always be a minority who abuses the confidences of others and thereby prompts ideas for the controlling of the less scrupulous competitors.

As serious as have the abuses been which men have perpetrated, however, they were but distractions in the free enterprise way of life, for the standard of living of most private enterprisers in the free world has risen steadily. Needs were satisfied and brought many new wants which required mass production methods to satisfy. Because of this great modification of man's environment, the performance of work and services became fractionalized, and more and more people functioned less and less as individual private enterprisers. These changes brought an altered emphasis to the free enterprise system, prompting employees and competitors of the successful companies to look to government to control and direct business. Employees developed associations and unions to strengthen their cause and ensure the private enterprise of their members. All these developments brought about some abuses which diverted the thinking of employees and employers from their basic purpose of working jointly to serve the consumer—the true purpose of private enterprise.

For these reasons, there is today a great need for a re-assessment of the case for freedom of enterprise and for a projection of what a new approach to making the citizen's personal private enterprise a stronger factor in our economy could do for all in the future.

The case for the free enterprise system is one of the oldest, most controversial, and most widely discussed concepts of human relations. That this should be so is natural because it is a way of life in which every citizen is involved. For all the familiarity which people claim to have with the basic principles of free enterprise, those concepts are neither as well understood as they should be nor as realistically appreciated as regards the personal responsibilities the system entails. With the rapid rise of industrialism, this inimical situation has become a key factor in the operation of the free enterprise system. Years ago the private enterpriser who owned a small business, and the employees with whom he operated it, were, through the force of rugged experience with the market, knowledgeable about the key to the success of the free enterprise system—providing the customer with products or services of good value. In those days, too, the customer was fairly well informed concerning the product or service he wanted to buy.

In contrast today so many factors involved in the successful operation of the free enterprise system have become very complicated. Basic to this situation has been the veritable explosion of knowledge which has occurred in the post-war years and the much less rapid growth of the background of experience needed to make use of the knowledge. In other words, men's wisdom (knowledge and the experience to use it), individually and collectively, is in a state of confusion—a veritable profusion of confusion as regards the choices which the mid-twentieth century free enterprise system offers them as private enterprisers.

It is important that this concept be appreciated in its broadest connotations. For the free enterprise market mechanism to work really successfully, the producer (which includes employees) must be wise regarding creating, producing, selling, and financing products and services, and the consumer must be wise regarding the products and services he needs and wants, their use, their purchase, payment, and financing. To document how far we are from such a state of perfection would take all of this volume and many others. To do so, however, would not be tackling the problems of making free enterprise work. It would merely be describing the symptoms of the problems of free enterprise with all the accompanying emotional ramifications and rationalizations. It is as inherent in the free enterprise system as private enterprise is in man himself that whatever man does, how he does it, and the results he achieves will always be short of perfection. Men are much better at analysis and criticism than they are at synthesis, which brings the matter home to roost. Because it is the private enterpriser's job to make free enterprise work—he cannot delegate the job to anyone else—it is his problem and his responsibility, and he can only blame himself if it doesn't work well. Making the system work is really everybody's job, and to do anything about it, each individual must perform his part. In doing it well, each will make his own lot better.

With this premise in mind, let us look at man's motives as a private enterpriser. The opening paragraphs of this chapter commented on profit and its place in the free enterprise system. Let us now be more specific.

The motivation to profit is an exceedingly powerful influence on man's thought and action, being closely akin to the key impulse of self-preservation. It is not, however, instinctive and is, therefore, subject to the maturing influences of knowledge and experience. The historian, in tracing the changes brought about through the profit motive, would record an evolution of human motivation. It ranges from the obverse of avarice to its aesthetic reverse of altruism. A spectrum exists between these two extremes which, through generations of education, understanding, and appreciation, has narrowed for most humans touched by western civilization to the gamut between selfish expediency and self-interest. All the motivations between these parameters are individualistic and are the sparks which make the world go 'round. It can thus be concluded that man's achievements, singular and collective, result from those motivations no matter what political, social, or economic system of human endeavor men organize.

Therefore, as a base for our discussion of free enterprise, the outer limits of the range of individual motivation current for most people should be detailed. In simplified profit motivation terms, "selfish expediency" denotes the individual's desire for benefits and satisfactions which take little account of the effect which those desires and actions have on others who also wish to profit by their own efforts. On the other hand, practising "self-interest", as the term is used in this chapter, means seeking benefits and satisfactions while having the enlightened outlook that, when others are able to prosper too because their efforts are not inhibited by what someone else is doing, the opportunities for all are improved. It is the philosophy of a good citizen who develops his talents for the maximum benefit of himself and society. Self-interest is truly a survival-of-the-fittest motivation, because the fittest in his wisdom would recognize that the inhibiting of others would in effect be inhibiting himself. Thus we see that being self-expedient in human relations is a profit of deterrence, whereas self-interest is a human relations profit of generation.

In the expanded sphere of man's world—one might almost say one world today—the influence of both self-expediency and self-interest can be very widespread. The last, almost fatal, example of expediency which degenerated into avarice for power, was the Second World War. Since that era, the breadth and depth of man's knowledge has expanded phenomenally, but man's experience is only by markedly slower steps learning how to make use of it. We are thus in a critical period of mankind's development. A private enterpriser's expediency dare not, through unrestrained competition in his business enterprises or by degenerating to avarice for power, bring about disastrous ends. The elixir is the acceleration of our learning practical experience which, with knowledge, becomes wisdom. Thankfully there is convincing evidence of such a trend. The world's largest service club encourages its members to recognize the wisdom of the adage, "He profits most who serves best." Now this is not a philosophy of do-goodism or just a service club's slogan. It is propounded as the key to man's profitable enjoyment of his life's work and activity in a free enterprise economy through the satisfactions he can gain from his private enterprise. There are many other influences at work bringing about this shift in motivation, but the limited progress of the whole concept underscores the truism that men in their millions learn slowly. It is, however, a certainty that all men will some day appreciate that their own private enterprise thrives on self-interest and withers through self-expediency .To achieve this wisdom must be the objective for the free enterprise system.

It is, therefore, patent that an economic system, organized to make the best use of the private enterprise of citizens, must be based on the understanding and appreciation of human relations and motivations as well as economic technology. Too, because private enterprising producers are also consumers, both parties to a transaction must be knowledgeable concerning the disciplines of the free enterprise system. The producer must know the economics of his job, and so must the consumer, and both must appreciate what constitutes compatible human relations. It is on such a foundation that free enterprise capitalism must rely in order to thrive.

Thus we may have arrived at a basic reason for the problems of trying to make free enterprise work successfully in our very complex world. It is the viability of the individual decisions which private enterprisers make that matters. There are literally millions of these which must be made in the free enterprise world every hour of every day. These decisions will reflect the private abilities, the knowledge and experience, and the profit motives of the participants. For these reasons, they will be in the interest of, indifferent to, or bad for, the operation of the free enterprise system. However, the important elements in this great maze of transactions is whether, on the average, the abilities of the private enterprisers are being used with more and more wisdom as time marches on, and whether personal self-interest is more evident in the decisions than selfish expediency. The evidence that such improvements are occurring indicates that men are developing an improved understanding and appreciation of the need to voluntarily control their own free choices. In so doing, they recognize that there are personally satisfying, and at the same time ethical, ways of carrying on their individual and collective private enterprise. It means too that they are becoming more conscious of their responsibilities and that the intelligent and efficient way to make free enterprise thrive is for each participant to follow a personally thought-out philosophy of business and code of ethics. Therein lies the link between human satisfactions and economic progress, and a framework for free enterprise and workable competition.

Thus the concept of each private enterpriser's having an understanding and an appreciation of his personal responsiblity for his statements and actions is at the crux of today's economic problems. There is an adage which says, "If each man sweeps before his own doorstep, the nation will be clean." Too, when a man is buyer, producer, seller, serviceman, and financier—that is, a complete private enterpriser in his own right in a free enterprise economy—a man can, by his experiences, appreciate his responsibilities. But today such a way of life is carried on by a minority of citizens—farmers, small retailers, and those single proprietors in service businesses. A second group, more important in the business world, has very significant levels of private enterprise responsibility but on a more specialized basis—managers, union leaders, supervisors, special project operators, salesmen, advertisers, etc. All are closely involved in their business function with the consumer's needs and wants.

However, today there is a drift away from individual responsibility for the largest number of people, who are operational employees of companies owned and managed by others. These employees perform a minor, yet essential, function in supplying the consumer's needs and wants of products and services. Because these very large numbers of individuals are remotely associated with the company's customers and perform only a small part of a group operation within a company, they have an underdeveloped sense of responsibility to the customer and of participation in the company's purposes. Most of them are merely performing their jobs for the monetary return to be gained. There is little thought on their part that they should be serving the customer well, because this is the way they wish to be served when they put on the customer's hat. To assist these employees to understand and appreciate that they do have a significant place as private enterprisers, being both producers and consumers, should be a responsibility of all others operating in the free enterprise system, as they have a better understanding and appreciation of its functioning. This is an important part of the jobs of company officers, managers, supervisors, and salesmen, as well as union officers, stewards, and others close to the rank and file of employees. Being a good example to other private enterprisers—the most effective training procedure—is a prime responsibility resting upon the heads of companies and unions.

So far the job of helping their employees and their members to better understand free enterprise has been performed indifferently by management and union leaders. And so most private enterprise employees, and many of the smaller entrepreneurs who have economic and psychological business problems beyond their capacities, look in frustration to governments for help. It is their hope that guidelines and legislation can be established to make owners and managers "desist" from taking advantage of them, and that tangible means can be provided by governments to improve their way of life, which they are certain is being "inhibited" by powerful forces in commerce, business, and industry. Such ideas have their origin in personal selfishness and in the individual's limited knowledge and experience. It is undoubtedly a fact that the private enterprise profit notions of most citizens have not advanced to the stage of self-regulation by reasoned policy. Ideologically, self-interest is the optimum point of personal motivation between unrestrained competition and governmental control. The former can be likened to the results of avaricious scheming, the latter to the epitome of laziness and helplessness. A vigorous and healthy free enterprise system cannot thrive on either of these expedient motivations but will be viable only if a majority of private enterprisers believe in self-interest.

No economic system allowing freedom to private enterprises will work as efficiently as it should if only a small minority of the people involved understand it and are trying to make it work. The decisions of the majority, if inimical to the success of the system because they are not knowledgeable about what they are doing, can undo a good which it has taken a generation to achieve. A little knowledge is indeed a dangerous thing. Only in an authoritarian state can a minority of private enterprisers control a majority, and then only after the majority have themselves all but ceased to be private enterprisers. Such an economic system can achieve successes and even some outstanding accomplishments in the fields of activity for which the minority set standards and encourage the citizens engaged in the pursuits. The great mass of people will, however, have to limit their private enterprise to what they are allowed to do and will do that effectively at their peril.

With these thoughts as background, let us now return to the concept of government intervention in business. As previously stated, because of the confusion introduced by the explosion of knowledge and the slow pick-up of experience, more and more people are less and less able to make their own intelligent choices and are looking to government, a body they feel they control, to make decisions for them and to prevent the more active private enterprisers from "taking advantage" of them. The fantasy that corporation profits are exhorbitantly high is just one manifestation of the erroneous belief that both employees and customers are being milched by capitalists. The false impression still persists despite its denial for a generation and innumerable corporate financial statements appearing in the public press. The dispelling of deeply rooted impressions from the human mind, even though they are untrue, is at the root of many human relations problems. The basic responsibility of democratic governments—to establish an environment of opportunity favourable to the activities of the citizens whom they represent—does, of course, include laws which govern the deportment of citizens and corporate entities as well as the policing of those laws, but does not include running the economy. It is, however, natural for the less well informed to look to a governing body to resolve what they feel are grievances against the behaviour of their more aggressive fellow citizens. As with so many of the good things in life, when this dependence is abused by enough people, political connotations develop.

There is an old saying, "Where there's smoke, there's fire," and this applies to the abuses a minority of men and corporations make of the power they possess. However, the market mechanism keeps most people and corporations seeking the public's patronage on a business-like, profitable basis. Too, in these enlightened days, by far the largest number of knowledgeable private enterprisers— be they individual or corporate—look upon their profit opportunities from a self-interest point of view. Their wisdom advises them that to do otherwise is to be short-sighted indeed. Because of the strength of the democratic process and because their contact with the market is usually several levels removed, a similar commendation cannot be given to the actions of many unions. Part of the responsibility for this situation, it must be acknowledged, lies in the fact that many businesses have not been as exemplary as they could have been in their own actions, nor have enough corporations stated and publicized their business philosophies, objectives, and policies so that employees and public could be better informed as to the long-term plans of business.

Thus, in the interests of the further development of the free enterprise system, the almost instinctive insistence of a large group of the less well-informed private enterprisers that the government do something for them becomes an issue and must be faced. What these citizens are really saying is that government should establish a planned economy which would afford a way of life less hazardous and more comfortable than they may be able to provide for themselves by being individual private enterprisers in a highly competitive world. Actually, the issue is broader than this; it is in reality central planning versus local planning. And because planning has often been poorly done, many men's hopes for improvement look to governmental action because, in their opinion, this seems a better way. The weakness in this idea is that planning is a process of mental synthesis at which man is not very good. Planners so often try to do their job by projecting the past into the future rather than breaking new ground. Planning must, of course, always be done in the light of knowledge and experience, but not by perpetuating the status quo. It is a matter of taking calculated risks. For this reason, planners of specific projects must be well-informed, experienced men, men who are never content to rest upon the laurels of their past achievements. When the occasion arises to choose the men in which to place confidence for such a job, for some reason the private enterprisers who work at manual jobs seem to prefer the elected politician to the men who employ them. Perhaps they feel they had a hand in electing their government representatives and thereby think they have some control over what they do.

Governments have extremely important functions to perform in establishing environments favourable to the development of the private enterprises of a nation's citizens. It is axiomatic that the future of free enterprise will depend in large measure on the understanding and appreciation parliamentarians have of the way the market system works and on their basing legislation on this wisdom. Parliament's job includes the planning and acting upon international, national, provincial, and municipal responsibilities which are outside the scope of private enterprise. It also includes such functions as the provision of national and provincial statistical services as well as research and exploration performances which are broader than the fields available to private consortiums. However, when it comes to intervening in the planning, administration, and control of business, government is getting outside its scope. Business thrives on competition motivated by the self-interest of private enterprisers, a situation which cannot be legislated or centrally planned into a healthy performance; nor can its results be simulated or improved by government intervention. For a government to have personnel qualified by knowledge and experience to effectively intervene, in even a few of the private enterprises which compose a free enterprise economy, would mean extending the official bureaucracy to several times its present unwieldy size. Engaging in centralized planning for private enterprise may seem a healthy and an innocuous approach to keeping competition from getting out of hand. However, intervention in any area of concern by government planning brings with it control of that area which, because it is controlled, quickly interferes with some other function. It does not require much compulsion before anything unplanned and uncontrolled is considered a menace to the whole state. Since governmental planning cannot be contained at any point, it soon deteriorates into no plan at all, leaving much inhibiting interference. Another degenerating influence is that a centralized body cannot adapt its plans and controls to localized requirements and wants. What is sauce for the goose does not always complement the gander. On the other hand, business enterprise is adaptable to the risks it encounters in planning and meeting market demands. Governments are not elected to direct the market nor are they capable of doing so.

The thought of planning brings to mind the premier function of private enterprise—creativity and innovation. The simplest form of creativity is doing things oneself; the highest form requires the genius of an Einstein. The average citizen who does a reasonably good job might be considered to be a bit above the lowest level. Yet it is when he does something creative that he really gains those personal satisfactions without which life would be a dull existence. Careful studies and extensive surveys come up with the knowledge that personal satisfaction is the great motivator, with monetary gain several rungs down the ladder. Now this is why being creative is the very essence of private enterprise—it strengthens our self-interest and profit motive and plays down expedience. Therefore, if private enterprise is to be the way of life for the great majority of citizens, the opportunity for some creativity and innovation must be built into what they are doing so the "do-it-oneself" urge is stimulated. This force is of particular importance to youth in its start into the competitive world, because it is then that the confusion and complexity of the market system suggests grasping at the mirage of an authoritarian world wrapped up in a nice, neat, easy-to-comprehend package. At that point, youth's private enterprise is at a low ebb.

What, then, are some possible solutions of these basic problems of making free enterprise work more effectively? No aim will come closer to the bullseye than a thorough re-assessment of the purposes of education. For years, the three R's seemed basic and still are; but the need for knowledge, understanding, experience, and appreciation is today so broad and so involving that only a completely new approach to education will do. It was stated earlier that planning must not be a projection of the trends of the past. It is most inadequate for young people to learn to understand things. They must learn, too, at an early age, to appreciate things. It is not sufficient for our youth to learn what was done and why people did things; all of them have to learn to understand and appreciate people themselves. Earlier comment in this chapter endeavoured to show that free enterprise would be as successful as private enterprise made it through the motivation of responsible self-interest. Therefore, to leave the gaining of these more personalized disciplines to post-academic absorption through the experiences of life continues the risk of a further languishing of the spirit of private enterprise. A rising level of wisdom is required to live successfully in the latter half of the twentieth century, and again by wisdom is meant knowledge plus the practical experience to adapt it to life. Knowledge without experience is not good enough, and experience without knowledge leaves modern man inadequately prepared to live successfully. If a citizen is to enjoy the right of private enterprise ensured him by the free enterprise system, he must understand and appreciate his hopes and aspirations and those of his fellow citizens and how private enterprise can bring these about.

What then can we do? The possibilities are so numerous and so great in scope that only one basic approach to improving the operation of the free enterprise system can be considered in this chapter.

Since the free enterprise system is really an organization structure within which private enterprisers can live and work, the basis of all education should provide an elementary and yet thorough understanding and appreciation of human thinking and relations between people. The purpose of education must be to inculcate a discipline as a self-discipline and not as discipline for perpetrated mistakes. The former is knowledge, and the latter experience; as has been said, both are required to make man wise. The young lad ten years of age needs to appreciate why he was punched on the nose by his classmate. It is not good enough to understand why— he must appreciate why. The basis for this wisdom should begin academically in the latter grades of public school. High school classes should include some elementary psychology of the individual and of groups so that youth does not enter the free enterprise world without some working knowledge of human relations. A most important part of this wisdom would be an awareness of the vital part individual satisfactions from work achievement can and must play in profit motivation.

The second basic wisdom obviously is a growing understanding and appreciation of why free enterprise is a natural organization structure for the work efforts of an individual private enterpriser. Too, a citizen must be aware of how he fits into the efforts of groups of private enterprisers and the economics of a country. He requires knowledge in this regard, not just post-educational experience. An appreciation of these understandings develops from exposure at an early age. To the minds of many people who are not involved in the market mechanism, free enterprise is characterized by an attitude of laissez-faire. To them, government control seems the obvious mechanism because it appears to make a

tight operational package. To the conscientious private enterpriser, neither laissez-faire nor a managed economy is the answer.
His knowledge and experience appreciates that in more intelligent
enterprise is to be found the solution of abuses and the plans for
man's better future. An intensive joint research should be made by
educators and businessmen as to how academic curricula could
provide a basic knowledge of private enterprise. The case history
method could be adapted early in a student's career to simulate
experience. To be sure, enlightened business would be interested
in providing much practical help. Co-operative plans for university
students have given a cue to the value which can result from
business education collaboration.

A most important example of these vital matters is to be found
in the intercompany relationships of the third group of private
enterprisers—the operative employees of corporate businesses. For
a citizen to be a good employee in a free enterprise economy,
he must be a private enterpriser who understands what both he
and the company are trying to do. To be effective, communications must be made through and to minds which are receptive and
which understand and appreciate. The foremen or section supervisors are the managerial employees directly responsible for the
work efforts of the large numbers of the third group. How information is received and how it is passed on depends on the wisdom
of the participants and, of equal importance, on the level of
human relations employed in the contacts between the members of
a team. A foreman or supervisor is almost required to be a practicing psychologist to perform his responsibilities efficiently and in
the interests of the free enterprise system. An appreciation of good
human relations is basic to all private enterprisers, because our
way of life will only improve significantly through the confidence
people can have in each other. It is ignorance and selfish expedience which cause most misunderstandings. With these conditions,
it will surely be agreed that a most effective means of instilling
some basic wisdom concerning a citizen's place as a private enterpriser should be found in exposing youth to these concepts in their
late public and secondary educational studies. Acquaintance with
such wisdom at an early age should be the most certain way to
ensure that these concepts become a basic factor in our way of
life. The results of the Junior Achievement Movement is one of
the best proofs of this premise.

As young people expand their participation in a free enterprise economy, there should be no higher aspiration than to be creative. Creativity and productivity need to be appreciated as the two functions which give private enterprisers their capability to serve consumers and earn optimum profit. To have a growing working awareness of these capabilities is a more sophisticated wisdom which will develop as the education program advances. However, all young people leaving the academic environment should have learned something of these concepts. They should have learned, too, that there is nothing creative in being provided with something by others, and that satisfactions come only from what one earns for oneself.

The contents of an academic curricula for the teaching of private enterprise require study and innovation of a high order. Education being one of the most important elements of man's adolescent environment, the modifications made throughout the last generation in elementary and secondary education were designed to fit the secondary or vocational school student for his place in the industrial, trade, or commercial world. His capabilities have in this way been oriented to job performance. Making such changes is like using yesterday's methods to solve yesterday's problems, and the range of knowledge is not broad enough for the needs of the latter twentieth century. The highly important matters of understanding and appreciating the free enterprise system and the psychology of people in both job and social relations have received a backhand of attention, almost as though they were of minor importance. Picking up such knowledge and experience it was thought could be left to rubbing shoulders with the world. Actually, these disciplines are the more basic considerations, and their absence from the curricula during the postwar years can, in this writer's personal opinion, account for much of the internal unrest in private enterprise business in the sixties. Business officers and managers and officers of unions should feel a reponsibility to aid in the rectification of this situation which is inimical to the self-interest of both groups. Governments must face their responsibilities in this regard, too. Education must and can contribute to harmonious relations among all citizens.

In the interests of stemming the growth of misunderstandings between management and labour which seem again to be on the increase, other academic opportunities are needed in addition to the long-term proposals just made. All of today's work force lacks the disciplines suggested, and it will be their understanding and appreciation which will be of vital importance to labour and management co-operation and peace over the next half generation. The night school and university extramural curricula could offer these subjects as essential adult education and as refresher courses for the oncoming employees. In the interests of strengthening the free enterprise system, no time should be lost in exploring the possibilities to be found in our educational system.

The educational opportunities just referred to could and would be available to all private enterprisers in modern business. Supplementary to these facilities, business could add in-plant courses and unions, in-field courses to round out the experience required to make the new knowledge truly practical. Careful study of the many excellent business and trade papers and periodicals should be encouraged by both groups. Of value, too, is the participation of the managerial personnel of both small and large companies in the major business associations. Through these organizations, the exchange and dissemination of business knowledge and experience have contributed much to improve the level of the philosophical outlook of private enterprisers.

The last several paragraphs have pointed to academic and extramural educational activities to be effectively integrated into our way of life and accepted by our citizens. It is proposed that these means could, to a most significant degree, resolve the basic problems of the free enterprise system inherent in the limited wisdom of the participants. So frequently the statement is made concerning the resolving of our industrial problems that better use should be made of the country's manpower. This is sound advice, but the emphasis is wrong, for manpower is employed, not used. What is important is that the average man have improved comprehensions so that the work he does and the decisions he makes will be better suited to the goals he understands and appreciates as being good for him and his fellow countrymen. His capabilities will then be employed more effectively.

One final and extremely important concept is needed to ensure that a growing educational level may be put to optimum use. In a free enterprise system, the terms of reference and the scope of governments must be clearly delineated. The action of the members of government are usually guided by constitutions which have to do with how a nation is organized and operated—not with the objectives towards which citizens can employ their enterprise. In the free enterprise system, private enterprisers choose their own objectives and their own plans. Nevertheless, throughout those objectives and plans, there should be thematic ideas which indicate optimum purposes. Navigators going to their separate objectives would have great difficulty if they did not have the north star to enable them to guide themselves. To a similar purpose, governments can provide leadership concepts for private enterprise and an environment favourable to their objectives. Truly stimulating leadership providing indicative objectives and plans has regretfully been in conspicuously short supply at the time it was most needed to meet the growing complexities of our social economies. On the contrary, the trend of government activity has been to decide upon operational objectives and to make plans and choices to implement them, giving the reason that, in so doing, political obligations were being fulfilled. Nothing could be more decimating to a free enterprise economy or to private enterprise.

If the suggested broad educational activities to raise the level of economic and human relations, understanding, and appreciation are successfully brought into being over the next generation, it is essential that the enhanced capabilities of our citizens be afforded a stimulating environment of opportunity and some indicative objectives and planning. Therein lie the main governmental responsibilities pertaining to private enterprise in a free enterprise society. If these functions are well established and government's responsibilities in the non-private sectors are well handled, private enterprise can make its way to higher and higher standards of personal wellbeing in a free enterprise economy.

This chapter has thus far covered numerous pages to propose a very simple and practical approach to resolving, in the long term, the problems which today plague the free enterprise system. For such problems, there is no panacea, and aspirin tablets for specific aches and pains are of little value. It is so because relations between people are the most complex of man's activities and are the basic ingredients of the free enterprise system's workings. Keeping these relations on the rails, and progressing, calls for personal effort in the right direction, by which is meant being motivated by self-interest more than by selfish expediency. Such an orientation grows best, not by the pressure of laws, but by understanding and appreciation—the products of knowledge supplemented by example after example over a number of years. The old adage of more haste meaning less speed applies—and rushing things causes more confusion, too. Nevertheless, there is no time to be lost.

Having been presumptuous enough to re-assess the case for free enterprise in the light of modern times, the application of the concepts to our Canadian scene could be a useful exercise. While Canadians have private enterprise roots in the soil of free enterprise, there are more inhibiting influences at work stunting the development of the system in our country than are to be found in most other economies. Canada and Canadians are closely associated with the major powers of this world of ours. We want to be members of the big league, but have been on the fringe of acceptance for a generation. We want to have a standard of living equal to our friendly neighbours to the south, and yet we haven't earned their level by our accomplishments. For these and numerous other reasons, we try to keep up with the American Joneses and have thereby been distracted from developing in keeping with our own abilities and the truly wonderful facilities and natural resources available to us. Many details of happenstance have kept us unprepared to make use of our opportunities.

These seem rather anomalous statements to make in the light of the outstanding progress the Canadian economy has made and the developments which have occurred in the postwar years. However, if the reasons for our achievements are tracked down, it will be found that both Canadian and American private enterprise have been responsible, with our cousins to the south playing the major part. We have been inept in that we have taken our good fortune and our accomplishments for granted and do not really appreciate how we acquired them. The American standard of living should really be a wonderful stimulant for us as private enterprisers, urging us to achieve for ourselves. Actually it seems to work in reverse, and we almost feel that, because the Americans have something, it should automatically be available for us without our having to earn it.

Because of our close contacts and interest in the United States, many Canadians feel that we could do no better than to be as dynamic as our cousins to the south. We do bask in the American sunshine—yet it is our dependence upon the Americans and looking to American accomplishments that has caused us to have a national inferiority complex. What the Americans do, we should do and be happy about it. The thought of Canada becoming a better place in which to live and work than the United States does not seem to occur to most Canadians. This means that we Canadians are trying to live by United States standards rather than by objectives we have set for ourselves. We are thus in a constant state of frustration with a pall of inferiority over us. Actually, one of the best traits of our neighbours we do not emulate as enthusiastically as we should is this—they are the world's best exponents of the free enterprise system. If we followed their example, their private enterprise leadership would surely be challenged. On the other hand, we have adopted from them their impatience, which is a usefully applied stimulator for the accomplishment of short-term projects, but, for the long-term result of building Canada into a leading nation in the mid-twentieth century, the patience of dedicated patriots is needed.

In an attempt to escape from our discomfiture and to show that we can do something better than our cousins, our governments have embarked on welfare programs of the most advanced character. Obviously, no one objects to welfare measures, and they are properly governmental responsibilities; but when all political parties, regardless of cost and with little concern for the real need, clamor for increased services, the matter becomes more political than altruisic. These "benefits" provide an inordinate drain on the Canadian pocketbook through taxes—money which could usefully be spent in improving our ability to create and produce for ourselves and the export market. It is an undoubted fact that the Canadian economy is underdeveloped in relation to its potential. At such a stage in a nation's growth, overdoing welfare syphons off job opportunities by heavy taxes and, at the same time, erodes the personal private enterprise initiative of many of the recipients. A parallel to this situation, and equally deterring to the competitiveness of the Canadian economy on the export market, are the Canadian employee benefits in which regard we are almost world leaders. No one would obstruct the providing of any reasonable benefits so long as they are earned and do not deteriorate the long-term interests of Canadian private enterprisers, both corporate and personal. These private enterprise criteria are certainly not being observed in the welfare and benefits being "arranged for" Canadians by our parliamentarians and our labour leaders. The best of welfare programs will never make Canada a land of opportunity.

These thoughts lead to further questions concerning the state of the Canadian environment and how conducive it is to the economic development of Canadian enterprises. This subject is mammoth and can be studied from many viewpoints. Let us, therefore, confine our attention to what the environment has been doing to the private enterprise of Canadians which is the subject of this chapter.

Literally for generations, the talk of freer trade or of reciprocity of trade with the United States has had high priority in public and government circles. Imports of consumer and industrial products have for years been encouraged in order to favour exports of raw and natural resource materials. Such thinking has expanded our materials economy and attracted outside capital in abundance which has meant substantial external control of those industries. Moderate tariffs and the possibilities of trade with the Commonwealth on a preferential basis also attracted outside capital for the production of consumer and industrial products. Currently over 60% of our manufacturing capacity in the country is controlled from beyond our borders. The long-term effect of these situations on the private enterprise of Canadians has been degenerative. Many individuals have been discouraged by the really difficult prospect of starting new small industrial operations which could later be the backbone of the economy. It is a fact that most of those which have started operating have sought foreign assistance, particularly in the field of creative work.

Frequently heard is the proposal that Canadian private enterprisers should start new Canadian businesses in fields in which Canadians can be more knowledgeable and experienced than the businessmen of other countries. If there ever was a red herring, this is one of the more obvious. The idea is impractical until the performance of Canadian creative work is much more enthusiastically adopted by Canadian business and our economy encourages such work by the sincere patronage of domestic efforts. The proposal will never provide a base for the building of a balanced industrial economy in our country. Many Canadians, discouraged with the prospects of their own enterprises in the Canadian environment, have sold their equity to foreign interests. Too, some of these same citizens, other disillusioned persons, and some expedient operators have been investing in American equities rather than keeping money in Canada where it is vitally needed. On a dollar per capita basis, Canadians own more American business equity than Americans do of Canadian enterprises. Because Canadians seem to want to bask in the American sun, our governments have for years fostered continentalism first, internationalism second, and nationalism third. The connotations of the former two have been lauded, whereas nationalism has been downgraded as selfish and expedient—almost a dirty word. Looked at critically as an environment for an underdeveloped country, enlightened nationalism is good and is really the providing of a reasonable opportunity to citizens to engage in the private enterprise of their choice. Absentee ownership and control tends to discourage domestic private enterprise.

There is one other influence chilling to Canadian private enterprise; that is the extensive infiltration of American unionism into the control of our labour forces. Unionism practicing private enterprise self-interest has and can do much for an economy, but when selfish expediency takes control and "sells" a membership on such practices, the long-term good of an economy suffers. The completely unrealistic wage increases which currently have virtually been forced by political expediency, and which are far beyond the possible gains in productivity, resprescent a complete lack of understanding of the functioning of a free enterprise economy. It will be nothing short of a miracle if the effectiveness of the Canadian economy is not set back half a decade by the inappropriate and untimely government action. Too, Canadian business is being intimidated by foreign interests to pay wage rates comparable to those prevailing in the mature, developed industries of the foreign land, despite the fact that the basic living costs are lower in Canada. Such a practice does not make good private enterprise sense and, rating those workers who accept less than parity as a second-class citizen, is degrading to the honest efforts of sincere private enterprise employees and employers. Canadian union leaders have a responsibility to truly be private enterprisers in a free enterprise economy.

The current inflationary trend in Canada is a first-class example of the ineptness which characterizes governmental attempts to control private enterprise. The wage increases referred to above were "arranged" by decisions of the federal government for a small group of employees, under federal jurisdiction. The percentage figure became a nationwide criterion for all labour negotiations in process and pending for both public service and private enterprise. As events transpired, in a number of cases the union membership itself demanded the government percentage increases, leaving no jurisdiction to their own leaders or negotiators and virtually voting "thumbs down" on any lesser "offering" without the proposal's having been made.

The wage increase was of such a proportion that no private enterprise could agree to pay it without a significant increase in selling prices. Yet another department of government initiated the reconsideration of some price increases necessitated by higher wages on the basis that inflation must be controlled. There could not be a much clearer indication that the government was much more interested in the large number of hourly rated employees than they were in either shareholders or the future development of industry. After private enterprise decided to provide an exemplary action as an anti-inflationary move, the public credit was taken by the government almost implying that industry had "knuckled under" to a demand. The government is not often so inconsistent in economic matters as to allow the right hand to do something the left hand does not know about. Too, in recognizing the inflationary trend, some peculiar accusations have been made by top labour leaders and left wing parliamentary members. The one which was so obviously untrue and misleading was to the effect that it was the large increases in business profits, not the additional wages, which were feeding the fires of inflation. Such a statement could be proved incorrect by a grade eleven high school student with an interest in mathematics, if he had the facts.

The purpose of these few paragraphs on inflation is to point out that neither parliamentarians nor government economists can control inflation once too much money starts chasing too few goods, which is the ultimate accelerator. Actually, the one bright hope of containing inflationary pressures is a higher level of understanding and appreciation of the basic operation of the free enterprise system by the average Canadian. Only by having such improved comprehension and self-control can the millions of people making free enterprise decisions orient their thinking and actions so that economic measures can be effective in limiting the inflationary spiral.

By many influences, Americans and other nationals have, through their own private enterprise and their own self-interest, really been too good to Canadians. Too much has been done for us, and creative work has been so readily available from others for a fee that our initiative has been dampened, and we have relied on supplied ingenuity rather than creating our own. By these statements there is meant no disparagement of the American or United Kingdom contributions to the growth and development of Canadian natural resources and primary industries, and the employment thereby afforded our citizens. The subject of our discussion pertains to the viability of private enterprise in our free economy. Operating in such an environment, there is little wonder that many Canadians have found it easier to let others run the show, less risky to sell their own operations and invest in foreign equities, more interesting to emigrate to the United States, and, lastly, for the third group, more "content" to rely on a security provided by the government than on the cumulated results of their own efforts. By so doing, however, we abrogate our responsibilities as Canadian private enterprisers to make free enterprise work well in Canada.

The development of the Canadian free enterprise social economy has been greatly inhibited by selfishly expedient thinking. The "brain drain" which has resulted in approximately six million people leaving Canada for the United States since the latter part of the nineteenth century, has stemmed directly from such thinking. While Canada has been exceedingly fortunate in the immigration of many well-trained people from Europe and other countries, the loss of even one of those new Canadians, or one of our own Canadian born and trained citizens, detracts from our development. The one bright hope on the Canadian economic horizon which can help rectify the "drain" is the incentive provided by our federal government in 1963 to stimulate research and development in Canadian business. More environmental stimulants of this sort are required if the Canadian economy and our private enterprises are to develop effectively in the highly complex and competitive world of the latter half of the twentieh century through the employment of our growing population in domestic private enterprise.

Thinking of the expanding of employment opportunities highlights the essential place of Canadian youth in our home-based enterprises. It is essential that our young people with both a broader range and more educational facilities available today, be recognized through having the opportunity to prove themselves. They are all potential private enterprisers. So frequently youth is considered too immature to carry responsibilities and must await a turn at the better job until management feels a move should be made. Generally speaking, youth's interests in educational availabilities are not taken as seriously as they should be by the academic pundits or businessmen. In a recent survey of opinion, 94% of the high school students responding expressed the opinion that there should be some study of economics in secondary schools. Proper attention to the thinking of our young people is essential if we wish to keep their outlook resilient. Nothing can stultify private enterprise more effectively than to close the door on the more distant Canadian scene. To the ambitious private enterpriser, the view across our southern border has for years been inspiring and enticing.

All these symptoms of our Canadian disinclination to consider where we are going add up to the diagnosis that, as a people, we are exercising insufficient private enterprise to make our free enterprise system work as effectively as it could or should. We are a virile northern people—industrious, creative, and possessed of growing skills and ambitions. We have been blessed with almost a superabundance of natural resources—far beyond most other nations. We have an interesting history of political stability and have been responsible in our obligations. Our heritage is a potential for social and economic development, available in such inviting opportunity to no other nation. Yet we seem unable to rise in our personal freedom of choice and action to the challenge of creating an economy with a natural balance and an independent vitality. There seems to be an apathy and a bowing to the leadership of others which continues to sap our initiative and our private enterprise, as well as our will to face the need to compete effectively. We are today close to a choice of path. We urgently need to find within ourselves the spirit of the pioneer and the leadership of a vision of what Canadians can do, of what Canada can become, in order to choose the road to high national endeavour through freedom of enterprise.

In the postwar years, outstanding group statesmanship in our parliaments has not been at an objective level to effectively enthuse our citizens to really be Canadian private enterprisers. Because of this lack, our people have been practicing less self-interest than is required to make Canada a great, independent nation in the second century of our Confederation. In the purely economic sense, there is fortunately a new source of guidance; the Economic Council of Canada is making available the understanding and appreciation of the objectives we need. The first and second groups of Canadian private enterprisers referred to earlier are beginning to look to the longer term of Canada's future as indicated by the Council. However, the third group, until they are much wiser concerning private enterprise, require leadership to be in the form of more personalized examples. Businessmen, supervisors, labour leaders, professional citizens, including teachers and university professors, and, last but not least, our elected members of parliament must provide examples now and for the long foreseeable future. Good examples of this kind are being provided, but they are in inadequate numbers. Too, the overall impression made on the public by the examples has not as yet reached the level of confidence necessary to be an effective guide to the millions of citizens who must decide upon the choices involved in making free enterprise work. Only part of the responsiblity for this situation can be placed on the shoulders of those who are trying to be exemplary. The comprehension of the average citizen must take a major portion of the blame. Again, there is clearly a need to make available educational opportunities to learn much more about private enterprise and human psychology.

Canadians should be able to undertake the making of our choice of path, if there is introduced, with true sincerity of purpose, the very salutary provision in our environment to make possible the gaining of an appreciation of the basics of freedom of enterprise and of human relations. The knowledge learned will not only provide understanding, but can route many of the inhibiting misconceptions rampant in Canada today. To be private enterprisers, our citizens must understand the place of work and productivity, the relationship between wages and our standard of living. They must be aware that self-interest is the enlightened way of life, and that freedom of choice and responsiblity go hand-in-hand. As well, to be Canadians, our citizens must play their part in Canadian enterprise and growth and not be content with minimal selfishly expedient performance.

The theme of Expo '67, the World Fair of our Centennial Year, is "Man and His World". The broad vista of Canada's social and economic future in the world of tomorrow will be presented in attractive visual concepts and spectaculars for the world to see and should do much to stimulate the private enterprise spirit and the national pride of our citizens. It is to be hoped that such will be the Fair's most helpful contribution to our Canadian way of life, because the opportunities afforded by our heritage must not be lost to others by default.

These fine perceptions arise from the wisdom people acquire as adolescents and adults. They beget quality to the behaviour of our citizens. They make possible the implementation of economic policies and practices designed for the long-term interests of the public. Because they result in self-motivation, they make freedom of enterprise possible—an attitude of mind which restrictions and compulsions by governments will never originate. The Economic Council of Canada has reported its well-researched opinion that the economic future of our nation depends on the wisdom of all levels of management and labour. The Council's purport of being wise of course pertains to the level of technical sophistication concerning our complex economic world. With this finding, all of us surely agree.

The premise proposed in this chapter is this: Of equal importance to the future of our democracy is the wisdom of the average Canadian concerning private enterprise and human relations. It is a sad commentary on the level of private enterprise understanding when the opinion can be expressed concerning the current Canadian inflation that there is only one thing which will knock a little sense into people's heads, and that is a depression which really hurts. In our modern world of hyper-competition, corporate private enterprise will only be truly successful through the close and understanding involvement of its employee private enterprises. For Canadians to achieve a stature which appreciates and welcomes cooperative freedom of enterprise is surely the foundation upon which we can ensure our heritage of being "The True North Strong and Free."

The Economy
is People

Dalton K. Camp

THE CANADIAN IMAGE

Dalton Camp

Dalton Camp was born at Woodstock, New Brunswick, in 1920. He has attended universities in Canada, the United States, and England, and holds degrees from the University of New Brunswick and Columbia University. In 1963 he was Chairman of the Progressive Conservative National Organization Committee, and in 1964 he organized the National Conference of Canadian Goals. In 1964, and again in 1966, he was elected President of the Progressive Conservative Association of Canada.

A nation's character is revealed in the heat of great events, in the response of its chosen and representative leaders to crisis and challenge.

Thus, Mr. Mackenzie King, writing personally to Neville Chamberlain on the Munich settlement, September 30, 1937, informed Britain's Prime Minister, "the heart of Canada is rejoicing tonight," and expressed his "unbounded admiration" while predicting that the "achievements" at Munich would give Chamberlain "an abiding and illustrious place among the great conciliators . . . the whole world will continue to honour."

Two years later Canada was at war. Mr. King could then declare it "the supreme endeavor of my leadership of my party, and my leadership of the government of this country . . . that when the amount of decision came all should see the issue itself that our national effort might be marked by unity of purpose, of heart and of endeavor."

For such an exertion, some were reconciled, some reluctant, and still others would remain throughout highly resistant. The Conservative Leader, Mr. Manion: "Sir, we are bound to participate in this war. We are British subjects, we are part of the British Empire . . . we should pledge ourselves here today to do our duty by Canada and the Empire."

The C.C.F. Leader, Mr. Coldwell, expressed reluctance. The war, he said, represented "the same struggle for trade supremacy and political domination which caused the last war" and recommended, on behalf of his party, that Canada should "defend her own shores, but her assistance overseas should be limited to economic aid and must not include conscription of manpower or the sending of any expeditionary force. . . ."

As luck would have it, nothing could prevent a good part of another generation of Canadians cheerfully and willingly—for there was no other way—investing its life's blood in a world war, inspired by the leadership of a British Prime Minister, and finding, in the end, perhaps by surprise, that it was a struggle against evil far more sinister than that which appeared to exist in the minds of their politicians.

But this Canada of 1939, of isolation and nostalgic loyalties, of astigmatic politicians, of a general population profoundly generous in impulse and intuitively tolerant despite its obvious internal ambivalence, this Canada no longer exists. It, too, perished in the Second World War, submerged by a miraculous technology, overwhelmed by a world of new urgencies which emphasized new values as well as fresh revelations.

The patterns of history changed. So did the historians. Canada's W. L. Morton, who has not only written but seen most of Canada's modern history, marks the demise of "the old Canada" without mourning, except to say that "its corpse cumbers the ground." He adds, "Yet, what makes us stumble is not a corpse, but a chrysalis. . . . A new Canada is struggling from the shattered husk into fresh life, a life of larger views and of more dynamic spirit than the old."

Can we trust major historians as minor prophets? Whether we can or not, we should, with pertinence, confirm the unformed presence of a new nation, so that when we search for the Canadian identity, as so many are doing, we know it cannot be what it was and will not be what it now is. What it will be we can only guess.

Perhaps there is a twilight period between the Canada that was and will be. Between Mr. Manion's reassertion of a Canada peopled by "British subjects" and "part of the British Empire," and Mr. Diefenbaker's stubborn posture on continued South African membership in the Commonwealth, there is the measurable and growing gulf between realism and sentiment, even within the body of Conservative thought. Or between Mr. Cardin's impassioned speech against conscription ("Where are your concessions, you British Canadians, in favour of French Canadians? What have you ever done to preserve unity between the two great races in Canada?") and the pre-emptive brusqueness of the late Lesage administration over a whole range of federal-provincial and French-English relationships, since further simplified in Daniel Johnson's choice, "égalité ou indépendance."

In Canada, the more things change, the *less* they remain the same, with the sole exception of our politics.

What is new about Canada is its unaccustomed affluence, its relative worldliness, the hastening awareness of some national shape and dimension, brought on by television and the jet, which has created the first serious challenge to the long-established order of Canadian politics, divisively parochial and sectional. And, certainly, in addition to all these, there is the ubiquitous new majority—the youth, the best educated of all Canadian generations, and the least conditioned by history's inhibitions.

The life force of the nation, its political system, has yet to yield to accomodate these new phenomena. There is the suspicion, of course, that the changes are disorderly and dangerous. Where some see the Canadian society in a state of flux, others see it aimlessly drifting; where some see the happy prospect of a new Canadianism, Professor Charles Taylor finds the nation seized by a "paralytic continentalism." Where some see the first signs of a new political dynamism, Mr. Taylor bemoans "the failure of nerve . . . of large sections of the electorate today."

Most will agree, however, that "the problem is political." With much simplicity it might be said that nations become what their politicians make of them. Hitler's Germany and Stalin's Russia are extreme examples. While nothing can change our climate, our geography, or our past, our image is formed by the priorities, motives and imperatives of our society as ordered by our political leaders, selected by their parties, and confirmed by the Canadian voter.

What does change is our attitude towards those parts of the Canadian circumstance that are fixed. In 1913, Kaiser Wilhelm thought it "inhuman" that anyone should be an immigrant to Canada, with its forbidding northern climate. Pride aside, many Canadians would have agreed.

Thus did the world enjoy the image of this hardy Johnny Canuck, who spent half of each year preparing for, and the rest enduring, the Canadian winter, who spent those long, black nights in a vast, silent land where neighborliness gave way to claustrophobia and a brooding sense of the conspiratorial presence of a harsh nature. Today football is played in Winnipeg before cheering thousands on the frozen ground of a snowbanked field. Canada's construction and building industry works the year round. The handy euphemistic phrase, "seasonal employment," is no longer an acceptable apologia for government.

Now Canadians in astounding numbers hurtle south in jets or remain to revel in their own winter season, while oldsters tell one another that winters are not what they used to be, when, in fact, they are the same. But the obsession is gone, and with it the rhythm of putting things up or down and the winter habit of enforced isolation.

If we have mastered our climate, we have, at the same time, become uneasy about our geography. If one could superimpose Canada's traditional parties, one over the other, they would form a cross—the historic direction of one running east and west, and the other north and south. And the dialogue, once spiced with patriotic sentiment, has now become heavily weighted by the ingredients of the moral economists, who attribute the loss of the national soul to the Americanization of the national economy.

In a world grown accustomed to new proportions of power

and size, the Canadian uneasily finds himself smaller, with satisfactory definitions of "middle power" or "sovereign state" harder to find. Geography has placed us beside a colossus. Canadians who feared its appetite for half a century now fear its indifference. It is beyond living memory since "manifest destiny" has been a credible slogan in the mouth of an American politician, or a reasonable fear in the breast of a Canadian patriot. Instead commerce, a materialistic culture, pervasive technology and a continental concept of affluence have all combined to lull the latent spirit of Canadian nationalism.

We are more intimidated than threatened, more overcome by what we imagine can happen than overwhelmed by reality. But Canadians cannot be fully persuaded that gravity is conspiratorial. Dr. George Grant laments a nation, and notes the defeat of Canadian nationalism. Technology, he argues, is merging the two North American nations and, as well, the world. It is almost a liberal plot because, as a consequence, conservatism becomes impossible "as a viable political ideology." And since conservatism is the custodian of the nation's traditions, standards and institutions, the loss of the ethos marks the loss of the state.

There is enough in recent Canadian history to suggest this. Dr. Grant, with incontestable sincerity, equates "men who felt deeply about the Commonwealth" with those who opposed Britain's first attempts to enter the Common Market; those who fought to preserve the Red Ensign are upholders of "basic principles." In defeats such as this the nation was "lost". That it should be lamented depends more on your generation than upon your politics.

Dr. Grant's lost Canadianism was already lost on a majority of his fellow citizens, whatever their political loyalties. It represented a nationalism that was the impossible dream of the colonial mind. The hosts of new Canadians saw it as alien, rising generations looked upon it as sadly irrelevant, and a vital part of the nation, the French Canadians, found it divisive.

The Canadian identity? We were, as a nation, more unique for a lack of it. Some believed there was such a thing, largely because it was their own. But even where it existed, while it existed, it could not survive; it did not grow, but withered, even while many continued to worship the barren branch or the husk. The question then, as the poet Earle Birney asked, was:

Parents unmarried and living abroad,
Relatives keen to bag the estate,
Schizophrenia not excluded,
Will he learn to grow up before it's too late?

Claude
Jodoin

UNIONS IN THE FUTURE

Claude Jodoin
*Claude Jodoin was born in 1913 at Westmount, Québec, and
received his education in Westmount and Montréal. For more
than thirty years he has played a prominent role in Labour
activities, as organizer, manager, and executive officer. Mr. Jodoin
became the first president of the Canadian Labour Congress at
its founding convention in 1956, and has been re-elected
at succeeding conventions.*

Any consideration of the role of unions in Canada's future is
obviously speculative. But one fact is certain; unions will have a
place in the future, and probably a more important place than at
present or in the past.

The primary functions of a trade union are in the sphere of
employee-employer relationships, and as long as those relationships continue on anything like the basis that now exists, there will
be a need for employees to co-operate through their own organizations. It is the contention of the labour movement that this is of
mutual advantage. It seems quite apparent that it is to the advan-

tage of the employee who, particularly in view of the increasing size of most companies, becomes little more than one small cog in a big machine. It is also to the advantage of the employer, a fact that will become increasingly apparent with the growing complexity of labour-management relations.

Collective bargaining as we practice it in this country has, despite its weaknesses, proved its worth. The organization of employees into unions and the introduction of collective bargaining have been the keys to the introduction of a truly democratic system, and we must nurture and preserve it if we are to preserve democracy itself.

It seems typical of human nature that the failures attract attention while the day-to-day successes pass almost unnoticed. This is certainly the case with collective bargaining. For every dispute that goes to the ultimate end of a strike there are almost a hundred that are settled by mutual agreement and without any interference in work.

The practice of collective bargaining has a relatively limited history; and yet now, before it can be regarded as having reached full maturity, it is being exposed to the unusually strong stresses and strains of a period in which changes are being introduced at an unprecedented rate. It is, however, quite obvious that collective bargaining, properly used, can be one of the most valuable means of facilitating adjustment to these changes. It is possible that many important changes may be necessary in both attitudes and practices of bargaining if this challenge is to be met; but it must be met if our society is to reap the benefits of the new knowledge and technical potential that is becoming available.

The occasional voices that are heard asking whether the union movement has a future appear to originate more from wishful thinking than from factual study. Union membership in this country is now at an all-time high with a record number of men and women holding union cards. At the same time, a large number of groups which have traditionally regarded themselves as having little or no common interest with unions are showing a very keen interest in establishing a relationship. The trend in this direction is something that has not been previously experienced.

These developments are likely to contribute to the changes which, it seems certain, the labour movement will go through in the years immediately ahead. Some of these will no doubt be related to the changing nature of the labour force itself. A great deal has been said and written about the increase in "white collar workers". This is a term which can be defined in many ways, but there is no doubt that the nature of a great many jobs is changing rapidly. It has been said with a good deal of truth that factories are becoming more like offices and offices more like factories. With the increasing dependence of office operations on mechanical equipment, the similarity grows. Heavy expenditures on very complex equipment are leading to the introduction of more shift work for office employees, as management is naturally hesitant to see apparatus representing such a large investment lying idle for long periods. There is a growing realization among many office employees that the situations and problems that confront them are in a great many respects identical with those confronting their fellow employees in the factory.

This new realization of a common interest among employees extends beyond the office to technical and professional groups. In May, 1966, a group of 18 professional organizations made a formal submission to the Ontario Government seeking legislation to give bargaining rights to professional employees. This awareness of the value and importance of being in a position to bargain collectively has been spreading among many professional groups at an amazing rate.

Teachers' organizations have become noticeably more militant and have directed their attention to collective action to establish better wages and working conditions; and they have achieved a good deal of success. Nurses have displayed a realization that organization to obtain tangible recognition of the highly important service they perform is not necessarily in conflict with professional ethics. It may be said as an aside that this is hardly surprising because the medical profession has long displayed a high degree of ability to advance the economic interests of its members. Some sections of the medical profession are now openly using the words "collective bargaining", both with regard to the members of the profession who are employees and with regard to the discussions between the self-employed and the administrators of pre-paid medical plans.

Very active discussions have been taking place in the engineering profession concerning the whole matter of collective bargaining and its possible application to engineers.

In the white collar field there has been a major development with regard to the civil service; the federal government has implemented the principle of collective bargaining for its employees. This is a long overdue step but, nevertheless, a highly significant one. These civil service groups have formally affiliated with the Canadian Labour Congress, thereby demonstrating their recognition of a common interest with other groups already engaged in collective bargaining.

The action of the Ontario government early in 1966 in revising labour legislation by removing a major barrier to the recognition of unions by municipal bodies is still further evidence of this very marked trend. Prior to this amendment it had been possible for municipalities to opt out of the province's labour legislation and so handicap the efforts of the municipality's employees to enjoy normal collective bargaining rights. This section of the Ontario Labour Relations Act had long been a bone of contention with the labour movement. Its removal paved the way for organization of civil employees and negotiations in a normal manner.

To point to these examples—and there are many others—is not to suggest that professional people are hammering at the door in an effort to force their way into trade unions as we now know them. It is true, however, that a very considerable number of people who fall into the white collar category have shown, and in many cases exercised, a desire to become affiliated with the labour movement. Beyond this, a number of groups in the professional category have made approaches and established informal relationships with our organizations.

It is, perhaps, too early to forecast with any degree of accuracy just where this development will take us, what the relationships will be in the future, and what effect all this will have on the labour movement as a whole.

The trend is, however, unmistakable, and on reflection, hardly surprising. Employees are employees regardless of the colour of their collar, the title of their classification, or their income. As employees they are required to meet firmly established conditions. Their hours of work are clearly defined, as are their salaries, vacation provisions, pensions, insurance plans and innumerable other conditions of employment. These are all matters that are at the nub of collective bargaining, and the interest being shown by these new groups is nothing more than a recognition of one of the established facts of economic life—that employees can best protect their personal interests by acting as a group.

No discussion of the changes taking place in the labour force would be complete without reference to the great influx of young people. This is bound to have a marked influence on several aspects of our economic life for the next few years at least. We have been told that Canada faces, on a per capita basis, the heaviest influx of young people into the labour market of any industrialized country. This development is already being reflected in our trade unions. We are finding an increasing number of young people becoming active in our organizations. They reflect the steadily rising educational standard of Canadian workers, and it has been suggested in some quarters that they have contributed to an apparent upsurge in militancy.

The necessity for a continual flow of new blood is recognized by all progressive trade unionists, and the Canadian Labour Congress has organized and is conducting an extensive adult educational program to meet this need. It is an aspect of union activity which is likely to be further expanded in the years ahead.

Presuming that there is a general acceptance of the assumption that collective bargaining will continue to have a place in our economic life, then attention may properly be turned to the nature of this bargaining, particularly as it is likely to differ from that now practiced.

The changes that are confronting us, and that are likely to continue to confront us in the future at an increased pace, are by no means limited to the people who comprise the labour force. Tremendous changes have already taken place in the nature of jobs, and this development is certain to continue far into the future.

Only a few years ago it was assumed that the average individual would take part in some form of educational program for a more or less established period, then take employment and remain on the job for the rest of his working life. In the future this pattern will no longer be valid. It appears that very few workers, and probably none who achieve any degree of success, will be able to go through their working life without periodically undergoing some form of retraining or updating. There is strong support for those who predict that most young people entering the labour force today will probably change their occupation several times before they reach retirement.

These developments are clearly going to have a very marked effect on the whole field of labour-management relations. In many industries there has already been a positive illustration of the effect of these changes on employment conditions and on actual employment of individuals; as a result there is a growing sense of insecurity among many workers. A prime example is, of course, employment problems on the railways and the circumstances which led to the important enquiry conducted by Mr. Justice Samuel Freedman.

The issues and the findings dealt with in the Freedman Report are fundamental to the whole future of collective bargaining and employer-employee relations. The basic issue had been defined earlier by Dr. John Deutsch, Chairman of the Economic Council of Canada, in these words:

> We are confronted with the problem of how to deal with dis-placement and dislocation, with the need for retraining, with the development of new skills, with the survival of an enter-prise and the investment of new capital, with material and human losses, and with the problem of how to distribute new benefits between wages, social welfare and leisure. These are complex and rapidly changing issues which cannot be tackled successfully unless, first, there is mutual concern and mutual recognition of the legitimate role of each party; second, there is a realization that neither the responsibility nor the cost of adjustment can be imposed solely upon one of the parties or let fall upon the weak; and third, there is a comprehension of the need for objective analysis, for information, for prior study, for consultation and forward planning, and for a readi-ness to deal with realities.

That definition gives some idea of the scope of the problems which must be met and dealt with if we are to take advantage of the great advances that are opening to us.

There are, of course, very wide differences of opinion as to the eventual effect of automation and all other forms of technological change. Opinions have varied, from forecasts that a minute frac-tion of the present labour force will be required, to the other extreme of continuing labour shortages. At this stage none of the proponents of these positions seem to present completely convincing arguments. No one really knows. However, we do know that very significant changes are already taking place and will undoubtedly continue to take place, affecting a large number of employees. To meet these new circumstances, fundamental changes are going to be required in at least some of the traditional approaches to labour-management relations. Moreover, the impact of these changes extends beyond those persons immediately concerned. Mr. Justice Freedman made reference to this when he said,

> A wise and benevolent employer may protect the present job holder either by retaining him in it until his retirement or by assigning him to another job. But what of the new entrant into the industry? For him the former job no longer exists. "Silent firing" is what this state of affairs is sometimes called. This new member of the labour force may perhaps have a different job available to him. But he may have to go elsewhere to obtain it, and so even in such cases some hardship would result from the technological change.

The various aspects of this sweeping development led Mr. Justice Freedman to this basic conclusion:

> The old concept of labour as a commodity simply will not suffice; it is at once wrong and dangerous. Here there is a responsibility upon the entrepreneur who introduces technological change to see that it is not effected at the expense of his working force. That is the human aspect of the technological challenge and it must not be ignored. There are responsibilities upon labour as well. Perhaps chief among them is not to use its organized strength in blind and willful resistance to technological advances. Labour must recognize the constructive role of technology in the general welfare and the economic strength of the nation. Nor should it insist upon unreasonably high rewards or excessive safeguards as the price of its acceptance of change. Stubborn opposition to measures of progress can only hurt the nation, labour not least of all. There is a challenge here to labour leadership.

This is a challenge which progressive labour leadership is both ready and anxious to meet. The constructive role of technology is recognized by the vast majority of trade unionists and with it comes the challenge to see that its benefits are fairly shared. This will continue to be a fundamental task of trade unions in the years ahead, and the very circumstances which Mr. Justice Freedman outlined draw attention again to the continuing need for trade unions as part of our economic and social structure.

Mr. Justice Freedman's report also drew attention to the fact that whole communities are likely to feel the impact of these changes. In some instances this has already happened. This fact, again, makes it important that voices from all sides be clearly heard. It has become very apparent that one of the greatest danger spots in these situations comes through a breakdown in communications. Sound employer-employee relations on a well organized basis can do a great deal to strengthen communications, to provide a means for prior discussion and to avoid unnecessary misunderstandings.

Governments can, and must, play an important role in research and in assisting both labour and management in meeting their mutual problems; but the parties primarily concerned are labour and management, and the issues that arise must eventually be solved between them.

It is becoming increasingly evident that it is impossible to write into collective agreements clauses which cover every possible eventuality; and this inability becomes more apparent with the growing complexity of labour problems and with the rapidity of change. This means that some provision has to be made for dealing, in an equitable manner, with matters that arise between contract negotiation periods.

It also means that provision must be made in collective agreements for dealing with situations which arise from these new conditions. The greater the degree to which one can anticipate particular situations, the greater the success is likely to be in meeting these problems. Studies have shown that there is a considerable time lapse between the decision-making period for new equipment and its actual introduction. We must learn to make better use of this time in preparing the human adjustments which the new equipment or process requires.

There is obviously no pat, overall solution. It is inevitable that there will be wide variations in the circumstances, in the impact of change and in the remedies required. There are, however, a number of approaches which can prove useful in one situation or another.

Severance pay plans are one of the most common and simple

methods of providing some cushioning effect to workers who see their jobs disappear. At the same time, severance pay does not tackle the basic problem. At best it is a means of helping the worker through a temporary difficulty. If his difficulty in obtaining new employment turns out to be more than temporary, then its effectiveness is lost.

There is what is sometimes called the "red circle" job. This means that the worker on a job that is affected is protected. He personally does not suffer a loss of pay; whatever adjustment needs to be made in the classification is made when he is eventually replaced.

The portability of pension plans, private as well as public, can be an important factor in helping a worker to adjust, as can the portability of insurance and other social benefits.

There is naturally a good deal of speculation concerning hours and the likelihood that we will see a further reduction in the work week. This is very likely to happen, though it must be remembered that workers cannot be expected to accept corresponding reductions in their earnings. It seems at least as likely that the working life of employees will be steadily reduced. In recent years we have seen a definite trend toward extension of education, and it is quite apparent that this is essential if young men and women are to adequately prepare themselves for a career. This means that they enter the labour force later than they otherwise would.

At the other end of the scale there is a marked trend toward earlier retirement. In a number of instances in which technological change has created a pool of redundant workers, special inducements have been given to workers who agree to retire earlier than they had originally anticipated. Some reports indicate that such measures have met with considerable success. A pattern of longer vacation periods and additional statutory holidays has been firmly established in the Canadian collective bargaining picture.

All these matters, of course, fall within the scope of the general social and economic pattern of the country; but the great majority of them are also subject to collective bargaining. Experience has shown that most have been very actively dealt with in the bargaining relationship between employers and unions. In fact, in a great many cases, it is through bargaining that these measures were first introduced; subsequently they were more generally accepted. This fact again underlines the important function which unions will inevitably play in the business perspective of the country.

The question of the type of trade union structure necessary to meet future needs is at present being carefully studied by the Canadian Labour Congress. Over the years the Canadian labour movement has evolved from a number of completely independent and isolated groups to a large structure. Four-fifths of the organized workers in Canada are members of unions affiliated with the Canadian Labour Congress, which is, in effect, a federation of unions. As part of its structure it in turn charters provincial bodies, provincial federations of labour, community organizations, and labour councils.

Each of the more than one hundred affiliated unions retains complete autonomy in its bargaining relationship with employers and in managing its own affairs, as long as it stays within the terms of the Congress constitution dealing with corruption, etc. One inevitable development has been a blurring of jurisdictional lines and the operation of more than one union in a particular field. This has sometimes led to complicated situations with repercussions both within the labour movement and without.

This whole matter has been studied by the labour movement over a period of years and, gradually, some approaches have been developed to smooth out inter-union relations. None, however, has provided a final answer and this fact, coupled with the new demands of union organization, has led to the more intensive study which is now being undertaken.

What the outcome will be remains to be seen; but this development is important because of its recognition of the readiness of the labour movement to confront and adjust to changing situations.

While the multiplicity of unions has, quite properly, given rise to concern, there is evidence of a strengthening of the relationship between unions and, in some instances, of a merger of unions with common interests. This greater degree of co-operation appears to be spreading on a world-wide scale. A large part of the Canadian labour movement has long been active in the international field through the affiliation of the Canadian Labour Congress with the International Confederation of Free Trade Unions. By this means Canadian union members have given considerable assistance to workers in developing parts of the world, in organizing their own democratic trade unions and in introducing collective bargaining.

This type of relationship is now going a step further in certain industries. Recent world conferences have been held by union members in two industries: electrical manufacturing and automobile manufacturing. The extension of big corporations in both these industries, as in many others, makes it essential that the workers' organizations keep pace by establishing a good working relationship among themselves. Here, once again, we see the trade union movement evolving to meet a new situation.

Beyond the day-to-day matters that are dealt with in the normal employer-employee relationship there is the role of the labour movement as a social force. This is a function which will undoubtedly continue as far as we can see into the future. In recent years great strides have been made in the provision of social services; but certainly the Canadian labour movement does not feel that the ultimate goal has been reached. In this respect, as with our bargaining objectives, what we seek is, as Sam Gompers once said, "More". We think this a worthy objective; the "more" we seek represents progress. When we lose that objective we are in danger of becoming a stagnant society.

It has long been the contention of the Canadian labour movement, at least as represented by the Canadian Labour Congress, that Canada has lagged behind in the provision of social services for its citizens. The introduction of a comprehensive national health plan is a prime example of this weakness.

It is only since the introduction of the Hall Report in 1965 that there has been general recognition of the practicality of a health plan to provide equal protection to all Canadians, despite the fact that such plans have been in effect in many other countries for a great many years.

There are many other loopholes in the structure of our social services. Our treatment of older citizens through an entirely inadequate pension scheme has been nothing less than a national disgrace. It is possible to go on and on with such a list of deficiencies; but the point to be made here is that we must have continued pressure for improvement, not only to bring present provisions up to a more adequate standard but to ensure that people who are dependent on these services share in the general progress which we, as a nation, will continue to make.

This philosophy is a fundamental part of labour's growing interest in politics; but at the same time we, as trade unionists, recognize that a political party alone is not enough. We in the Canadian Labour Congress are giving increasing support to the New Democratic Party as the party which we find most clearly reflects the view of our organization. We take this position fully recognizing the democratic right of every one of our affiliates, and of every individual member, to exercise his own political prerogatives.

In exactly the same manner we, as an autonomous organization, reserve the right to criticize the New Democratic Party or any other party. In exercising the rights and responsibilities of citizens we do not feel that we are in any way sacrificing our fundamental role as a trade union organization.

In summary, it appears certain that the labour movement in Canada is going to play an increasingly important role in the nation's affairs. Even some of the sharpest critics of trade unions frequently acknowledge that they have made a considerable contribution in the past. Those of us actively connected with the labour movement today look forward to an even greater contribution in the future.

David Kinnear

MERCHANDISING FOR TOMORROW'S CONSUMER

David Kinnear
  Born in 1909 at County Down, Northern Ireland, and educated in Belfast, David Kinnear came to Canada in 1928. The same year he joined the staff of the T. Eaton Company Limited, and in 1965 was appointed to his present position as Executive Vice-President and Chief Executive Officer of the Company.

In tackling a subject of this kind, it is perhaps advisable for the writer to ensure at the outset that he and the potential readers have the same understanding of the meaning of the title.

The term "merchandising" is generally accepted as the process of planning involved in having the right goods or services in the right quantities, at the right price, in the right place at the right time, and to accomplish this profitably. Successful merchandising requires the operator to be a keen observer of changing consumer wants, and to be able to determine with reasonable accuracy not only what goods or services will be in popular demand, but also where consumers will want to buy them—at a suburban store or downtown, in the home or through a catalogue by telephone; with what accompanying services, clerk service, self-selection, credit arrangements, delivery, etc.; and at what times of day, week, or month, noon-hours and evenings for downtown workers, week-days for housewives with school-age children, evenings and Satur-days for mothers with preschool children, Saturday for suburban families, etc.

The term "tomorrow" also requires clarification. Merchan-dising is really a forecasting business. Short term forecasting of consumer needs over several months is a regular procedure in the business. In so short a period, major changes are rare, and the forecast usually involves minor shifts in direction or rate of change. Week-to-week information on the trends of sales enables the merchant to spot significant demand trends and to provide for them in his buying of merchandise. On the other hand, long-term forecasts for merchandising, forecasts which typically run ten years or more into the future, are basically extrapolations or pro-jections into the future based on historical trends. The data used is drawn from the developments of a number of years in the past and is projected into a much longer future than is done by the short-term forecast. The long-term forecast suggests what life will be like ten or fifteen or twenty years hence if long-term trends in population, labour force participation, income growth, consump-tion, etc. continue at specified rates in the future. It deals with a time period so long that, even though the important events are probable, the prior knowledge is not of great value over either the short term or intermediate term, since the ups and downs of the intervening years may overshadow the importance of the long-term goal.

Consequently, the really difficult forecasts to make are the ones that concern those intervening years—the period from two to five years hence—tomorrow! They must take into account the changes of yesterday, of last year. Which of these infant emerging trends will take shape and cumulate into trends of significance over the next five years? Which will flash briefly and fade out of the picture?

Forecasts of tomorrow must scrutinize with equal care the longer-term trends of five, ten, twenty, or thirty years ago. For example, our economy continues to be influenced by the effects of the depression years of the 1930's. The low birth rate in those years has resulted in the years after 1955 in a smaller proportion of persons in their twenties and early thirties, the ages when most couples have their children. Consequently through most of the 1950's and into the early 1960's, the number of marriages each year changed little. Over the next five years the number of marriages will be climbing significantly, with considerable effects expected on consumer demand. Another effect of the depression is that it produced a set of values, relating to many aspects of consumer needs, different from that possessed by the individuals whose work experience has been confined to the postwar period of an economy continually expanding except for short-term recessions.

So the influences that will shape the nature of consumer demand two to five years hence are mostly all around us now. In the complexity of our ever-changing society the trick is to distinguish which changes are important, to anticipate them and act on them. Technological development, new products, war, international and federal-provincial economic agreements, all produce change in our social and economic environment, as do people's values and tastes, their living and working conditions; so also do social, political, and religious upheavals. Some of these changes that escape recognition as infant trends of significance will undoubtedly cause substantial departures from projected long-term trends and bring grief to forecasters.

It may be considered extremely presumptuous for anyone to attempt to predict correctly even one or two of the important shifts in consumer demand that will occur over the next five years. Nevertheless, such predictions must be made and acted upon if a business is to enjoy future growth and not gradually dwindle away because all of its energies were concentrated on serving existing consumer wants. This short treatise attempts to examine some of the more significant factors that seem destined to shape the course of merchandising over the period suggested as "tomorrow." It does not attempt to deal with factors like international and national political events, duration of the war in Viet Nam, which are too uncertain and cannot induce logical action by business.

The topics that are discussed are the economic environment, the social environment, the influence of young adults, the technological environment, and the implications for merchandising.

THE ECONOMIC ENVIRONMENT

Will Canada's economy be expanding in the next five years as it has in the past five? Can consumers expect to enjoy the same sort of growth in incomes and living standards? Or are we likely to become becalmed in a period of recession or stagnation during which the economy will record little real growth?

After the end of World War I, the North American economy enjoyed a period of expansion until 1929, then a deep depression during the early thirties, followed by a slow recovery which gained momentum as the country converted to an all-out wartime economy in 1941. Prior to the end of World War II, the opinion was widely held that this war also would be followed by a severe dislocation of the economy, declining prices, and serious unemployment. Instead the economy entered a period of sustained growth as it strove to satisfy the unfilled wants of consumers and of business that had accumulated during the war years because of the underconsumption of the depression years. This growth in the economy extended, except for a few short term recessions, to 1957, by which time most of the post-depression, postwar backlog of demand had been satisfied. Through 1957 to 1961 the economy remained in the doldrums, then surged ahead in a resumption of the expansion from 1962 to 1966.

Now questions are being raised. Did we really escape a postwar deflation this time? Was it the 1957-1961 period, or was this merely a period of consolidation in the major business expansion that extended from 1945 to 1966? And are we going to experience our postwar world-wide deflation over the next few years?

The balance of payments difficulties of Canada, the United States, the United Kingdom, and other countries have come to be recognized as symptoms that the international monetary system requires an overhaul in order to provide international exchange liquidity sufficient to accommodate the growth in world trade. In the past, similar problems of international monetary liquidity have been resolved only after a crisis—in 1930, in 1921, and in 1907. It is not surprising, therefore, that warnings of a possible global deflation have been made over the past year or more by such responsible people as Prime Minister Harold Wilson and the International Monetary Fund itself.

While such warnings are justified—the danger exists—one

must give considerable weight to the ability of governments to deal satisfactorily with the situation. An important influence on future economic trends as compared with past has been the new role of increased government direction of domestic economies, using tools and information on the operation of the economy that just were not available in prior years. Acting through world organizations like the International Monetary Fund and World Bank, nations also appear to have achieved a degree of international cooperation now that they did not possess in 1930 or 1920, enabling them to deal successfully with the problem of international monetary liquidity. In assessing the economic environment of the late 1960's, therefore, we have confidence that the world's nations will reach a solution to the problem before a crisis exists and so avoid a worldwide deflationary period.

Given this assurance, we can look for the North American economy, and the economy of Canada in particular, to experience a new wave of expansion founded on the unparalleled increase in the proportion of young adults now beginning to move into the age groups between 18 and 30 years, and particularly those of 20 to 24 years. This increase occurs as a result of the uptrend in births during World War II and the sharp upsurge that followed in the years 1945 to 1948.

During the past sixteen years we have seen the tremendous impact of this upsurge in the explosive demand for expanded educational facilities—first in public schools, then in secondary schools, and now in universities and colleges. Now the wave is pushing on into the country's labour force. The first report of the Economic Council of Canada forecast that in the years 1965 to 1970 we should see 1,035,000 persons added to the labour force. This compares with 687,000 added in the years 1960 to 1965, and with 795,000 added in the preceding five-year period, 1955 to 1960, when immigration swelled the natural growth. Under conditions of favourable employment, we may anticipate that this major expansion of the labour force will have an impact on the production and consumption of goods similar to the impact already experienced on educational facilities.

When planning on a short-term, year-to-year basis, it is easy to lose sight of the economic consequences of abnormal growth in a particular market that become clearly visible when viewed over a five-year period. An idea may be gained by comparing the past and estimated growth in the number of persons in the 20 - 24 year age group.

5-Year Period	Numbers of persons 20-24 years of age
1950 - 55	15,800
1955 - 60	55,900
1960 - 65	208,700
1965 - 70	434,000

Estimates provided by the Economic Council of Canada report, **Population and Labour Force Projections to 1970** (December, 1964).

THE SOCIAL ENVIRONMENT

What kind of a society will we be living in by 1970 or 1971? How will people be living? How will social values, status symbols, consumer wants change? Hindsight is of considerable assistance in revealing how far we have progressed in the past, and from such information deductions about future trends may be made.

Probably the most outstanding change in the past twenty years or so has been the "rags to riches" evolution of the North American consumer. Canadians have not yet attained the degree of affluence of their neighbours to the south, yet the change has been remarkable nonetheless. By and large most people today are better off financially that at any time in our history. Family income has risen not only because of the general increase in wages and salaries, but also because of the increasing participation of married women in the work force, providing a second source of income for the household. More significant has been the gain in *discretionary* income in recent years; that is, in income available for spending after the necessities of life have been provided for. Continued enlargement of government and private welfare benefits, including family allowances, prepaid medical and hospital care, old-age pensions, and unemployment insurance, have eased the moral compulsion to "save for a rainy day" and released an expanding volume of spending power for use in discretionary ways. There is a leverage factor operating here. Once a family attains an income sufficient to cover its essential needs and provide for some discretionary spending, further additions to income become solely additions to discretionary income, so that discretionary income increases faster percentagewise than total income.

While the growth in family incomes has made possible the purchase of a better living standard, many other factors have combined to shape the kind and type of goods or services that consumers want. Among these factors have been the changing age distribution of the population, with an increasing proportion (37% in 1961) in the younger ages having no experience of working conditions of the depression; the growth in education, bringing with it more sophisticated tastes and a greater range of intellectual leisure activity; the injection of European culture and customs brought to Canada by the huge influx of immigrants who have come since World War II; the much wider participation in adult education; the increasing urbanization of the population; the increased speed and impact of mass communication through television, which instantly brings American culture and customs into most Canadian homes; the improvement of automobile and airline transportation, which has brought about enormous increases in travel; the changing working conditions, especially the shortening work week and the expanding participation of women in the work force.

The important change in the consumer wrought by these influences has been an increasing sophistication which demands much greater variety of product, better quality, and styling that is "fashion-right".

In contrast to the single mass market of the 1930's and 1940's, a market plagued by low incomes and by the experience of living through the depression years, we now have a stratified market dominated by an entirely new upper middle income market, which is the largest and most powerful consumer group. It is comprised mainly of urban people trained in executive, managerial, and professional occupations and successful entrepreneurs who enjoy incomes of over $7,000 annually. It now accounts for approximately 50% of the market and is growing in importance. In addition, at the top of the scale is an expanding top income group, which comprises about 20% of the market. In contrast, the former lower middle income group, which used to make up about 50% of families, is now reduced to only 25%, and below this is the marginal subsistence group of low income who either cannot or will not find the means of self-support. It all adds up to the fact that today just about 70% of the consumer market can be considered as upper or upper middle class, and it is from this segment mainly that the demand has come for better quality in all its forms: quality of design, construction, and material; quality in performance; quality in packaging and advertising; quality in store appearance and decor.

The growth in demand for better quality merchandise is evidenced in many ways. Better quality may be equated with better intrinsic quality—a better technical design that results in more convenience and longer, trouble-free performance. Thus a hand lawn mower is replaced by a power mower, which is replaced by a riding mower. Refrigerators are now frost-free; electric irons must have automatic heat controls for different fabrics and be easily switched from "dry" to "steam"; cameras are equipped with semi-automatic or fully automatic devices to give correct exposures; cars with automatic transmissions account for an increasing market share and must have a "50,000 mile" power train guarantee; drip-dry clothing and permanent-crease apparel gain favour.

In another sense the demand for better quality has taken the form of a reaching out for merchandise of greater artistic elegance —a move away from purely utilitarian values toward the more decorative, away from gaudiness to simple elegance in design. It is difficult to find an area of consumer interest where this demand for better taste is not apparent. The architectural design and furnishings of the modern home or apartment; the simpler, cleaner design of Scandinavian furniture; the mounting demand for finer fabrics in men's clothing; the growing consumption of gourmet foods and wines; the enormous growth in sale of classical records, stereo, and works of art; all these are but a few examples of the demand for better quality merchandise.

Social scientists view the growing desire for merchandise associated with more gracious living as an expression of a change in the value systems of our society away from rugged individualism and indifference to comfort towards more civilized virtues and culture. It is a trend that should expand more rapidly in the years of our "tomorrow".

Quality of product is closely aligned with quality of service, as witness the long-term warranties issued by the automobile manufacturers. With more leisure we have multiplied our leisure time activities, with the result that we seem to have less time to enjoy them. So we stress the convenience and trouble-free attributes of products and services and resent those that fail to fulfil this requisite and subtract time from our leisure activities.

In the retail area, today's consumer demands a higher quality of personal service, a better quality of processing his purchases. Store decor is an important factor to the quality-conscious shopper, and retailers are striving to upgrade store appearance to meet this growing appreciation of good design.

Along with the new demand for quality has come a new insistence on variety and assortment with all its attendant problems for manufacturer, distributor, and retailer. This desire for "something different" probably stems from the increasing urge for greater expression of individuality, which more affluent and younger consumers tend to possess in great degree because fostering individuality in children has been part of our culture. Many examples may be cited to illustrate the tremendous proliferation of variety that has marked consumer demand in recent years.

Only ten years ago the classification "bed sheets" would have been considered a fairly staple item in one of our larger stores. To have a balanced assortment in it would require keeping in stock white sheets in four qualities, each in four different sizes, and in two brands. This would have represented a total of 32 stockkeeping units. Then we would have carried hemstitched sheets, again white, in two qualities, four sizes, two brands, which would be an additional 16 stockkeeping units. If you go into the sheet department of this store today, you will find again the four qualities, four sizes, two brands of white sheets, but you will also find a similar assortment of sheets in a number of solid colours, an assortment in coloured stripes, and an assortment of four printed patterns in four colours. Moreover, you will find not only flat sheets, but fitted or contour sheets that come in two sizes for twin and full-size beds, and in white, solid colours, stripes, and prints. In addition, the department is probably testing consumer reaction to two or three additional patterns of coloured sheets. In total, where the retailer had to worry about 48 stockkeeping units ten or fifteen years ago, he now has to consider a total of 616 stockkeeping units in trying to keep a balanced assortment.

In women's fashion the inventory complications created by

the demand for variety are even more striking. Ten years ago women's sportswear apparel was considered basic, and a large part of the volume was transacted on very few styles. Our store did a substantial sweater business with 30 styles, more or less basics, in cashmere, lambswool, botany, shetland, and nylon. On the average, each style would be stocked in 6 colours and 4 styles, so in total there would be 720 stockkeeping units to make up the assortment. With the big change to synthetics, and with consumer demand for variety, our largest stores must stock by style, yarn, weight, and price; so that whereas we carried 30 styles in 1955, today we carry approximately 175 styles. Again assuming an average of 6 colours and 4 sizes for each style, this means a total of 4,200 stockkeeping units in only one classification of merchandise. Think how the multiplication of assortments inflate the inventories of the typical large department store that carries on business in as many as 1,500 to 2,500 classifications.

Not too many years ago ski slacks were considered as an essentially functional garment. Three or four basic ski slacks were quite sufficient to satisfy most customers. However, ski wear has now become a fashion item, and we must carry twenty basic styles in various synthetics, stretch fabrics, blends, wools, and cotton, to say nothing of the wide variety of prints and textures.

Certainly over the next few years the growing affluence of consumers will extend the already strong demand for better quality merchandise and services and for continued diversification of product, and will augment their insistence on merchandise that possesses more elegance, more "fashion-rightness". There will be one important difference, however, and that is the acceleration in the influence of the young people in our population. Not only is their spending important, but their influence on all purchasing will be magnified.

THE INFLUENCE OF YOUNG ADULTS

As has been noted previously, we are moving into a period characterized by an unprecedented expansion in the broad 18-30 year old group. It is recognized that the 30-60 year old group of consumers remains the most important class of consumers; they form the largest segment in numbers, they have the highest incomes, they make most of the family purchasing decisions, they are the backbone of the consumer market. But they tend to have a conservative, "middle-aged" outlook. So it is primarily to the young that we must look for innovation.

As teenagers in previous years and in the present, this large new youth market has caused quite a stir. In merchandising, entire new lines of apparel, accessories, and cosmetics have been created to serve their wants, and they have contributed substantially to the great expansion in sales of such merchandise as sporting goods, records, and radios.

Not only are they important as consumers, but they exert a disproportionate influence on family living and family purchasing. Probably no topic has received more discussion among parents and educators than how to understand and get along with teenagers. They are credited with everything from the trend in sports cars to the popularity of the pizza. Consider their influence on the music and entertainment of the day. Consider also who started the trend to women's boots, textured stockings, pale lipstick and eye make-up, shorter skirts, stretch pants, and the bikini. Nowadays mothers tend to dress like their daughters rather than vice versa, and fathers wear the narrow trousers first adopted by their sons and are even making motions to join their youngsters in the trend to motorcycle riding.

Now many of this group are moving up into the age group that accounts for the bulk of marriages, household formations, and home purchases, and which spends a higher proportion of personal income on apparel, cars, and recreation equipment. In the light of past experience it appears certain that their influence will produce considerable changes both in the type and design of products and in the way they are sold. Consequently marketers would be well advised to examine their characteristics and try to anticipate the changes that will occur. By and large these young people are the trendmakers of our tomorrow.

Young people starting married life today want to start in the style of living they have been accustomed to at home. They are brought up to regard good housing, home furnishings, household appliances, television and stereo, and an automobile as essential possessions that they should have right from the start of married life. An increasing proportion of the new brides are postponing children and going to work for a few years to acquire these "essentials". Having experience only of an expanding economy, they are confident of their income prospects and willing to make their purchases by the use of consumer credit based on income expectations rather than on current income. Moreover, they may acquire their possessions from parents or other relatives as well as from their own earnings.

Today's youth is better educated than that of previous generations. Young people have been able to indulge to a greater extent in travel, through the use of the automobile and the airlines. They have been allowed more freedom in their relations with others outside the home; they have participated more in frank discussions dealing with many aspects of life. Consequently youngsters today are more knowledgeable and sophisticated than those of past generations. They display better taste and demand higher quality in the things they buy.

Young people are more mobile and tend to gravitate to the larger urban areas both for employment opportunities and for enjoyment of the other aspects of urban life. A greater proportion of them prefer to live in the central city area, where there is more to see and do than in the suburbs. Hence the years ahead should experience a quickening in the past trend of movement of population to urban centres and a continuation of demand for new, modern highrise apartments, centrally located. Since modern apartments are equipped with household appliances, a greater proportion of spending will be directed to furniture, home furnishings, stereo, and television than to stoves and refrigerators.

The young also participate considerably more in leisure time activities than people in the middle age groups. Expanding sales in recent years of equipment for such activities as skiing, boating, underwater diving, camping should receive further stimulation. And because young people want to discover things, grow in learning, and have new experiences, we can expect them to be a growing market for travel tours, particularly since the development of charter packaged tours and new "jumbo-jet" aircraft will lower the cost of such travel in the future.

Those who wish to merchandise successfully for tomorrow's customers should conduct research to define the psychological background and motivations of the current crop of young adults. For example, young people live today in a period when many time-honoured beliefs, customs, and traditions of our way of living are being questioned, challenged, and often discarded. They are under more pressure, therefore, to seek a worthwhile standard of values they can identify with.

For the young marrieds this sense of uncertainty is heightened by the new responsibilities they assume. When it comes to buying products they are faced with a larger variety and a greater misery of choice than in other generations. Moreover, because they spent less time in the home as youngsters, they haven't learned from their parents the "tricks" of homemaking. The young bride is confused by terms like sirloin, porterhouse, wing steak; and the young husband isn't sure whether he should use an oil-base or water-base paint on the walls and woodwork. However, they like to discover and learn things for themselves. Consequently, they will be influenced to buy where the sales person's approach is that of helping to solve their problem, of educating them in the use of the product and what it will do for them, of providing assurance that they have made the right choice. They will be equally influenced to avoid the sales approach which by any means, intended or otherwise, displays a lack of interest in their problem or exposes them to embarrassment because they lack knowledge of the product. Self-selection is not the answer; it avoids exposure to embarrassment but it contributes nothing to the other real needs of the young customer. Perhaps just as television is being used successfully to educate in schools, so it may replace salesmen in educating and instructing consumers in stores.

The greater participation of young adults in leisure time activities leaves them less time for shopping and causes them to be more insistent on quick, efficient completion of the transaction. They want related merchandise grouped together for easy, logical selection. In large department stores a trend has started to reclassify and rearrange merchandise so it is oriented to the customers' needs rather than to the requirements of the buying function. It may be foreseen that this trend will be accelerated by the growth and influence of the young adult market.

THE TECHNOLOGICAL ENVIRONMENT

More rapid change in our way of living and in our consumer wants is being fostered by more rapid technological development. Both result from two factors. First, the amount of money being spent on research in North America has greatly expanded in recent years. Second, nowadays new inventions and new technology are put into general use in a shorter period than in prior decades. For example, from the time they were invented it took 33 years for the vacuum tube and 18 years for the X-ray tube to receive general application. But it took only 10 years for the nuclear reactor, only 5 years for radar, and less than 3 years for the transistor.

Most of us are aware of the more obvious technological changes that act directly to change our way of living—colour television, world-wide T.V. projection by satellite, electronic data processing and digital computers, supersonic jet aircraft, Xerox copying machines, fast-frozen foods. Generally, however, we are ignorant of the many lesser known technological developments that promise to greatly change our health, diets, and work productivity over the longer term; for example, lasers, ultrasonics, negative-ion machines, solar energy conversion systems. The writer may be excused, therefore, if he claims no more than general knowledge of technological developments and confines his remarks to a few of these inventions that promise to have significant effects over the next few years.

Colour television may provide us with entirely new concepts of the use of colour in textiles for apparel and home decoration. Certainly it should stimulate the already growing trend to increased use of colour in consumer products. In the same way satellite transmission of international T.V. programs will bring the customs and cultures of other countries into our homes and induce new changes in the products we buy.

One other major technological advance of the next few years will be the wider development of the use of computers. The number of computers in use in Canada has increased from 4 in 1957 to 1,440 in 1966. Constant improvements are being made in the computer itself, but probably more important will be the progress made in the ability of management to implement computers so that the maximum advantages they afford can be realized. This is particularly the case with computer application in merchandising, as will be discussed in the next section.

Perhaps also the construction of new expressways and subways and new high-rise apartments in our major cities may be regarded as technological innovations that will induce changes in our patterns of travel and our shopping habits, and will force changes in industrial and commercial locations. On the one hand, these improved transportation facilities in and near metropolitan areas attract the movement of industry and of residences further away from the central city. From considerations of convenience, larger, more complete shopping facilities are encouraged to follow this movement—providing theatres, auditoriums for community meetings, doctors', lawyers', and dentists' offices, as well as retail and other customer service outlets.

On the other hand, the improved transportation facilities provide easier access to the central business district and afford the opportunity for the downtown area to supply the shopping goods and specialty goods needs of the entire population in the metropolitan area. Twenty years ago when our major cities were smaller, more compact, and well served by public transport, and when automobile ownership was substantially less, the downtown stores attempted to cater to all the merchandise needs of the population; now downtown retailers must re-align their merchandise mix and become the dominant centre for shopping goods and specialty goods—the better quality and more costly items of apparel, furniture, and home furnishings, goods which are purchased less frequently and for which people are willing to travel away from their community shopping centres to find wider assortments.

It is indeed fortunate that development of these new transportation facilities, providing easier access to the central business district from all parts of the metropolitan area, coincide with large-scale replanning of the downtown shopping core in these cities.

THE IMPLICATIONS FOR MERCHANDISING

Fortunately changes in consumer markets do not take place overnight but evolve gradually over a period of years. Over the past ten years retailers and suppliers of merchandise have generally responded with action appropriate to the changes in markets that evolved during those years.

During the early 1950's, as urban populations expanded and people were once again able to buy new cars in volume, thousands moved out into the suburbs to find a better living environment for their families. Retailers moved out with them—first in limited service neighbourhood centres which became obsolete as popula-

tion enlarged to the point where it could support a larger commu-
nity-type centre. This latter centre typically contained a 20,000
square foot food market, a 20,000 square foot junior department
store, as well as 25 to 50 other retail stores and retail service
establishments. Next came the regional type centre, containing a
department store branch of 120,000—200,000 square feet and other
stores on a 30 or 40 acre site. More recently to serve the still expanding suburban population these are being succeeded by the
larger regional centres, occupying 50 to 100 acres and containing
two large department stores. The Yorkdale centre in Toronto
which opened in February 1964 is of this type. It has about
650,000 square feet of department store space, 400,000 square feet of
other retail space, and includes two theatres, professional offices,
banking facilities, and other services.

As working habits changed, and in particular, as an increasing
proportion of married women began to work full time (10% of all
married women in 1951 to over 27% in 1965), retail stores responded by extending their shopping hours to provide first one
night opening, then from two to five nights for the shopping convenience of these working women and their families.

The growth in demand over the past ten years for merchandise
of quality, for products of better technical design that are less
complicated to use, for products in good taste that replace ornate-
ness with simple elegance, for products that are more artistic and
colourful has induced response in retailers and suppliers of retailers, too. They have endeavoured to satisfy the ever-increasing
demand of the consumer for a greater and yet greater variety of
assortment from which to choose.

The expanding demand for products for recreation in particular, where the consumer looks to the retailer for specialized and
technical advice on the use of the product, has fostered a tremendous increase in the number of specialty shops. For example, from
1951 to 1961, the number of camera shops in Canada increased
from 165 to 409; marine supplies and boat shops from a negligi-
ble number to 405; sporting goods stores from 449 to 803; stores
specializing in floor coverings, upholstery and interior decorating
from 359 to 719. Over the same period, by way of contrast, the
smaller general merchandise stores, geared to carry limited assortments of a wide range of merchandise of a standard quality and
price and out of pace with the changed demand, have lost ground

to the newer specialty stores, the department and variety stores. Their numbers decreased from 3,646 in 1951 to 851 in 1961.

In their presentation on the selling floor, retailers have endeavoured to meet the public's growing appreciation of good design and tasteful decor. They have spent millions of dollars in remodelling their premises and invested many more millions in new stores. In both cases they have supplemented their own merchandising acumen with the talents of architects and designers to create new and exciting environments for the presentation of merchandise. In new suburban shopping centres and in downtown areas, enclosed, air-conditioned malls, tastefully decorated, giving access to well-planned, merchandise co-ordinated shops of all kinds, make shopping an aesthetically pleasing experience. Within the large department stores specialty boutiques have been created to cater to the needs of the more discriminating shoppers.

Product packaging, wrapping paper, shopping bags, delivery trucks, advertising format—in fact all media by which the store and the product are presented to the consumer—have been scrutinized similarly and to some degree have been redesigned to project the image of good design and better quality.

There are three important forward steps that must be taken over the next few years if marketing in this country is to successfully move the volume of consumer goods required to maintain continued prosperity.*

First of all, the functions of the retailer and the supplier must be more closely co-ordinated so that the marketing process can become more efficient and distribution costs lower. The second step requires the re-creation of the central business districts in our cities. Third, marketers must be prepared with the right merchandise and service profile to meet the needs of the fast-growing young adult segment of the market. It is the writer's belief that action in these three areas will be the major concern of those engaged in the merchandising process over the next several years. Let us examine each of these areas.

Through the 1950's and 1960's, changes in consumer buying

---

*It is sometimes not realized that consumer spending for goods and services accounts for approximately 65% of total demand. In this affluent age failure of the economy to attain the goals set for it by The Economic Council may be due more to under consumption of goods through marketing inefficiency than to any other single cause.

habits have occurred with greater rapidity than in previous decades. In revising his operation to remain in tune with new consumer demands and at the same time maintain competitive prices, the retailer has had to extend his ingenuity to the utmost to hold down operating costs and maintain an adequate profit margin. For example, the growing participation of married women in the labour force has created a corresponding growth in demand for evening shopping hours. According to a Department of Labour Survey, in 1941 only 5 out of every 100 married women were working. By 1951 this had increased to 10 in 100, and by mid-1966 28 of each 100 married women were working. With so many married women working full time, stores have had to establish evening shopping hours—at first one night a week, then two nights, and then in suburban stores four and five nights a week. Such night openings have resulted in a higher utilization of capital invested in plant and inventory; but in both small and large retail outlets they have also provided management with a continuing problem of maintaining adequate supervision of part time employees in order to give a satisfactory level of customer service without adding to costs.

The considerable investment in new branch stores, in remodelling existing stores, in upgrading interior decor, packaging, wrapping, advertising etc. which has been made in answer to new consumer demands for a more attractive presentation of the merchandise is an investment of a long term nature. Over the short term, it tends to increase operating costs.

Finally, and most important, costs of the retailer have been increased by the necessity of handling the grossly expanded inventory forced on him by public demand for greater variety of assortments. There are two parts to his problem. First there is the increased difficulty of having the right merchandise; the retailer must avoid on the one hand the lost sales potential that results from out-of-stock positions, and on the other hand the excessively costly merchandise without popular appeal that must finally be marked down and sold at a loss. The other part of the problem involves the increased complexity and expense of the actual physical handling of the merchandise and the attendant paper work in moving the merchandise from the supplier to the retail store and out to the customer's home. These are problems of greater significance to the large department store and chain store organizations than to small retailers. Evidence of their effect on profit is seen in the slowdown in inventory turnover experienced by department stores in the U.S. and Canada. The report of operating figures of these stores by the National Retail Merchants Association showed that average stock was turned 4.3 times during the year 1956 but by 1963 it had fallen to 3.4 times and has remained at near this level in 1964 and 1965.

In an effort to cope with the vastly increased complexity of business that has resulted from the awesome expansion in the variety of merchandise assortments and from the establishment of suburban branch stores, the more progressive firms have been changing and streamlining their organizations and investing substantial funds in new materials, handling equipment, and electronic data processing equipment.

There has been a general trend towards eliminating costly free services and improving the gross mark-up by emphasizing the growth in profitable sales rather than striving merely for a growing sales volume.

At the present stage of this revolution in retailing, this struggle to provide for the new demands of the increasingly affluent consumers market, the score card is of a mixed nature. Some outstanding retail firms have managed to cope successfully with the new complexity of the business and achieve a notable record of success. On the whole the record of large scale retailers, be they department stores, chain variety, food or drug chains, indicates that the major achievements in reducing distribution costs and gaining satisfactory profit still remain in the future.

Possibly also the record of suppliers of consumer products has achieved a none too favourable record in this regard. It was revealed at the annual conference of the National Retail Merchants Association in 1964 that 95% of new products introduced were unsuccessful at the retail level. Just think of the waste in developing, producing, distributing, and promoting these products! It is obvious that producers must work more closely with retailers and other distributors in researching the market to determine just what new products have at least a good chance of selling.

The foremost necessity in merchandising for tomorrow is solving the problems of merchandising in a way that will satisfy the enormously assorted needs of an increasingly quality-conscious, even more discriminating market, and at the same time bring handling and selling costs down to a level where this can be accomplished profitably. The big costs of distribution are due to a misjudgment of demand. The merchandise that does not sell must be purchased, shipped and received, marked and placed on the selling floor where it occupies valuable space; it may be advertised and require sales people's time to show it. And when it must be marked down and sold at a loss, all of these costs must be loaded on the merchandise that does sell readily.

It is clear, therefore, that new and more satisfactory concepts and techniques of merchandising must be developed to make distribution of consumer products an efficient and profitable undertaking. Retailers must be able to forecast and specify more precisely their merchandise requirements; suppliers must assume the responsibility of scheduling production to meet demand and to guarantee delivery of merchandise free of defects. Obviously retailers and suppliers are going to have to work in close concert rather than at arms length.

The new techniques are going to have to involve the use of data processing and computers in order to develop the information needed by management with sufficient speed and to handle most of the paper work involved in ordering, shipping, receiving, delivering the merchandise, and billing the customer. Already experiments are underway to link the computer of the manufacturer with that of the retailer and to handle much of the ordering and processing automatically.

The rate of progress in developing new techniques of merchandising over the next five years will depend on the degree of success achieved in the re-organization and re-education of management and employees to change their working attitudes and methods to allow the computer to function properly.

In the area of downtown renewal, plans are already well-formulated in several of our larger cities for large scale, imaginative projects that will restore the downtown business district as the heart and soul and pride of the city. As already mentioned, in the large cities the downtown shopping core has a revised merchandising function which the suburban shopping centre complements rather than competes with directly. This function is to provide a lively, competitive retail aggregation that offers shopping goods and specialty goods assortments for the entire metro area, that caters to the shopping requirements of the downtown working population and also to the population residing in the central city area. The plans for the new downtown shopping areas are designed to provide for this new function and to create downtown a place that will re-establish the pleasures of shopping, a place for people to come to enjoy themselves, with space to move freely and leisurely and with things that delight the eye, entertain, and educate.

Naturally, because the scope of these projects involves many more interests than those of the merchants, the road to completion is necessarily a slow one. But the next few years should see material progress made in these areas. It is fortunate indeed that the new expressways and mass transit facilities in these cities are being constructed simultaneously to improve downtown-suburban transportation and augment the initial success of the new downtowns of tomorrow.

The third area claiming the attention of retailers and suppliers over the next few years lies in providing for the needs of the expanding group of young marrieds. An indication of these needs has already been given in this article. The important point is that this change in the consumer market is now underway and the major impact will take place over a short span of years. It is evident already in the steady expansion in sales of automobiles, in the sharp demand for new apartment dwellings, and in the persistent uptrend in the use of consumer credit. Those firms that will prosper from the new trends will be those that adequately research the needs of this market and employ imaginative new concepts to put their findings into use.

Sen. M. Wallace McCutcheon

CANADIAN BUSINESSMEN: RELUCTANT POLITICIANS

Senator McCutcheon
Born in London, Ontario, Senator McCutcheon graduated
from the University of Toronto with a Bachelor of Arts degree
in 1926. After attending Osgoode Hall, he was called to the
Bar of Ontario in 1930. Senator McCutcheon served as Director
and/or Officer of a number of industrial and financial
companies until 1962, when he was appointed Senator and
Minister-without-Portfolio of the Government of Canada.
In 1963 he served as Minister of Trade and Commerce.

The editor of *Canadian Business Perspectives* asserts that Canadian businessmen lack a total perspective of the business environment. If what the editor says is true, in what area does the deficiency exist? Where is the lack?

My answer—and the answer which I believe is implied in the very topics selected for this book—is that business executives, making recommendations or acting on them in their managerial role, do so with, at best, a superficial knowledge of the origin, objectives, and implications of political policies and decisions.

I also contend that the political level, making decisions which affect or concern business, is doing so ever more remotely from the realities of business operations and objectives in the 1960's. Business and politics, making decisions which affect each other's objectives and operations, decisions which affect our whole society, are doing so on the basis of a growing ignorance of each other.

Few of those who recommend, make, debate, or administer political decisions have more than a nodding acquaintance with business management, much less its complexities in the 1960's. Few of those who share responsibility for business decisions are aware of, or much interested in, the subtleties of the democratic political process.

That business executives are afflicted with a certain tunnel vision when it comes to political policy and decision making is demonstrated in the approach taken by business in its representations to governments and parliaments. Almost invariably, the approach is a form of *special pleading*—asking for the exemption of this industry or that, or this situation or that, from some tax or statute; protesting the adverse effect of this decision or that on a particular company, industry, or area. Seldom, if ever, is there a discussion of the broad objectives of political policy; almost never is there a positive suggestion as to how a given political objective might be better achieved.

That the political level is encumbered by superficial and outdated information about Canadian business in the 1960's is all too evident in the many complications, the unnecessary anomalies, the incredibly naive assumptions that are found or implied in some of the "new" legislation that has been passed in this decade. Quite aside from the argument over the principle of the Canada Pension Plan or the Canada Labour Code, for example, the definitions, details, and regulations written into such statutes as these require contortions of accountancy and administrative gymnastics on the part of both business and government that are weird and wonderful to contemplate. In the end, a perplexed business community and an embarrassed civil service manage to agree on some semantic liberties which enable them both to interpret certain provisions in ways which make possible a sensible application of the statute or regulation in question.

There is a wasteland of ignorance separating government and

business, the two power centres in our society. It is essential to overcome this ignorance if nothing else, to make effective communication possible. Somehow we must arrive at a better understanding of each other's roles, objectives, and limitations, a more thorough understanding of each other's motives and machinery. Otherwise, neither government nor business will make its maximum contribution to the whole society.

Clearly, it is impractical to think in terms of encouraging more politicians, civil servants, and others at the political level to become *involved* in business. In passing, however, it might be worth noting that the political process, and the society it serves, would benefit from some organized effort to keep politicians and bureaucrats more in touch with business trends, developments, and techniques.

The concern of this article is to encourage businessmen to become involved in the political process *as citizens*. This is one way in which those at both the political and business levels could acquire a more extensive knowledge and appreciation of the role of the other.

Contrary to what some businessmen think, legislation doesn't just *happen*, merely because politicians and bureaucrats are trying to justify their existence by devising new ways in which the political level can intervene in the worlds of commerce, labour, the arts, or education. Legislation is based on some concept of the country's needs as articulated by people on the political level; and this concept depends for its very life on a consensus arrived at on a more popular basis, usually within the framework of a political party. Whether the wider consensus or the concept comes first is immaterial to this article. The fact is that legislative action almost always is the last stage. When this stage is undertaken, the political people are reasonably certain of the concept, and confident about the consensus of support that exists. Miscalculation, especially of the latter, can be fatal, particularly if your opponents—having calculated correctly—are in a position to exploit your mistake.

Political leadership in Canada is not quite as responsible, nor as responsive, to the rank and file of its parties as it might be. In other words, our democratic process is not as popularly based as it is supposed to be, ideally. Nevertheless, most politicians will agree that the attainment of a popular consensus on a given policy must

begin with one's own party members and supporters. The successful political party, after all, is a good cross-section of the population of the country.

Who are the people who comprise what is referred to as "the
Party"? They are, of course, the elected Members of Parliament;
the national and regional executives; those who serve on policy,
organization, finance, publicity, and other committees; the executives of the party at the constituency level. "The Party" also includes the hundreds of men and women who have committed
themselves as active supporters to a particular party, and who give
their services to the political process at one or several of the
various stages, from the drafting of policy resolutions to the display of campaign literature, from the raising of money to the
distribution of placards. Imperfect though it is, the party system
gives each of them an opportunity to raise his voice, to have his
"say" on the public issues that concern him. It gives him an
opportunity to become involved, to participate more actively in
the political process—the choosing of candidates, the formulation
and presentation of policy—than his neighbour who does no more
than cast a vote on election day.

Political preference and activity is personal, a matter of individual choice, conscience, and responsibility. Corporations, professions, and ethnic groups don't belong, *as* corporations, professions or ethnic groups. Our political parties are made up of individuals who join as individuals, not as representatives of their
occupational or religious status or interest. To be sure, our major
political parties are usually representative, using the word in a
statistical sense, of the age, sex, ethnic, geographical, and occupational groups in the country. And every party member—the M.P.
trying to persuade his caucus to adopt a particular course, or
debating the Budget in the Commons, the party executive trying to
influence parliamentary leaders on a given issue; the party worker,
warning against the danger of a particular course of action—each
is conditioned and influenced by his own background, experience,
occupation, and environment.

There is but a handful of businessmen who can be counted
among the thousands of Canadians actively involved in this process, either as candidates, elected members, or committed party
executives and supporters. Business executives as a group are
under-represented in the list of the approximately 1,000 candi-

dates whose names are on the ballots at federal elections; consequently, they are underrepresented among the 265 who become Members of Parliament. Even more significant is the fact, which would be acknowledged by anyone familiar with our national politics, that business executives are among the least interested or active Canadians in political activity of any kind. They are conspicuously scarce among the party executives at the national, regional, or local level; among the delegates to party conventions; on policy, organization, finance, or publicity committees; indeed, among the citizens who occasionally attend a political meeting. In this sense, it is not as "reluctant politicans" that I criticize Canadian businessmen, but as *reluctant citizens*.

In smaller communities, local merchants do tend to accept some responsibility for leadership. You will find them in respectable numbers as delegates to party conventions, serving on local, regional, or national committees, and as political candidates. Many also devote a good deal of time and effort as part-time mayors, reeves, councillors, members of district school boards, and other volunteer civic work.

The most consistent truants from political responsiblity are the managers and executives from our middle- and large-sized corporations. As for their abstention from politics at the elective level, a glance at the statistics of Members of Parliament by occupation is interesting. Before the turn of the century, there were as many as twenty Members in a particular parliament who classed themselves as "executives". This number has decreased to a handful for most of this century.

In the 1963-65 Parliament, there were five Members who classed themselves as "managers", and there have never been more than twelve (usually four or five) in any Parliament since 1867. In the 1963-65 Parliament, there were seven who designated themselves "industrialists". Except for one Parliament (1949-53) when there were ten, there have seldom been more than four or five Members in this category. The number who listed themselves as "manufacturers" has declined from a high of eighteen in the 1911-17 Parliament to none in the 1963-65 House. The numbers so listed in the 40's and 50's has fluctuated between seven (1945-49) to zero (1957-58).

The number of economists employed in private industry has been growing since the War, and one might have thought that this might produce a group with an interest in public policy that would lead them to seek public office. There were two Members who listed themselves as "economists" in the 1958-62 Parliament, four in the 1962-63, and three in the 1963-65 House. Even here, many of the "economists", upon closer examination, turn out to have been engaged not in private industry, but in government service or in academic life.

These statistics are not entirely conclusive. Members list their own occupations, and Mr. Winters, for example, lists himself as an engineer, which he is. However, he has been a senior executive of a number of Canadian companies, particularly between 1957 and 1965, but there is no mention of these associations in his official biography in the Parliamentary Guide. Mr. J. R. Nicholson might list himself as a lawyer, although he too has had extensive experience in business. But it is clear from the statistics, and from personal observation, that Members with experience as business executives are vastly outnumbered by lawyers, doctors, teachers, smaller merchants, farmers, fishermen, and, on occasion, by clergymen. And, as I have pointed out on the basis of my own experience and that of others in political life, business executives are equally scarce in the ranks of active Party members and supporters.

There is, then, a discernible pattern of disinterest in politics on the part of Canadian business executives, particularly middle and senior management. The implications are serious for government, business, and society as a whole.

First, this virtual abstention from the political process on the part of business executives is one of the basic causes of the lack of knowledge that the political decisionmakers and the business decisionmakers have of one another and of one another's problems and objectives.

Second, it deprives the country of a useful human resource, especially at the policy-making level. I do not suggest that the talents of businessmen are apt to be more valuable in this respect than those of citizens drawn from other occupations; the point is that businessmen, like others, do have their own special experience and qualifications which enable them to bring a particular insight or perspective to political issues or problems.

Third, it means that those who recommend or make some of the most important economic decisions in the country are not participating in any meaningful way in the development of political, social, or even overall economic policies and goals.

My regret is not so much that their abstention from activity deprives our parliament and our politics of a "business point of view". I do not believe there is a "business point of view", or for that matter a labour point of view or an agricultural point of view, on most of the real issues that have to be resolved in this country. Moreover, no Member of Parliament is elected to represent any narrower interest than that of the public good, nor should anyone participate in political activity of any kind with anything less as a motive. To be sure, it is important that our parties and our politics should be representative of the broad spectrum of society, but political parties are composed of individuals, not of representatives of the professions or occupations.

Fourth, business executives and managers in medium- and large-sized corporations are becoming a larger group numerically, more important in the development and execution of company policy, with increasing numbers of employees under their influence. These include some of the best minds and skills turned out from our universities every spring, recruited avidly by our corporations.

Judged by the involvement of their inhabitants in the world of democratic politics, our corporation offices might as well be great monasteries of glass and stone. The organization man is a political celibate.

The attitude of the "organization man in general" to the larger society was described ten years ago by Willian H. Whyte, and is worth quoting in the present context:

> If ever there was a generation of technicians, theirs is it. No generation has been so well equipped, psychologically as well as technically, to cope with the intricacies of vast organizations; none has been so well equipped to lead a meaningful community life; and none probably will be so adaptable to the constant shifts in environment that organization life is so increasingly demanding of them. In the better sense of the word, they are becoming the interchangeables of our society and they accept the role with understanding. They are all, as they say, in the same boat.
> But where is the boat going? No one seems to have the faintest idea; nor, for that matter, do they see much point in even

raising the question. Once people liked to think, at least, that they were in control of their destinies, but few of the younger organization people cherish such notions. Most see themselves as objects more acted upon than acting—and their future, therefore, determined as much by the system as by themselves.

To the extent that the political process determines where "the boat" is going, the organization man has very little to say about it. Political involvement ("becoming mixed up in politics" is the phrase most often used by senior executives to describe the phenomenon), either elective or non-elective, is discouraged by most of our corporate employers. I am fearful that our large corporations are developing a generation of non-citizens. They will leave politics and government to the politicians, or, perhaps as bad, to the bureaucrats.

Most companies can supply a lengthy list of "practical" reasons which make political activity by its executives undesirable. Senior executives do not welcome any disruption of their carefully charted corporate plans. They do not relish the loss of a key middle, or even junior, executive who may be contemplating a venture into politics as a candidate. After he has served his term of office, there is no guarantee, and in fact, there is little likelihood that he will be able to pick up his corporation career where he left it four years previously. And it is often implied by senior executives that politics is somehow "bad" for business.

Political activity of a non-elective kind may pose fewer hazards to the career of the individual executive, but it is certainly not encouraged by the corporation. Executives are encouraged to discharge their civic duty (and, incidentally, to promote the public relations of the company) by participating in all the "safe" and "non-partisan" causes—church, service clubs, youth work, and so on.

All of these are worthwhile, but it is hard to understand why companies do not offer as much encouragement to executives and employees to take an active part in the political process. "Politics is bad for business . . . . . we have to deal with people of every political party as our customers, so we can't take a stand." Of course they can't. Nobody is asking the corporation to become involved in politics, as a corporation. What is being suggested is that the company provide a minimum encouragement to those of its executives who do wish to take a personal stand—to do so without jeopardizing their positions and careers with the company. But contrast the position of the executive who asks for a week away from the office to attend an out-of-town service club, or fraternal convention with that of his colleague who might make a similar request for the purpose of attending a political gathering, or working at an election campaign. The fraternal, charitable, or service activity is looked upon as complementary to the business career of the rising executive and, therefore, desirable. Political involvement, "getting mixed up in politics", is regarded as competing with, disruptive of, and somehow hostile to the interests of the executive and the company.

Again and again, one hears senior executives exulting in and exalting the virtue of something called "good corporate citizenship". It is hard to ascertain exactly what this is, beyond obeying the laws of the land, accepting government "guidelines" gracefully lest they be imposed by statute, and taking a constructive interest in the community which the corporation serves. I am not denigrating "good corporate citizenship". I observe only that it is as yet very vaguely defined. Whatever it is, it is not a substitute for the exercise of personal responsibility as a citizen.

If it is accepted that corporation executives of all ranks are reluctant to involve themselves actively in the political process, and if it is accepted that it is important to awaken some interest and activity, the obvious question is whether there is anything that a corporation as a corporation can legitimately do about it.

I believe there is. As a starting point, a company might issue a clear statement of company policy, stating first of all that the company as a company does not have any particular political preference, but that it recognizes the importance of political parties and the political process, and urges its executives to join one or other of the parties as an active supporter, to take part in its deliberations and become identified with it for the time and to the extent that the individual feels the party merits his support. The statement should then outline in some detail the conditions under which the elective ambitions of any executive may be accommodated—what leave of absence for campaigning, what leave of absence for holding elective office, what protection may be granted to the executive's seniority if he is elected, and under what conditions he may be able to return to the corporation if and when he leaves politics.

It should not be too difficult to outline what arrangements may be made for executives who, though not standing as candidates, wish to take an active part in the affairs of the parties. Attendance at political conventions out of town, time given to party committees, either at election time or between elections, can surely be accommodated by most corporations. The only guideline I would suggest in this context is that the arrangements should be at least as generous as those made for executives who take part in other community, charitable or fraternal activities. The most general rule of thumb seems to be, "If you are interested in politics, be interested on your own time". To many senior executives, political activity by their subordinates is regarded almost as unfavourably as moonlighting.

Fortunately, there are one or two companies in Canada, and a few more in the United States, that have troubled themselves to establish a clear policy which encourages political activity on the part of executives, and outlines the ways in which the company can accommodate it. There are perhaps three or four companies in Canada where such provisions are written into collective agreements with their employees. Senior people in the labour movement have advised me that whether the provision is written into a company-union contract or not, there is usually no difficulty in arranging the minimum accommodation for any union member who wishes to stand as a candidate—a leave of absence without loss of seniority from his job. Companies have not seemed willing or eager to make the same provisions for their executives.

At the University of Toronto, a directive was issued in July, 1966, which outlined the conditions under which the University can accommodate the entry of faculty members into elective politics. Leaves of absence are granted for campaigning at the federal, provincial, or municipal level, and up to a maximum of four years, to hold elective public office. Other universities have issued similar directives.

Some companies have gone—or tried to go—even farther. There are cases in the United States where companies actually provide forms for their executives and employees to list, if they wish, the political party they would be willing to support. The company turns these file cards over to the appropriate party. This is a very practical gesture, and one which I am inclined to favour as a politician; as a businessman, however, I acknowledge that the whole precedure could smack of coercion by the company, or an attempt to pry into the political beliefs of executives and other employees. For this reason, perhaps it is not to be recommended. Still other companies have provided "political education" courses. Here again, there is always the danger that such courses will either be accused, or will in fact be guilty, of trying to proselytize for a particular party or ideology. An alternative is to encourage executives and employees to attend after-hours courses in politics and government conducted by universities; and/or to take part in seminars and conferences sponsored by such organizations as the Canadian Institute of Public Affairs, the Canadian Institute of International Affairs or the Canadian Association of Adult Education.

In any case, there are some precedents that are worthwhile examining, if senior company executives are willing to take this situation seriously. In my view the failure of business executives to take an active part in the political process, either because of personal disinterest, the apathy of their superiors or active discouragement of the corporation, requires some positive response from the corporations that employ them. The very least a company president can do is to begin by asking himself whether company policy and attitude at the top, either expressed or implied, are in any way responsible for the disinterest of less senior executives.

Businessmen spend a great deal of time *reacting* to policies and decisions formulated by government. How the policies originated or were developed is a mystery to them. What the purpose is, is lost on them. What the effect of the policy is, is considered in the most narrow and subjective terms. I am not pleading for a stronger "business lobby" in government or political parties. The point to be made here is that if business executives involved themselves more actively in politics *as citizens* they would have a much better understanding of the "hows" and "whys" of political decisions *as businessmen.*

It is also worth mentioning, because it is important, that if business executives ignore politics, it is true that politics and politicians are almost equally ignorant of business, business decision-making, and business executives. The implications of this mutual ignorance in the Canada of the 1960's can be somewhat staggering.

It must be admitted that political parties and government are much less imaginative and perhaps even less persistent than they should be in attempting to attract business executives to politics, both elective and non-elective. Not much effort has been made to obtain leaves of absence for younger executives who might serve, for instance, on ministers' staffs in Ottawa, or at the headquarters of political parties, or as research, organizational, or "idea" men with party caucuses. Given some initiative on the part of the politicians, and a willingness to contribute on the part of the corporations, it might even be possible to explore the idea of "sabbaticals" for executives who might be interested in working in such capacities.

The medium- and large-sized corporation exerts a remarkable influence on the lives of its "organization men". It is perhaps not quite as direct or as personal as the influence exerted by the employer in another age who had a handful of employees who were the sons of his father's employees. But the influence is nevertheless potent and pervasive. The explanations for it have filled volumes of both scholarly and popular literature.

Citizenship, and its responsibilities, are personal. And until business begins to encourage rather than discourage or merely tolerate the active involvement of its executives and employees in the whole political process, there will remain a gulf between politics and business, two of the vital power centres of our society.

This gulf, only partially bridged by briefs, brochures, and occasional personal contacts, does not make for better politics and government. And it is bad business.

Howard

Ross

O.B.E., C.A., M.A. (Oxon), LL.D., D.Acc.

THE CONTINUING PROBLEMS OF
BUSINESS EDUCATION

Howard Ross

  *Howard Ross was born in Montréal in 1907, and obtained his
early education there. He holds a Bachelor's degree from McGill
University, a Master's degree from Oxford, and has received
numerous honorary conferments. As a prominent chartered
accountant, university governor, and member of a number of
enquiries on higher education, Mr. Ross has pursued a dual career
in business and education. He is the present Chancellor of
McGill University, Montréal.*

Any discussion of higher education is complicated by the fact that
education is both an end in itself and a vital factor in economic
growth. Our universities have a well-recognized obligation to train
people for the professions and for leadership in business, in government, and in other spheres. However, as the Commission on Financing Higher Education in Canada (the Bladen Commission)
points out, "We must not fall into the totalitarian way of thinking
of people merely as instruments, to be developed as the community

needs them; rather must we think of the community as an instrument for developing the talents of individuals." The Massey and Gordon Commissions have emphasized the same points; as did the famous Robbins Report in England when it stated, "... we do not believe that modern societies can achieve their aims of economic growth and higher cultural standards without making the most of the talents of their citizens. This is obviously necessary if we are to compete with other highly developed countries in an era of rapid technological and social advance. . . . But beyond that, education ministers intimately to ultimate ends, in developing man's capacity to understand, to contemplate and to create".

It would be difficult enough to plan in the educational sphere and to assess progress if we had before us the relatively straightforward objective of contributing to economic growth and welfare. It is much more complicated still when we must remember the twofold nature of education.

UNIVERSITES IN CANADA

In most things we tend to follow patterns established in the United Kingdom or in the United States. In our universities we are perhaps closer to the American tradition. Here, as in the United States, universities were founded in the early days by religious bodies and later by state or provincial governments. Naturally, the conditions being so similar, the same pattern emerged. The tradition in both countries has been for governing boards composed of "laymen", as contrasted with the government by academics that is characteristic of at least the older English universities.

There is probably no area where contrasts are sharper between university education in the United Kingdom and in the United States than in the field of business education. The original tradition at Oxford and Cambridge concentrated on classical studies. Even English literature was not accepted as a subject for teaching until late in the nineteenth century, and to this day the idea of teaching specifically "business" subjects must be contemplated with reluctance, although Oxford has just established courses in "management studies". It is not surprising that, as McGill's Donald Armstrong has pointed out, there were no college professors amongst the heroes of the Industrial Revolution.

However, great changes are occurring in all countries today, and three reports of high prestige have appeared recently in the United Kingdom, urging the case for business education at the university level. The National Economic Development Council and two Royal Commissions (Franks and Robbins) concur and speak with respect of what the Robbins Report alludes to as "the great business schools of the United States".

Leadership in business education has certainly always come from the United States. There had been undergraduate teaching in this field for many years when Harvard founded its famous School of Business in 1914. The pattern, which we have closely followed in Canada, has varied somewhat from university to university, sometimes being at the graduate and sometimes at the undergraduate level, in either "Schools" or "Faculties". Both "Commerce" and "Business" are common titles.

It is interesting to speculate on the extent to which the undisputed industrial leadership of the United States today is attributable to the early recognition in that country of the importance for business of the role of universities in business education.

In Canada we have followed, with characteristic sluggishness, the American tradition, as we have generally done over the entire field of university education. In the United States about twice as many people, proportionately, attend university. Moreover, there is an interesting relationship between the countries. The percentage of students of university age who attend universities in Canada today is almost exactly the same as the percentage in the United States fifteen years ago—and this fifteen-year lag has persisted for a considerable period. The trend is so generally recognized that future projections of university "population" in Canada can be quite confidently made by simply assuming that the Canadian percentage of attendance will continue to run fifteen years behind the American. However, while half as many Canadians go to university, the comparison is even more disparate in M.B.A. courses, as approximately seven times as many Americans, per capita, are enrolled in such courses.

It is impossible to get very far into a discussion of university topics without becoming involved in statistics. In fact the serious task of predicting the demand for education in the future has come to be known in university circles as the "Numbers Game". Whenever statistics of university attendance are used, however, it should be understood that they are inevitably very rough. In Canada education is a provincial matter, and there are basic differences in the school systems from one province to another. In Ontario senior matriculation is required for college entrance, while the English-speaking universities in Québec more frequently admit students at junior matriculation level, or one year earlier than in the Ontario system. On the other hand, the French-speaking universities in Québec are part of a system which includes classical college, to which there is no counterpart elsewhere. For these and other reasons, it is dangerous to make interprovincial comparisons without great caution. In the international field there are, of course, more serious differences still.

NEED OF UNIVERSITY GRADUATES IN BUSINESS

It is surprising how relatively little serious study there has been of the relationship between university education and business careers. Even in the United States, where much more work has been done on the matter, a study of business education financed by the Carnegie Foundation in 1959 complained that little information was available. There are some quite superficial studies, such as comparisons between the earning power of graduates and non-graduates, but these are not conclusive. Those going to university tend to be from select groups who would be expected to earn more than the average even if they did not go to university.

However difficult it may be to document the point, there can be no doubt of the validity of the general conclusion that training for business in universities is of overwhelming importance. All countries today are terribly dependent on steady economic growth. The maintenance of full employment, the raising of standards of living, the stability of foreign exchanges, the financing of the "welfare state"—all of these programs depend for success on increased productivity, and anything which caters to this becomes an essential objective. There is no doubt that one of the most important factors in the battle for increased productivity is better training. The Economic Council of Canada, in its *Second Annual Review* has concentrated heavily on this thesis, as the following quotations indicate:

> ... Education is a crucially important factor contributing to economic growth and to rising living standards. ... It has long been recognized that education possesses intrinsic value

as a factor enhancing the quality and enjoyment of life of individuals, as well as the quality and energy of a whole society. We fully appreciate this fundamental value of education and we would not wish to detract in any way from the basic view that education is a means of enlarging man's understanding, stimulating his creative talents, ennobling his aspirations, and enriching human experience. But education also has economic aspects whose character and dimensions have only more recently become a matter of interest and careful study, and it is primarily certain economic aspects of education which are the special focus of attention in this Chapter. . . . Intensified efforts in these critical areas of education will require a great enlargement of resources for education. But as already emphasized, the rate of economic return to education is very high.

. . . There is a general need to upgrade and bring up to date the education and skill qualifications of the existing labour force, including management and professional workers.

OVEREMPHASIS?

Paradoxically, while university training for business is essential and must be encouraged, there are many cases in which it is overdone. As is so frequently the case, this subject has been investigated most thoroughly in the United States. John Keats in his book, *The Sheepskin Psychosis*, has a good deal to say about overemphasis on the college degree. His case histories undoubtedly parallel examples that could be discovered in Canada. His thesis is that there are many people in universities now who should not be there, because a degree has, sometimes quite inappropriately, become a requirement for certain jobs. The reason for this may simply be that hiring someone with a degree simplifies a personnel manager's life. It can save him a good deal of tedious investigation if an applicant has this acceptable hallmark.

WHAT KIND OF EDUCATION FOR THE PROFESSIONS?

We might now consider what kind of education is required for modern business, and the companion question, who should provide it.

If we look first at education for the professions, we find in Canada several well-developed patterns. In subjects such as medicine and law a reasonable degree of standardization has been achieved. In these cases university education is supplemented by an established tradition of training on the job. In engineering the pattern is almost equally well-developed, and in accounting a good deal of progress has been made towards an accepted pattern. Education being a provincial matter, however, we must expect some diversity from province to province.

The accounting profession illustrates how our systems of professional education have developed through co-operation between universities and professional societies. When the first accounting institutes were founded nearly a hundred years ago, the apprenticeship method of training was adopted according to the Scottish tradition. This remained the only road to professional qualification until the 1920's, when recognition began to be accorded the recently established undergraduate course leading to the degree of Bachelor of Commerce. A considerably reduced period of apprenticeship and training was accepted for those who held this college degree. At present there are two roads to the Chartered Accountant degree, one through high school education and five years of registration as a student-in-accounts in a public accounting firm, and the other through a Bachelor of Commerce degree with a shorter period of training (varying somewhat in length from one province to another). A recent decision of the Canadian Institute of Chartered Accountants has set 1970 as the target date by which all candidates for the C.A. degree will require a qualifying college degree at the Bachelor level.

The history of the accounting profession illustrates the normal tendency toward increased reliance on university training.

WHAT KIND OF EDUCATION FOR BUSINESS IN GENERAL?

When we turn from professional education we face the bewildering variety of the business world. This includes not only commerce, industry and finance, but other areas of increasing importance from a management viewpoint, such as government departments, crown corporations, public utilities, and a wide range of institutional and non-profit organizations.

There has been, in fact, a marked change in the career pattern of Canadian university graduates over the past twenty-five years. A generation ago the typical graduate headed almost automatically for business or the professions, whereas today graduates aim as well for careers in government, social service, teaching, or research. It is interesting to note that, in this respect at least, we are following the English precedent, as a university education has always been regarded in England as a prelude to service to Church or State or as a training for teachers.

If we accept the fact that our universities have a responsibility to train good managers, we encounter the next problem of what kind of training is appropriate. There are those who argue that the best preparation for management is a broad education in the liberal arts, leaving specialized skills to be acquired later through post-graduate studies or through practical experience in the actual work of management. This will undoubtedly always remain one road to business success, but an alternative route through specifically "Commerce" courses has been well established.

Such courses normally offer a wide variety of subjects which are deemed to be generally useful in business, such as accounting, commercial law, economics, mathematics, psychology, and so on. At some universities separate Faculties have been established, while at others the Commerce degree is granted under authority of the Faculty of Arts, usually through a "School" which is in effect a subordinate grouping in the Faculty.

Graduate courses have been established generally in the American pattern, with the degree of M.B.A. granted after a one- or two-year course. Less emphasis tends to be placed on accounting than in the undergraduate courses, and more on marketing and scientific or mathematical approaches to business.

BUSINESS COURSES AT CANADIAN UNIVERSITIES

Of Canada's fifty universities, twenty-eight are members of the Association of Canadian Schools of Business and offer undergraduate or graduate degrees or both. The list of members is as follows:

Alberta	McGill	St. Francis Xavier
Bishop's	McMaster	Saint Mary's
British Columbia	Memorial	Saskatchewan
Carleton	Moncton	Sherbrooke
Dalhousie	Mount Allison	Sir George Williams
Ecole des Hautes	Mount Saint Vincent	Toronto
Etudes Commerciales		

Laval	Ottawa	Waterloo
Loyola	Queen's	Western Ontario
Manitoba	St. Dunstan's	Windsor
New Brunswick		

CRITICISMS

Critical studies of business education have been much more thoroughgoing in the United States, indicating once again the leadership of that country in this field. Two serious studies came to fruition in 1959 with the reports of committees set up by the Ford and the Carnegie Foundations. These studies not only produced comprehensive analyses of the current situation, but stirred up a tremendous amount of critical discussion. It has been claimed that many of the reforms recommended in such reports were already well in progress. The fact remains that about that time the whole subject of business education began to be examined with a new thoroughness.

The conclusions of these American reports can be assumed to be valid for Canada too. Perhaps the theme of both reports is summed up in the Ford Foundation Study, which concludes, "The blunt fact is that the majority of students currently studying for the (business) masters degree are enrolled in makeshift programs which are generally unsatisfactory." Some of the points made to support this conclusion were:

Academic standards. It is interesting that the great problem stressed in both reports is that of improving academic standards. Both graduate and undergraduate schools are criticized for the lack of rigour in admission standards and in course content. Broader and tougher courses are recommended.

Research. Another point that receives emphasis is the importance of research. The admonition is reiterated that knowledge must not merely be passed on to students, but new territory must be explored and researched. The courses must constitute a significant intellectual adventure. They cannot be justified unless new ideas are developed.

Breadth. It is the simple-minded notion, perhaps not unnaturally, of many businessmen that university business education should produce graduates well-trained for the job which the businessman hires them to do. This is an inadequate concept. Students are not trained to do their first job effectively; their education must be aimed at producing graduates who have learned how to continue self-education throughout their working lives. Thus the teaching of specific techniques is not the proper function of a university. Nor is it desirable to encourage the present tendency to proliferate new specialties, one after another. One of the dangers besetting university education is a trend towards building up too many areas beyond their true academic worth. As the Carnegie Foundation Report says, "Chief attention needs to be placed on fostering qualities of clear analysis, imaginative reasoning, and balanced judgment and on strengthening those qualities through repeated application to business-type situations."

Flexibility. The variety of business careers means that business education must aim at great flexibility. This is all the more true when business education is used, as it should be open to be used, by those who intend careers in government and other non-business fields.

Cooperation by the different types of institutions. There are a number of different kinds of institutions interested in business education. These include universities, professional institutes, junior colleges, technical schools, and so on. There is a tremendous job of co-ordinating to be done so that each of these institutions can play its proper part. Certain subjects are appropriate for university teaching and others are much better handled by technical schools; we have a great deal to do in Canada to sort out the responsibilities of different groups.

THE FUTURE OF BUSINESS EDUCATION

It is not difficult to guess some future trends. Everyone expects a great increase in university education. All trends are in that direction, and there is no reason to expect a change. It is also safe to assume that business education will grow at an even faster rate than higher education in general. It has been estimated that one in every five students now majoring in some subject in the United States is majoring in business. The figure would not be as high in Canada, but here again we tend to follow American trends.

If we assume a rapid increase in enrolment, we must expect major problems in financing and staffing. University professors are highly mobile, and Canadian universities have a particularly difficult problem in competing so directly with American universities, which have larger resources. Problems of financing and staffing are going to get worse instead of better; and they are bad enough now.

Another trend will be towards more graduate study and research. It has been calculated that, while Canada ranks second among the world's nations in standard of living, it is fourteenth in expenditure on research per capita. More research in the business field may be expected along with increased research in other areas.

Another well-established trend is for universities to be drawn more closely into business and government life. The space-age demands more of universities in coping with problems of survival.

Viewing these various trends, we may conclude that our business education will be increasingly oriented towards mathematical approaches, computer science and scientific disciplines in general.

OUR CHANGING WORLD

All of the foregoing trends can be summed up by saying that we live in a world of fantastically rapid change. The implications for education are quite clear: When things change rapidly, education must be continuous throughout one's career. The problem of the future will not be the university dropout but the university graduate who doesn't keep up to date.

One result of the need for such continuing education will be the rapid growth of extension studies at universities. Many Canadian universities now have a registration in their extension department of the same magnitude as their regular daytime registration. In this extension work, courses in business and accounting predominate. While some cultural subjects are taught, the big pressure is for more business courses.

PROBLEMS OF CONTROL

The need for more business education is easy to predict. It is much harder to foresee precisely what kind of courses will be required. For example, take the basic question of who is to decide what kinds of education we should stress. Increasingly, governments are paying the shot, and it is a pretty sound principle that he who pays the piper calls the tune. But governments in Canada have shown no indication of being able to cope with this sort of decision. Most of us would be gravely alarmed if government sought to plan and control our system of higher education.

It might be assumed that the businessman knows what he wants and can decide the form our business education should take. However, the businessman is not free from bias. It would be natural for him to want someone trained to be immediately useful, whereas this is not the kind of training which is recommended by those who have made the serious studies referred to above. The safest course is to leave planning to the academics, who are professionals in this field, although undoubtedly they will need help and advice from the business and professional communities.

At university level the aim should be to develop a liberal education in subjects relevant to business rather than to produce ready-made managers. Beyond this very general conclusion, planning will have to proceed with great caution.

It is easy to decide that there must be some planning, for it would be quite irresponsible not to look ahead at all. However, it is easy to overdo planning, and the zeal and dogmatism of some planners can be terrifying. It might at first be assumed that we must plan now to produce the business and professional men we will need ten years hence, but this immediately raises the question of deciding what conditions will be like at that time. For example, should we not start by estimating, say, the number of electrical engineers that will be needed ten years from now? This presents a couple of serious problems. In the first place, such estimates must be very rough indeed, subject to all sorts of qualifications. In the second place, it is hard to imagine, in a country with our traditions, that someone who wanted to be an electrical engineer could be told that we had already provided for the anticipated number of electrical engineers required, and that he should report for training, say, as an actuary or dentist, where more people were needed. This kind of direction doesn't seem to fit this country, and it is inevitable that planning for the future must remain rough and tentative.

Directions
for Destiny

John Deutsch

SOME BASIC ECONOMIC TRENDS IN CANADA

John J. Deutsch
  John J. Deutsch was born in 1911 at Quinton, Saskatchewan.
Since his graduation from Queen's University in 1935, Mr.
Deutsch has had a distinguished career both as an economic
advisor and member of a number of royal commissions and
government departments, and as a university educator and
administrator. In 1963 he received his present appointment as
Chairman of the Economic Council of Canada.

The Canadian economy is in the midst of a period of rapid change. There are forces at work which are having profound effects on the way all of us live and make our living.

In this article I shall review briefly some of the basic changes which we can expect to influence developments in the Canadian economy over the next five to ten years, changes which will play a large part in determining the framework in which business will operate as Canada embarks on its second century of Confederation.

These basic factors are:

a spectacular increase in the size of our working population and the growing importance of the younger age groups in the labour force;

the rising demands for knowledge, education, and skills;

the continued movement out of rural areas, and the continued rapid growth of our large cities and their suburbs;

the achievement of further substantial increases in income levels and in standards of living, and the growing importance of services, recreation, and leisure;

the importance of the important new developments in world trade.

The most striking feature over the remainder of this decade and in the early 1970's will continue to be the rapid growth of our labour force. The numbers of people seeking work are increasing faster than the total population. Indeed, the rate of labour force growth is now faster in Canada than in any other industrially advanced country. It is, for example, 50 per cent faster than in the United States, and about four to five times faster than in Western Europe.

Two basic factors are contributing to this rapid expansion of our labour force. The most important is the very high birth rates in the 1940's; almost half of our population is under 25 years of age, and in the years immediately ahead the numbers of young Canadians entering the labour force will be roughly double the numbers reaching retirement age. The second feature is the growing numbers of married women seeking jobs. In 1950 only one of every ten married women was in the labour force; by 1970, it is expected that nearly a third will be at work. This will have significant effects on average family incomes, on the way in which families live, and on consumer spending patterns.

If we succeed in maintaining high levels of employment, the number of Canadians at work in 1970 will have increased by about one million in the space of only five years. To do this, however, will require that we continue to achieve very rapid economic growth over the remainder of this decade.

There is little doubt that the factors that have brought about the most far-reaching changes in our society in this century have been the advances in education, scientific knowledge and technology, and the effect which these have had on our productivity. We have now become accustomed to a life of rapid scientific and economic change—but we need not look back very far before we see a world vastly different from our own. For centuries the changes in man's living standards proceeded relatively slowly. Even at the time of Confederation, more than half the population of Northwestern Europe and North America still lived on farms, and few farmers were able to produce more food than they needed for themselves and their families. Most manufacturing activities were still in the handicraft stage. Communications and transportation were slow and uncertain; the steam engine was still in an early stage of development, the internal combustion engine was unknown, and the electric motor and generator were still more than a quarter of a century away. In the 1860's the muscles of men and animals still provided virtually all the energy available for economic activity.

The natural resources that support today's high living standards have always been available, but they yielded no benefits until the appropriate knowledge and techniques had been developed to process and market them. We are now living in the age of the computer and of nuclear energy, an age when the stock of knowledge is increasing at an exponential rate and the application of our growing technological capabilities is affecting whole ranges of occupations and industries.

This application of improved technology has contributed at least as much as, if not more than, increases in the numbers of workers and capital to the great economic expansion which has occurred in the world's industrial countries in this generation. In the past Canada has depended almost wholly on other countries for its technology and know-how. The attainment of our economic goals now calls for a much larger Canadian effort in research and in the use of the latest available techniques. It is not good enough simply to rely upon rich natural resources.

Today the vast majority of our people live in cities and towns, and they find their work in factories, in stores, in offices, and in an ever-expanding variety of services. At the same time, the jobs for which physical energy is the primary requirement are declining, and those which involve rising levels of education and skill are increasing. The trend towards rising skill requirements has extended into agriculture and our other primary industries. At present fewer than 10 per cent of Canada's labour force is employed in agriculture, and the average farmer produces enough food for 30 other people. Commercial farming has itself become a large-scale and highly mechanized business which calls for rising levels of investment, managerial and technical competence. Similar forces are at work in forestry, fishing, and mining.

The average man now on the job in Canada has at least 40 per cent more basic education than was the case at the turn of the century. Over the period from 1911 to 1961 the proportion of the male labour force with only elementary school education has declined from 75 to about 45 per cent, while the share of those with university degrees has more than doubled.

But this improvement was less than it could—or should—have been. Even at the beginning of this decade, almost half of our male workers had received no high school education. The advance in the educational attainment of workers in the United States has been more rapid, and there has been a widening educational gap between our two countries. This gap widened particularly at the secondary school level during the 1920's and 1930's, and since the war it has been growing mainly at the university level. Studies prepared for the Economic Council indicate that this has been a not inconsiderable factor in the difference in average incomes between Canada and the United States.

In the past Canada has been able to rely upon immigration to fill many gaps in our inventory of skills. The demand for skills, however, is rising very rapidly throughout the world, and not least in those countries from which we have drawn large numbers of highly trained workers in the past. Everywhere these skills are in short supply. Of course, we can and should increase our efforts to attract such skilled workers from abroad and to retain the ones we have. But in the longer run, the much larger part of the solution must be found in educating and training more of our own young people in the skills needed by a modern economy.

In the years ahead we can expect not only an increasing enrolment of our young people in schools and colleges, but also that many more members of the existing labour force will be seeking ways to improve their skills and earning power. Nevertheless, there is likely to continue to be a shortage of experienced professional, managerial, and technically skilled manpower. Although the total supply of manpower in Canada will increase by an unprecedented amount over the period 1966-70, there will be no increase in the male labour force in the critically important 30-45 age group. In addition, there is evidence to suggest that the average educational attainments of present managerial personnel in Canada are very significantly lower than in the United States; in fact, the average differences between the two countries in this group appear to be wider than in almost all other major categories of the labour force.

The shortage of qualified people for middle-management positions in Canada is already acute and will have important implications for the availability of senior management for many years to come. We will have to devote a great deal more attention and planning to meeting the management needs of the future. This will have to include opportunities for bright young people to move ahead as quickly as they can, and more adequate provisions for continuing education and training for those already at work. In short it will entail making the most efficient use of the scarce skills which are available.

At the same time, the rapid economic expansion which we require will continue to involve a very large volume of new capital investment in the Canadian economy. Canada is a very large user of capital, especially in periods of rapid growth and development; indeed, the amounts of capital used per worker are generally higher in Canada than in the United States or in any other large industrial country.

When the Economic Council began its work in 1963, a number of factors pointed to the need for a particularly high level of investment over the balance of the 1960's. There was the requirement to make up the deficiencies in capacity which had developed during the period of relatively high unemployment; there was the need to modernize equipment and to provide increasing productive capacity so as to create employment opportunities for our very rapidly growing labour force. Finally, there are also the vast investments which have to be made in housing, in utilities, in educational and transportation facilities, and in the other requirements of a society which is undergoing urbanization and industrialization at what is really a spectacular rate.

The recent very high *rates* of increase in construction cannot be repeated indefinitely. However, this industry must continue to expand in order to build all the facilities which we will need in the future. The most urgent task now, therefore is, to increase as quickly as possible the capacities and the manpower resources of this basic industry to the levels which are likely to be required for the much larger economy of the future.

If Canada's enormous capital requirements are to be met, the Council indicated there will also have to be high rates of savings. However, while Canadians might be expected to provide rising amounts of savings, it was anticipated that domestic sources alone would not be sufficient in the years immediately ahead. Unless Canada were to reduce its growth below what would be required for full employment and adequate levels of productivity, there would have to be some continued inflow of foreign capital for some time to come.

In the years ahead there will continue to be a strong trend for more Canadians to find their work and make their homes in relatively large urban centres and their suburbs. The knitting together of many specialized and closely interrelated activities in concentrated geographic areas is a fundamental feature of highly industrialized societies. It provides the advantages of economies of scale and specialization, larger markets, and more useful pools of skills. It contributes to the achievement of higher incomes and higher standards of living. The movements of our own population in search of these better opportunities have dwarfed even the large numbers of new Canadians received through immigration from other countries. In fact, for several decades the population of our cities and towns has been increasing relatively more rapidly than that of similar communities in the United States. So far in the 1960's, the number of Canadians living in our largest urban centres has grown twice as fast as the population of the rest of the country. We can expect the strong trend towards increasing urbanization to continue into the future.

Consequently one of the most pressing needs of our times is to ensure that our burgeoning cities are good places in which to work and live. A new and higher degree of urgency must be attached to solving the problems of air and water pollution, traffic congestion, and meeting the needs for more adequate recreational and cultural services.

It also means making greater efforts to provide adequate housing. The rate of family formation, which was 60,000 a year in the early part of this decade, will reach 125,000 a year by the early 1970's. This will call for more houses and more apartments. We shall also have to devote a great deal more attention to urban renewal and to the problem of making better use of the deteriorating central areas of many of our cities.

Our growing economy has already made possible spectacular increases in the average real income of Canadians. Over the past 35 years consumer expenditures per capita have nearly doubled. Since the war the increase has been roughly one third. The maintenance of full employment with rising productivity can mean further significant improvements in our standard of living by 1970. If we achieve the gains which are possible, total production will have expanded by roughly 50 per cent, and average incomes per capita by more than 20 per cent, in only seven years.

However, not all of our increased productive capabilities will be devoted to raising our consumption of goods and services. A significant part will go to shortening the work week and to expanding the time for recreation, entertainment and cultural activities—not to mention commuting. As the regular work week continues to decline, we can expect further time will be available for all these activities.

Another area of growing concern to Canadians is the need to find ways to encourage greater regional participation in the progress of the national economy. There have been large and persistent disparities in the levels of income and in the rates of growth among the major regions of Canada. For many decades Canadians living in Ontario and westward have generally had incomes that on the average are substantially above the Canadian average, while incomes in large parts of Quebec and in the Atlantic Provinces have remained far below the average.

Our experience makes it clear that the persistent problem of regional imbalance will not be overcome by temporary expedients or by simple make-work projects; nor will we be able to solve it by measures which attempt to slow down the growth of the high-income areas merely to transfer incomes to areas of slower growth. Instead, serious efforts will have to be made to get at the basic problems which confront the low-income regions, such as levels of education, lack of capital, low productivity, and inadequate access to markets. If these basic problems are tackled effectively, the low-income regions can improve their performance in a way which will raise, and not reduce, the levels of employment and output in the country as a whole.

Nevertheless, there will always be Canadians in every region who, because of age or other circumstances, will not be able to participate directly in employment and whose poverty will become more acute and more obvious as general income levels rise. The public will ultimately have to decide what degree of assistance it is prepared to give and what form it should take. But in our increasingly affluent society there will be growing scope for more energetic measures to attack the remaining problems of poverty. I think that in the decade ahead this problem will occupy more of our attention and concern.

The future progress of the Canadian economy will also reflect the important new trends in world trade and the way we respond to these new developments. In Canada we exchange almost half of the physical goods we produce for the products of other countries. This has allowed us to enjoy significantly higher incomes than we could otherwise afford. At the same time, the scales of output and degrees of specialization in much of Canadian secondary industry are inefficient by present-day standards. We are trying to produce too great a variety of bits and pieces for a restricted market. We will only get better economies of scale and specialization by promoting the development of larger markets. These must include the foreign market as well as the home market. It is, therefore, essential that we arrange our affairs to take advantage of the rapid changes which are occurring in the world around us.

One of the most striking developments in the postwar period has been the rapid expansion in trade among the leading industrial countries. Trade among these nations has been expanding more rapidly than their total production, and manufactured goods and highly processed products have been the fastest growing elements in this trade.

This dynamic expansion reflects a number of basic factors. First of all, there has been, since the war, a growing economic interdependence and co-operation among the leading industrial countries. While there are still significant barriers to trade, substantial reductions have been made by the large industrial countries, and these countries have come to represent what is essentially one vast market for a great many products. The present Kennedy Round of tariff negotiations is an effort to make further important progress in reducing trade barriers. The development of larger markets is providing opportunities for increasingly specialized production of many goods which can be produced efficiently only on a large scale. There have also been widespread improvements in the quality of manufactured goods, along with the appearance of many new products. Frequently these involve the application of large amounts of skill and technology but relatively decreasing amounts of raw materials. The great advances in transportation and communications are reducing the old barriers of time and space which formerly provided shelter from external competition. More and more the relative efficiency of processing and manufacturing techniques is becoming the main factor in determining the course of a nation's trade. Finally, the sustained economic growth in many leading industrial countries has brought rising levels of affluence, and these countries are determined to continue these rapid improvements in their productivity and living standards. Increasingly this is providing rich international markets for sophisticated consumer and industrial goods which formerly were confined largely to North America.

To maintain our economic progress will require that we participate fully in the dynamic growth of the trade in processed and industrial products. This means improving upon our past performance. We have not been keeping pace with other leading industrial countries. To a significant extent this reflects the structure of our trade. Traditionally our exports have been concentrated in food products and unprocessed materials, and world markets for these products have been expanding relatively slowly. We should do everything possible to maintain and improve our share of trade in these basic commodities, but this alone will not be adequate to enable us to reach our employment and production goals. We shall have to make greater efforts than in the past to raise our exports of the more highly processed materials. It is in this area that the largest opportunities in the years immediately ahead are likely to exist.

As a consequence, the Economic Council has called for a new emphasis in our commercial policy. It has recommended that Canada take the maximum advantage of the Kennedy Round to create opportunities for rising exports in manufactured and processed products, as well as improved outlets for our more traditional exports. Such a new emphasis would require a somewhat different attitude and approach in trade negotiations than those used in the past.

At the same time, there are strong indications that we are

moving into a new situation with respect to trade in food. The degree to which the world food situation has changed has become apparent only recently. One of the symptoms of this change has been the reduction of world food surpluses which had been so bothersome in the 1950's and early 1960's. These new developments have very important implications for Canada.

While trade in agricultural products has grown during the past decade, it has not grown as fast as trade in manufactured goods, and most of the increase in agricultural exports has come from the developed regions of the world.

In the less-developed countries, food production has increased considerably, but this increase has in the main been wiped out by further acceleration of population growth during the past decade. In addition to the problems encountered in the less-developed countries, there has also been the failure of Russian agriculture to achieve expected increases in output. This has resulted in substantial imports of agricultural products by the Soviet Union and Eastern European countries. We have experienced a coincidence of rapid increases in population, lagging output in the underdeveloped countries, and a failure of adequate production in the Communist countries.

Studies made by the F.A.O. indicate that the world's population may be double what it is now by the end of this century. In the past, food production has increased rapidly enough to enable some increase in overall per capita food consumption. The annual rate of increase in world agricultural production has averaged close to 2.0 per cent over the past 25 years, in comparison with a 1.5 per cent per annum increase in population. But the situation differs greatly between the advanced countries and the less-developed countries, in which almost two thirds of the world's population now live. The population in the less-developed countries has risen by about one quarter over the past decade. Over this same period agricultural production in these countries increased only by roughly the same amount. In the developed countries population increased by about one eighth, while their agricultural production has risen twice as fast. How the future needs of the less-developed countries are to be met is certainly one of the most perplexing problems facing the world today. In the developed countries agriculture has been going through a rapid transformation, with substantial increases in productivity. Similar increases have not been attained, however, in the agriculture of the less-developed countries whose populations are exploding.

These are the realities of the new world picture which confront us. Trade between the industrial countries has been growing much more rapidly than the trade of the less-developed countries. We must also recognize that the agriculture picture around the world is one of a very substantial degree of protection, and that progress in the direction of freer trade in agricultural products will be difficult and will require very special efforts. In the attention which is now being given to the international food and agricultural problems there are new opportunities for Canada both to play a large part and to offer leadership. As one of the relatively few countries potentially able to produce a substantial amount of food over and above its own requirements, our position is one of considerable importance. Many of the agricultural products that Canadian farmers are able to produce efficiently are those that would be in great demand if incomes could be raised in countries where they are now very low. Along with other countries, Canada will have to play a much larger part, by opening markets and by giving aid, to help the less-developed countries in their desperate efforts to achieve decent living standards and participate in the new possibilities for economic progress. The plight of the poor countries is one of the basic challenges which face all of us in the rich industrial countries of the world. The great population explosion which is now under way increases the urgency of this challenge.

I have mentioned very briefly some of the basic forces which are now affecting the Canadian economy and which are likely to influence events in the 1970's. The Economic Council has emphasized very strongly that the achievement of our basic economic goals—full employment, rapid growth, reasonable price stability, a viable balance of payments, and wider participation in our national progress—will be much more feasible if we can accomplish rising levels of productivity. In short, improvements in productivity are the essential means for real advances in living standards; there is no other way.

This calls for imagination, initiative, and enterprise in exploring new and better ways to use our economic resources and talents more usefully. The speed with which our economy is changing makes it all the more necessary for all of us to look ahead, to set objectives, to try to anticipate the problems which are likely to arise and to arrange our affairs so that we will be ready to take advantage of the opportunities which the future will offer.

Daniel Johnson

CANADA AND QUEBEC: CAN THIS MARRIAGE BE SAVED?

EXCERPTS FROM EQUALITY OR INDEPENDENCE

Daniel Johnson
Daniel Johnson was born at Danville, Québec, in 1915.
He studied law at the University of Montréal, and was admitted
to the bar in 1940. Mr. Johnson was first elected to the Québec
Legislative Assembly in 1946. In 1954 he was named parliamentary
assistant to Premier Maurice Duplessis, and two years later he
became Chairman of Committees and Deputy Speaker
of the Legislative Assembly. Mr. Johnson was elected
leader of the National Union Party in 1961, and Prime Minister
of Quebec in 1966.

FOREWORD

The history of the French-Canadian nation is above all the history of its constitutional struggles, the history of a people looking for a homeland.

With time the terminology has changed. What was once the

struggle for survival has become the fight for self-determination. But the reality has remained the same. As in past centuries, the French-Canadian nation intends to pursue its true vocation and maintain its identity. Today, as in 1763, we reject the possibility of assimilation and we affirm our right to remain ourselves and to develop freely on this North American continent where history and destiny have placed us. This determination to live, to live together and to live in French in this country that we have built, inspires our efforts and gives us no choice but to go on fighting. It gives a special quality and a unique grandeur to French-Canadian political life. It imposes continual choices and sacrifices on us. But it also obliges us to be stronger, bolder, and more vigilant.

So far we have tried to beat back all attacks. But two centuries after the conquest, we would certainly like our right to be what we are, namely a French nation in America, to be admitted once and for all. We want to be a nation free to work in peace towards our fulfilment, constitutionally endowed with the powers necessary for this development in all fields: cultural, social and economic. We want to see an end to rearguard actions, sterile combats, exhausting quarrels for crumbs of sovereignty. We are no longer satisfied with being tolerated. We want to be masters in our own house.

We are not waiting passively for our existence to be recognized. This book [*Equality or Independence*] bears witness to that fact: it sets forth principles and outlines solutions which, while respecting the rights of the two peoples that make up this country, will permit us to grow and prosper. I certainly do not claim to offer the reader a scientific treatise. This work is the fruit of my reflections, the synthesis of my political thought on the problem of the relations between the two peoples who form this country. Essentially, it is a summary of the ideas that I have repeated many times before various audiences.

As early as 1938, when I was president of the Students' Society of the University of Montréal, I told a group of Ontario university students that "this country will be bilingual and bi-ethnic or it will not survive". I have not changed my mind; and the day that I discovered a political party that had given itself the mission of promoting this ideal I became active in it. I fought for the reconquest of provincial autonomy because to me this was the first stage in the historical movement that has brought us to the crossroads where, today, we must make a definite choice. Every day the constitutional crisis is becoming more acute, and there is no chance whatsoever of its being resolved so long as the equality of the two founding peoples is not recognized.

During the debate on the Address in reply to the Speech from the Throne on January 16, 1962, I said: "You must realize that the next few years could well be the years of the last chance for the Canadian Confederation." The Laurendeau-Dunton Commission, in a preliminary report published three years after my own statement, admitted that Canada is passing through the greatest crisis in its history, and maintained that basic reforms are essential if the destruction of the country is to be prevented.

No reform can be basic and decisive unless it goes to the roots of the problem, unless it is founded on the realities of the country. In my opinion we need nothing less than a remaking of the Canadian constitution. It is in support of this thesis, that, without pretention, but with the most profound conviction, I offer my contribution.

WHAT IS A NATION?

I feel it is essential to begin by defining the word "nation".

There is obviously a misunderstanding about the meaning of this word, and English-speaking and French-speaking Canadians do not at all agree on its definition. This in itself is proof of the differences in our philosophic outlook and in our ways of thinking and speaking, differences which led Murray Ballantyne to say: "I am not quite the same person when I am speaking French." Our English-Canadian compatriots speak of Canada as a nation made up of two peoples, while the French conception is of a people made up of two nations. This is certainly more than a semantic quarrel, but there is no reason for mutual accusations of bad faith.

Behind this difference in the interpretation of a word lies an important philological distinction. A nation can be defined in two ways depending on the degree of evolution it has achieved. It can be a sociological phenomenon before being a political phenomenon, and its definition can depend on sociological content as much as on political reality. The confusion between the English definition and ours stems from the fact that in English the emphasis is on the political content of the word, while in French the emphasis is on the sociological content.

Let us start from the definition of "nation" that apears in the Larousse Dictionary: "A human community, usually occupying a common territory and which, as a result of a certain historic, linguistic, religious or even economic unity, has a desire to share a common way of life." This is the sociological definition of the word "nation". This is a clear, precise, common-sense definition. If we accept this description of a nation there is no doubt that there are two nations in Canada, two human communities, distinct in language, religion, culture, traditions, and historical evolution. Even in the provinces where they form the minority, each of the two naturally tends to group itself apart on a regional or local level in order to create a favorable milieu for its development.

It must be noted that the basic element of a nation is not race but culture. Whatever his name or ethnic origin, a person belongs to one nation or another depending on the cultural group he identifies with as a result of his roots, his education, his choice, his way of life, his way of thinking and expressing himself. I am thinking in particular of all the new Candians who have voluntarily joined the French-Canadian culture, by taste and by choice, and who are actively participating in its development and its enrichment. This is what I mean by a sociological phenomenon and this is how it helps define the idea of a nation.

It happens nevertheless—and this is only normal—that once a cultural community has reached a certain stage of development, and especially if it possesses certain undeniable historic rights, it seeks to identify itself with a political state. In order to develop in the direction dictated by its own peculiar character, a cultural group needs the framework, the institutions, and the powers that only a state which it directs can provide. Thus the nation, a sociological phenomenon, tends to coincide with the state, a political phenomenon. To the extent that it achieves this identification it becomes a nation-state. This is the case with most nations who have reached the final stage of their evolution.

I admit that the French-Canadian nation has not yet arrived at this final stage, and this is undoubtedly the reason why some still deny our right to the title of nation. But with all its strength the French-Canadian nation is working towards fulfilment at the level of the state, and its aspirations are perfectly normal and legitimate. A little later I shall demonstrate how and why the French Canadians are seeking to identify themselves with the State of Québec, the only state where they can claim to be masters of their own destiny and the only state they can use for the full growth and development of their society; while for its part, the English-Canadian nation is tending to make Ottawa the centre of its community life.

FEDERALISM

Essentially, federalism is the search for a point of equilibrium between unity and separation, between forces that tend to unite and those that tend to divide. This equilibrium cannot always be achieved in the same way, since the forces that must be reconciled vary greatly not only from one country to another, but also from one era to another within the same country. Federalism, therefore, can take on extremely diverse forms.

Thus the two most powerful countries in the world today, the United States and the Soviet Union, have federal constitutions. But these constitutions do not really resemble each other, since the United States is a relatively homogeneous country, while the Union of Soviet Socialist Republics includes people of very different nationalities and languages. Two of these federated republics, the Ukraine and Byelorussia, have even acquired a certain international status permitting them to be directly represented at the United Nations.

It is therefore not necessary in any given federation for all the federated territories to have exactly the same rights and responsibilities. It is precisely the specific genius of federalism that it is able to adapt itself to almost any situation.

TWO NATIONS ON THE MARCH

It is vital to note—because this is the main source of our problems—that all the provinces received exactly the same rights and responsibilities under the British North America Act. The special needs of Québec provided the starting point, since it was primarily because of Québec that a federal constitution was established rather than the unitary one which several people, including Sir John A. Macdonald, would have preferred. However, Québec did not receive any special status. Instead, all the provinces were cast in the same constitutional mold. *This amounted to basing confederation on the assumption that each province, and not only Québec, would behave as the home of a national community.* This, I believe, is the key to our present difficulties.

In short, it was presumed that all the provinces would develop in the same way. In the context of 1867 this idea was more realistic than it seems today. Ontario was the heir of Upper Canada, which had asked for and obtained its complete separation from Lower Canada in 1791. As for the Maritime Provinces, until then they had developed as distinct colonies without any organic relationship with central Canada. Therefore, all the original provinces had good reason to cling to their autonomy. Each entered confederation with a historical heritage, a body of traditions and special characteristics that made it a distinct community. In the first few years of confederation provincial autonomy was not an exclusively Québec affair. The other provinces were just as insistent on it as we were, and sometimes more so. Prince Edward Island valued its own special identity so much that it did not join confederation until 1870, after three years of reflection.

It was Ontario, under the leadership of Sir Oliver Mowat, that first joined the battle on the issue of provincial rights. And in 1887, during the first inter-provincial conference convened at Québec by Honoré Mercier, the delegates from Halifax inserted in the minutes a sort of reservation, in which they warned that they were participating in the discussions "without prejudice to the right of the government, the legislature and the people of Nova Scotia to adopt any line of conduct that might be considered advisable in the future with the aim of achieving the separation of this province from Canada". Further proof that separatism and the right to self-determination are not inventions of Québec.

The English-Canadian Nation

Later on, however, a phenomenon occurred that was to radically change the sociological face of the country. This was the gradual formation of a real English-Canadian nation.

With the help of the common structures set up in 1867, and thanks to the rapid progress in the means of communication, our English-speaking fellow citizens in the Maritimes, Ontario and the

West, who already shared the same culture, gradually acquired certain common customs and a desire to share a common way of life. The result has been a community whose cultural and economic aspirations are tending more and more to converge. Certainly, local peculiarities and divergent interests continue to exist in the various regions; but they are not of a kind on which to found a distinct national existence. It is quite understandable that this English-Canadian nation should tend to identify itself with a state. Nothing could be more normal or more legitimate. And, as I said in the first page of this book, the unity of a nation calls for the unity of a state. The assumption of the Fathers of Confederation that each province would behave as the homeland of its own national community has become obsolete. For all practical purposes, provincial autonomy is no longer a major concern for our English-speaking compatriots.

From now on the English-Canadian nation wants Ottawa to handle all important matters, even when these touch on particular national and cultural characteristics. They consider the Ottawa government as their national state. I would not dream of blaming them for what is, after all, a perfectly normal tendency. What inconvenience would they suffer, for example, if education were financed and controlled from Ottawa rather then from the provincial capital? The fact that they are in the majority in the federal parliament reassures them that they have nothing to fear. They can even see great advantages in the uniformization of teaching standards across Canada, since graduates from one province could then take advantage of career opportunities available from one end of the country to the other.

Therefore, I do not think that I am mistaken in saying that English Canadians have become a nation. There are still quite important differences in interests and even in attitudes among the English Canadians of the Maritimes, Ontario, the Prairies and the Pacific Coast; but these differences are not as important as those that distinguish English Canadians from French Canadians. One thing is certain. In spite of geography and in the face of pressure from certain interests, powerful forces and influences are working to strengthen the unity of the English-Canadian nation. *This is an objective whose nobility and grandeur we must certainly recognize.*

Instead of opposing these unifying tendencies as in the past,

English Canadians in the different regions of the country have come to consider the Ottawa government as their national government, and have themselves started to take the initiative in calling for its intervention in all important questions. As Professor Donald V. Smiley of the University of British Columbia has remarked, they are already acting as though they were living in a unitary state. The shared-cost programs, for example, are merely a detour to arrive at a unitary system behind a façade of federalism. The English-Canadian provinces do not even feel nostalgic about the fiscal freedom they have lost. For the most part they do not ask for new sources of revenue, but rather for federal subsidies. And they show little concern over the conditions that may be attached to such subsidies. They well know that the standards set by Ottawa are conceived with the majority interest in mind.

If the English provinces are trying as hard as possible to turn Ottawa into their national government, I do not see why we should want to stop them. The right to self-determination applies just as much to the English-Canadian nation as it does to the French-Canadian nation.

The French-Canadian Nation

On the other hand, it is no less clear that French Canadians want to make Québec their national state. And, here too, I do not see why anyone would want to prevent them from doing so. It is a logical development deriving from the very roots of culture.

I first realized the depth and seriousness of the constitutional problem the day that I decided to pursue my studies in French-Canadian institutions. In choosing this course I was following a perfectly natural inclination. But even so I was quite conscious of the inevitable implications of my decision. As with all the young people who continue to enroll in the colleges and universities of French Canada, I was in effect opting for one of the two cultures that are supposed to have an equal right to exist in this country. Moreover, a culture is more than a language. It is a philosophy of life. It is a way of seeing and thinking. Therefore, to choose the French culture is first and foremost to perform an act of faith, faith in the permanence and the increasing influence of this culture in Canada. For if the French culture has no future in our country, if it is destined eventually to disappear as some people claim, if it condemns those who live by it to be nothing more than second-class citizens who can go so far in life and no farther, then it is a complete waste of time and a tragic waste of energy to continue one's education in French-language institutions.

Yet to choose the French culture is even more than an act of faith. It is a pledge, a pledge to do everything possible so that Canadians of both cultural communities may have an equal chance to attain not only material success but also the total fulfilment of their personalities. Unlike the other provinces, ours aspires to sovereignty because it is the guardian of a unique culture. It is no longer enough for it to be master of its language, its schools, and its civil law; it must also be master of its economy so that it can organize it in terms of the unique French-Canadian culture. Consequently, it must have fiscal liberty as the key to all other liberties.

A PROBLEM OF COEXISTENCE

Essentially our task is to discover and put into practice the appropriate means of ensuring the harmonious coexistence of two national societies on the same territory. The two communities are profoundly different, not only in language and culture, but also in their outlook and thinking, their way of life, their traditions, their historical evolution, and the desire of each to share a common way of life. Each of the two groups intends to remain faithful to itself and to develop in the way indicated by its own special aspirations. Each has reached a stage of evolution that makes any attempt to weld them together to form a hybrid Canadianism quite unthinkable. No one can freely renounce his identity and become someone else. Nothing is more profoundly anchored in human nature than the instinct for self-preservation and continuity. To propose that some day there will be simply "Canadians" in this country—unhyphenated Canadians, *homogeneous Canadians*—amounts to an ideal of Utopianism, or to a secret wish for the assimilation of the other group.

There are, of course, resemblances, points of contact and common interest between Canadians of the two cultures. But to see only that and forget the rest is to distort the problem from the start. Any attempt to unify people who differ succeeds only in increasing the irritation and division between them. Those who would have unity at any price merely make union impossible. *For a union cannot exist at all if it does not first exist in the spirit and hearts of men.* If we are to create a climate of confidence and friendship among all Canadians, we must first recognize that each of our two national communities has a *natural right, a legitimate desire for self-determination.* Each must have all the freedom and means of action necessary to govern itself in everything that concerns its own life and special aspirations. Then and only then will they find it possible to create common structures together, and to adhere to them with eagerness and conviction because these structures will help each to achieve its destiny.

Internal Contradictions

Unfortunately, the constitution that governs us—or at least is supposed to govern us—no longer answers the needs of either English or French Canada. It was conceived a century ago in terms of the four original provinces which, at the time, looked upon themselves as the homes of four distinct peoples. It takes no account of the development of our two communities and *is now acting as a straightjacket on both of them.*

Every nation tends to identify itself with a state. To organize its life and to develop according to its own special genius, every nation needs a government to serve it. The roots of the French-Canadian nation in this country go back more than three centuries. As it enjoys a majority in the Québec government only, it is perfectly normal and natural that the French-Canadian nation should try to retain and even expand the freedoms, powers and means of action that were granted to this government in 1867. It is logical that French Canada should push with all its might in the direction of provincial autonomy, just as the English-Canadian nation is pushing toward centralization.

But because of an outdated constitution, conceived in terms of the realities of another century, the only way in which each nation can follow its natural bent is by frustrating the natural evolution of the other. Québec can preserve the freedoms essential to it as the principal home of a particular culture only by resisting with all its strength the political unification of English Canada. And, to provide itself with a strong central government as the political expression of its gradual integration, English-Canada must fight the autonomist demands of Québec with equal force.

These are the internal contradictions that are threatening to blow our country apart. Instead of co-ordinating the efforts of the forces at hand, the constitution is driving them to confront one another and to waste their energies in interminable conflicts. The tragedy is that under these conditions, each begins to believe in the ill will of the other. There are some English Canadians who sincerely believe that Québec wants to lead the rest of the country by the nose and impose French everywhere, even on those people who have no need of it. And there are French Canadians who with equal sincerity see political centralization as an attempt at genocide, a plot against their language and culture. The fact is that *both nations are simply victims of an obsolete constitution.*

TOWARDS A NEW BEGINNING

As we have seen, the main cause of our present difficulties lies in the lack of a constitution adapted to the political and sociological realities of modern Canada. Our country is made up of two cultural communities which, in different degrees and for different reasons, are frustrated in their development by the existing structures. In fact, because of these structures there is a danger that our two nations may come to look on each other as natural enemies, when in reality, considering the multitude of their common interests, they are natural allies. Our most urgent task is to put an end to this fatal misunderstanding before the position of either side becomes too rigid.

We often hear people say, "Let's forget what separates us and concentrate on what unites us." In my opinion this is tackling the problem at the wrong end. *It is precisely this obsession with unity, of which Durham was not the only victim, that is preventing a really profitable union.* Our first duty is to become clearly and resolutely aware of what divides us. Then it will become possible to unite what can be united.

In his book, *Conscience of Switzerland,* Gonzague de Reynold made the following observations, which apply very well to the Canadian problem and can help us considerably in our search for a solution:

"To unify is not to unite. To unify is material, to unite is moral. We unify things but we unite beings, and often in unifying things we disunite beings. A country can be unified to the point of having an administrative and political appearance of the most complete unity; but if it hides discontent, suffering, and disunity, it is nothing but a lie—an apparently solid piece of land, maintained as a garden, but under which a deep pit has been dug. It is easy to unify. All you need are jurists, bureaucrats and policemen. But it is difficult to unite. This requires intelligence, understanding and purpose. Uniting destroys nothing, but unifying does destroy something; and that something is unity".

This is the direction in which we must turn our search if we want positive results. History demonstrates the impossibility of merging or unifying our two nations. A forced unity that would do violence to nature would be the source of bickering and perpetual conflicts. *What is possible and desirable in a binational country is not national unity*—a term that will always remain ambiguous—*but a national union,* a national harmony founded on the respect of legitimate differences. On October 15, 1963, André Malraux said in Montréal: "I now know that you do not create universal brotherhood at the expense of patriotism, but rather with the help of patriotism, by building on it and with it." This is the situation with regard to Canadian brotherhood. We shall not be able to build it at the expense of national differences, but rather with their help, by building on them and with them.

A New Alliance

In our opinion we must make a new start and not try to patch over a constitution written a century ago in terms of the needs and realities of that era. It is easier to build a new machine than to repair one that has been allowed to get completely out of order. It will also be easier, and infinitely more inspiring, to construct a new constitution rather than repatriate one that has ceased to command respect and which will always remain the symbol of an era when Canada was still only a colony.

To be valid, the new constitution will have to solve the internal contradiction that tends to oppose English and French Canada within a legal framework that is poorly adapted to their respective needs and in which both are cramped for space. For situations of conflict it must substitute situations of co-operation. It must allow both nations to develop freely.

IS THIS THE TIME?

The reader is perhaps asking: Are present circumstances favourable for redrafting the constitution? My answer is yes. And I give the word "redrafting" its full meaning. We must draft anew and completely remake the constitution of the country. I believe that the time is ripe, and that it has become not only possible but imperative to give Canada a completely new constitution based on the alliance of two nations, each having all the sovereignty necessary to allow it to develop in the direction of its own destiny, and, as equal partners, working together in the management of their common interests. And that is not all. I believe that if we do not quickly seize the opportunity now before us to remake the constitution on this binational and bicultural basis, a split will become inevitable. Canada will break up into several fragments under the impact of new forces that we will be unable to control and integrate.

Let us first recall one principle: Constitutions are made for people, not people for constitutions. When circumstances have changed, when needs are no longer the same, when there is no longer harmony between reality and the legal structures of a country, it is not the citizens who should be adapted, by will or by force, to the obsolete institutions; it is the institutions that must be adapted to the new realities. Once again I refer to the testimony of Canon Groulx who said in Québec on June 7, 1964: "There are no forms of government that take precedence over a nation's right to life. Constitutions are neither absolute nor untouchable. The letter cannot kill the spirit".

AN EXPERT APPRAISAL

And indeed, many things have changed since 1867. At the beginning of 1935 a special committee of the House of Commons was formed at Ottawa to "study the best method by which the British North America Act may be amended." Representatives of all political ideologies participated, including Ernest Lapointe, Henri Bourassa, J. S. Woodsworth, and Onésime Gagnon. The committee called before it several specialists in constitutional problems including Arthur Beauchesne, then Clerk of the House of Commons and without any doubt the foremost Canadian authority on parliamentary law. Mr. Beauchesne's testimony, which is included in the committee's report, contains insights that must have seemed quite revolutionary at the time. He pointed out that the Canada of 1867 was much different from the Canada of 1935. Its population was a mere three million and the total budget of the Dominion scarcely exceeded 14 million dollars. Motor vehicles were still unknown; aviation was a dream. Indians, half-breeds, and fur traders comprised the whole population of the west. Our country was still a colony whose governor received lengthy instructions from the Colonial Office. We were not even authorized to negotiate our own treaties. We were garrisoned by English troops and "social reforms appeared as the last word in dangerous radicalism". After drawing a picture of the changes that had since occurred, Mr. Beauchesne concluded that Canada needed a constitution adapted to new conditions. To quote his words, "Amendments here and there would be mere patchwork which could not last. The people of 1935 are different from those of 1867. What we want is a new constitution."

A Constituent Assembly

And how should Canada proceed to provide itself with a new constitution? On this point Mr. Beauchesne is categorical. I quote him again:

> "It is idle to think that this can be done in the same formal way as an amendment to a public statute. The new constitution must leave nobody with a grievance. A spirit of conciliation should predominate. For these reasons the task must be entrusted to an independent body in which all the elements of the country will be represented. I, therefore, beg to suggest an imposing Constituent Assembly formed of eminent men coming from all parts of Canada. Provincial conferences, attended by a few ministers, would hardly satisfy public opinion."

Mr. Beauchesne suggested that this constituent assembly be formed of representatives of each province according to its importance. I do not share this opinion and I shall return to this point later on in this discussion. I believe that the constituent assembly should be made up of delegations from the two Canadian nations, joined by representatives of the other ethnic groups, and that it should draw up a charter of fundamental rights to be incorporated into the constitution in order to prevent any racial or religious discrimination.

Mr. Beauchesne also insisted that the assembly be convened in a city other than Ottawa—in Winnipeg, for example—to prevent it from being influenced by federal authorities. He even suggested a new name for our country, the Federated States of Canada.

All this, I repeat, happened in 1935. The depression and the war that followed were scarcely designed to encourage these fine projects. Instead of a constituent assembly, we had the notorious Rowell-Sirois Inquiry, which I am tempted to call an deconstituent assembly. In any case, the important thing is that as early as 1935 a specialist such as Mr. Beauchesne found that since 1867 the sociological environment had changed sufficiently in Canada to require a new constitution. Indeed, during the past quarter century a phenomenon has arisen that has made itself felt in our country as in all others, the phenomenon of the acceleration of history. Evolution has been even swifter and more profound from 1935 to 1967 than it was from 1867 to 1935. The same changes that make the adoption of a new constitution both possible and necessary for our country are taking place at the global level and at the Commonwealth level, as well as at the level of Canada and Québec.

Changes in the World

In his introduction to a volume called *Constitutions and Constitutional Trends since World War II,* Prof. Arnold J. Zurcher of New York University points out that more new constitutions have been written in the world since the end of the First World War than at any other time in history. If, as Valéry wrote, civilizations are mortal, constitutions are much more so. They are born and die according to the pace of social change, and their average life span has never been shorter than now. Therefore, it is not such a difficult and dangerous enterprise to rewrite a constitution. Countries much less developed than ours succeed in doing so without difficulty, and I do not see why Canadians should be incapable of doing the same.

THE INDEPENDENCE OF QUÉBEC

As assimilation has been definitely rejected and the status quo is capable of satisfying no one, and as we have refused to pursue a policy of superficial repairs and interminable begging, only two possible solutions remain: equality or independence, a new constitution or separation.

I believe that we must not reject the separatist solution a priori. It could happen, for reasons that have little or nothing to do with Québec, that total independence could become the only solution compatible with the survival and progress of the French-Canadian nation. I differ completely with the people who seem ready to sacrifice our culture in order to save Confederation. Without animosity I want to make it clear that Confederation is not an end in itself. However, if we try everything to make it equally inhabitable for our two cultural communities, and should our efforts prove hopeless, Confederation will no longer seem to us to be worth saving. There are some who want to preserve Confederation even if it means sacrificing Québec's autonomy. As for me, I am ready to preserve Québec's autonomy even if it means sacrificing Confederation.

In saying this I am merely adapting to the present context a doctrine that my party has always held. On at least two occasions Mr. Duplessis repeated in the Legislature what he had already proclaimed at the 1950 Federal-Provincial Conference: "If you do not want to respect the agreement of 1867, and if we are no longer wanted in Confederation, the Province of Québec will take the necessary measures to enable it to live by itself." On December 1, 1959, one month before his death, Paul Sauvé, while speaking of the need for a more equitable division of the sources of revenue, stated: "I say with all the sincerity at my command that if in 1962 the authorities of the country at large do not realize that this is a matter of life and death, I do not see how the Canadian Confederation can continue to function."

I am not, therefore, one of those who take the separatists lightly. It is really too easy to go to Toronto or elsewhere and reap applause by saying, for example, "Don't worry about our Québec separatists. They are just a handful of dreamers who would like to build a new Chinese or Berlin Wall around their province." Undoubtedly there are extremists everywhere. But the

separatists that I know—and there are some in my own party—
have never believed that in our era Québec could be self-sufficient
and ignore the rest of the continent. Independence is not autoc-
racy, and those who mix the two are doing it deliberately to
confuse the issue. Whatever degree of emancipation it has
achieved, every country must organize its economy in harmony
with the territories around it. If it is independent this will be done
by treaties and commercial agreements. The main thing is that
this process of harmonization should not always be accomplished
by others in terms of their own interests. It must be the result of
true co-operation. As I understand them, the separatists believe
that, under present circumstances, this co-operation is no longer
possible between the two cultural groups who share Canada. They
believe that political separation is a necessary prerequisite for any
future co-operation.

Those Who Are Frightened By Separatism

Some politicians, both French and English, pour forth
speeches and even insults in an effort to defeat separatism. I do
not think that this is the right way of going about it. *Verbal
violence seems to me to be quite as unjustifiable and ineffective as
other kinds of violence.* In my opinion, we will not prevent the
destruction of Canada by crusades and denunciations. The wea-
pons that must be used are understanding and justice.

Why do some people advocate the total independence of Québec? It is because they have had enough of begging and of patchwork compromises. It is because they have lost hope of ever
feeling at home everywhere in Canada. It is because they want to
escape from their minority status and their position of subordina-
tion. Youth is impatient. It searches for absolutes. It can never be
satisfied by half-measures, by crumbs and percentages of rights. It
wants solutions that are just, but also clear and basic.

Nevertheless, now as in the past, separatism does not seem to
me to be the only solution. In his recent book, *The Political
Choice of French Canada,* Philippe Garigue affirms that separatism would cause a rupture not only between English and
French Canada, but also within French Canada itself, since more
than a million French Canadians live outside Québec. This is a
possibility that we must consider. Moreover, as in 1791, sepa-

ratism would not solve the problem of the coexistence of two peoples on the same territory, for a large English-speaking minority with unquestioned historical rights inhabits our province.

Serious-minded separatists are the first to acknowledge that Québec could not, in any case, live in isolation, and that independence would by no means do away with the need for harmonious collaboration with the rest of the country and continent. What they say is this: Let us first become independent, and then it will be much easier to determine the conditions of this co-operation in a climate of equality. The argument has weight. However, in view of the perspective opened up by the creation of the Parliamentary Committee on the Constitution, before reconciling myself to the last resort of separatism I would prefer to try everything possible to enable the French-Canadian nation to feel at home throughout the whole of Canada, to feel that Canada really is *their* country. It seems to me that we can achieve equality through negotiation without necessarily going through the stage of independence which, needless to say, involves a certain number of risks that are rather hard to evaluate. For this reason, on May 13, 1964, I asked the Constitution Committee to prepare a study on the consequences of independence.

However, I continue to believe in the possibility of a dialogue and of establishing a new constitution for Canada that would institute at the summit, for the whole country, a really binational structure where the delegates of both cultural groups could work together on a basis of equality in the management of their common interests. I do not believe that this inspiring task is beyond the moral and intellectual strength of Canadians of either culture.

And besides, it is either that or separatism.

The French-Canadian nation, for three centuries in the process of formation, needs a climate of freedom if it is to develop its potential to the full. There can be no cultural equality without cultural autonomy. And there can be no cultural autonomy without political autonomy. The French-Canadian nation must have a homeland. If it is unable to achieve political recognition from one ocean to the other in a new and binational federalism, it will have no other choice but the independence of Québec. I fully realize that this is an extreme solution, a last resort. It is a little like a strike. But a union that is starting negotiations would be unwise to exclude from the outset the possibility of a strike, even if it sincerely hopes to avoid it. If it should turn out that secession were the only way for French Canadians to remain themselves and to stay French, then it would not only be their right, it would be their duty to be separatist.

A BINATIONAL CANADA

The idea of a resolutely binational Canada does not mean that all Canadians would have to speak both languages and participate in both cultures. Such an idea seems to me both utopian and senseless. It is not the citizen that must be binational; it is the country in its political, economic, and social structures. A binational Canada is a Canada that we can love and serve in English or in French, with the same rights and responsibilities whatever the province or region we choose to live in. In order to build a Canada that is equally suited to the fulfilment of both cultural communities, it is essential that both of them work together towards this goal, openly and in a climate of mutual confidence. For my part I have not lost hope that we can yet obtain the collaboration of our English-speaking compatriots. If we are to achieve this, each group must clearly establish its own objectives and make clear what it hopes for in the new order we must build.

Through the Constitution Committee, Québec intends to set forth its requirements, define its aims, and, in fact, specify the conditions for a new type of union. For its part, the Estates General of the French-Canadian nation could present the ideas of all the main French-Canadian organizations in Québec as well as in the rest of the country. In this way, the basic elements that must be conditions of our adhesion to a new federal pact would be clearly and objectively stipulated. This should have the effect of clearly defining the problem in the eyes of English-speaking Canadians. It is necessary because among our English-language compatriots many people are wondering just what French Canada wants. They realize that we are in a state of crisis and that we are dissatisfied with the present constitution. In general they are ready to listen, but they would first like to know what is wrong. Articles in several papers in the other provinces have asked French Canada to specify its goals. This is precisely the role of the Committee of the Legislature and of the Estates General.

Once the views and needs of French Canada have been specifically stated, the next step will be to get the dialogue under way with the other cultural group. Here we logically arrive at the idea of a *constituent assembly* in which the two basic elements of the country, together with representatives of other ethnic groups, would combine their ideas and building materials in order to construct a constitutional edifice perfectly adapted to the Canadian realities of today.

An Antidote to Americanism

We have every reason to assume that, for their part, our English-speaking compatriots want a strong and united Canada that is better able to withstand the attractions of Americanism.

How can an English-speaking Canadian of today, living and playing like an American, constantly bombarded by American radio, television, and magazines, how can he remain different from an American? The only way he can is by gaining a clearer conception of what makes Canada different. This is where the idea of a binational and bicultural Canada, as opposed to the American melting pot, comes in. Our partners need us, rooted as we have been in this country for more than three centuries, in order to intensify and deepen their own sense of Canadianism. They need us in order to see themselves clearly as Canadians. Consequently, they would not be helping themselves by pushing our backs to the wall of assimilation, or of what has been called, somewhat less brutally, enlightened integration. If the day should ever come when there were no more French Canadians in this country, it would be much more difficult to be a Canadian of any kind.

As for us, how long can we continue to work in English and play in American without losing our national identity? If we lose it, all Canada will be engulfed in Americanism.

Therefore, our English-speaking compatriots must understand clearly that by maintaining our own identity we are helping them to keep theirs. And if they really do want to keep it they must help us build a new constitution that will make Canada a truly binational country, and consequently different from its great southern neighbor.

The Seal Of The New Alliance

Some people have a mania for pinning down guilt. If relations between the two ethnic groups are difficult and complicated, they say it is the fault of the Fathers of Confederation, or of the English Canadians, or of the French Canadians. This unfortunate tendency is perhaps merely a way of looking for an alibi, of avoiding their own responsibilities. The past is the past. Those who created it doubtless acted according to their best conscience and with all the means at their disposal. It is a very grave injustice to judge men of yesterday in the context of today. Our responsibility today is to build the present, and as far as possible the future, with the means at our disposal, the means of today. It is not so much a struggle to be carried on as it is a task to be achieved together. *It is not a question of building a constitution against someone,* but simply of building one for Canadians— Canadians of both cultures. Its architecture must be conceived in such a way that English, French, and new Canadians all feel comfortable within it.

To build this joint edifice, this constitution which will be the seal of a new alliance, each of our two cultural groups must contribute its special qualities, its ideas, and its materials. I have infinite respect for the languages, customs, and special characteristics of the new Canadians of various origins. I want the new constitution of our country to include a charter of human rights that will make all of them first class citizens in Québec as well as in the rest of Canada. But the historic rights clearly acquired by the two cultural groups that form the foundation of our country are something else again. And this fact, too, must be carefully defined in the constitution.

Because of the numerical disparity between the two cultural groups in each province and in Canada as a whole, Canada can be binational only if it is organized in such a way as to effectively guarantee and protect the legal equality of these two elements everywhere. The indispensable instrument of this equality is the constitution. *In other words, we need in Canada an authority that surpasses that of a simple majority whenever the survival or the self-fulfilment of one nation or the other is at stake.*

The Test Of Equality

In my opinion this constitution should be conceived in such a way as to make Canada not only a federation of ten provinces, but also a federation of two nations, equal both in law and in fact. On this point I would refer you to the opinion of Philippe Garigue in *L'Option Politique du Canada Français.*

> "If federalism remains a possible solution to the problems of French Canada, it must be understood differently from the present federal system and must start from the principle that the French and English Canadians form two nations that co-exist and intermingle throughout Canada. Instead of the present organization based on the principle of "territorial" representation, and instead of government operation based on majority rule, Canadian federalism, if it is to be a workable solution, must start from a "national" representation on the basis of linguistic groups. Then federal organization would be an expression of both the separation and the collaboration of two nations, both represented in government on the basis of the linguistic aspect of their identity."

Therefore, the constitution should contain not only a charter of human rights, but also a charter of national rights. The first is essential to protect the fundamental rights of the individual in an era when the state is tending to interfere more and more in everybody's life. But its main purpose is to consider the individual as such, and not in terms of his culture or nationality. In a binational country we must also have a charter of national rights which will constitute the official recognition of Canada's English-French character and which will clearly state before any other statutory legal stipulation, the *fundamental principle of the equality of both languages and both cultures throughout Canada.*

The constitution of a binational Canada must necessarily establish precise legal guarantees for the members of either cultural group who are in a minority in any given area. And these guarantees must be exactly the same, whether they concern the English-speaking minority in Québec or the French-speaking minorities in the other provinces. *Equality cannot be conceived in any other way.* Specifically, this principle must be applied at the outset in the school system of each province. Wherever they are present in sufficient numbers, parents of either cultural group must have the right, recognized by the constitution, of organizing their own schools and of benefiting from grants equivalent to those available to the majority. Special grants should also be provided to permit isolated families to send children to schools of their own culture. *But above all it is essential that the same rules everywhere govern the rights of both national groups where they are in a minority.* This is the real test of equality.

CANADA OR QUÉBEC?

Will we obtain this equality? The answer does not depend on us alone. That is why I feel it would be premature at this time to concern ourselves unduly with the precise structural form a new constitutional system should take. Before deciding on the container, let us decide on the contents.

Some people talk of a special status for Québec, but carefully avoid any definition of what they mean by the term. Certainly it is a very convenient phrase that can mean almost anything. As I have already explained, there are many examples of federations where certain member states enjoy a special status. But I know of no case that could apply precisely to Canada. Our situation is unique. Other people talk of associate states, an interesting formula to be sure. But here, too, we must specify what we mean by it, since all sorts of associations are possible. The minority shareholder in a company is in a sense an associate.

The most important thing is to determine what powers are essential for the self-fulfilment of the French-Canadian nation. For nations as for individuals there are certain basic freedoms for which one does not beg and which can be the object of no compromises or deals. For the French-Canadian nation the right to self-determination is of this sort. It is a collective heritage that I feel has been established once and for all, and which I would never consent to discuss in any negotiations. What we want is more than the powers given us by the 1867 constitution. What we want, in fact, is the right to make our own decisions—or to have an equal voice in decisions—in all fields that concern our national life.

For after all, are we now masters in our own house when Ottawa alone regulates everything concerning radio and television, media which in our era are perhaps the most effective instruments of culture?

Are we masters in our own house when Ottawa refuses to protect by appropriate tariffs the products of certain industries that are vital to French Canada?

Are we masters in our own house when Ottawa can make use of immigration policies to change the ethnic balance to the point of reducing us to a minority status even in our own state of Québec?

Are we masters in our own house when a decision of the Bank of Canada can affect the credit of our businesses, our financial institutions, and even of the government of Québec itself?

Are we masters in our own house when federal taxes skim off the profits from the exploitation of the natural resources belonging to the Québec community, and, by the inequitable operation of the companies' tax, prevent us from planning our economy to meet our own special needs?

Are we masters in our own house when, through succession duties, the Federal Government can upset the whole economic basis of our civil code?

Are we masters in our own house when nationalization is the only method remaining open to us to bring back to Québec the taxes accruing from our basic industries?

Are we masters in our own house when the Supreme Court, all of whose judges are appointed by Ottawa, is the final interpreter of our French law and the only court to which we can submit our grievances against the Federal Government?

All these instruments are at the disposal of Ottawa for direct intervention in our national life. They are all situations that we must correct if we wish to determine our own national destiny. Federation, associate states, confederation, special status, republic, whatever it may turn out to be, the new constitutional regime must give the French-Canadian nation all the powers it needs to take its destiny into its own hands. After three centuries of toil, our nation is entitled to live in freedom. So much the better if it can feel at home from one ocean to the other, but this implies the recognition of its complete equality. Otherwise, we shall have to opt for the independence of Québec.

Canada or Québec? Wherever the French-Canadian nation finds its freedom, there will its homeland be.

Eric
Kierans

FOREIGN GUIDELINES AND CANADA'S ECONOMIC FUTURE

Eric Kierans
After graduating from Loyola College, Montréal, with a
Bachelor of Arts degree, Eric Kierans did graduate research
in economics at McGill University from 1947 to 1950. His
extensive business experience includes the founding and
control of several Canadian firms. Mr. Kierans has served
as Professor and Director of McGill's School of Commerce, as
President of the Montréal and Canadian Stock Exchanges, and
as Minister of Provincial Revenue for the province of
Québec. Elected MPP for Notre Dame de Grace in 1963, he
was appointed Minister of Health in 1965. In November,
1966, Mr. Kierans was elected President of La Fédération
Libérale du Québec.

In this second century of Confederation we Canadians must
have more confidence in ourselves. If we do, we will all be better
off. We have been a prudent and a cautious people, hesitating
too often to assert ourselves and to act positively and politically

when the occasion demands. Confederation itself was a creative act, a deliberate effort which we have not matched in our hundred years of history. Since 1867 we have backed into our present state of independence—not wholly complete with a constitution still resting in Westminster—by a series of withdrawals from the influence of the mother country. Never have we made an overt declaration that we are a society of millions with problems, aims and objectives which demand purely Canadian solutions based on a set of consistent political principles. The word "consistent" is important.

Canada and confidence should be interchangeable terms like Israel and independence. If Israel maintains personal freedoms and enterprise even though surrounded by enemies, why cannot Canadians assert the supremacy of politics over economics and commerce and so reduce the wild fears of living beside the American giant? Nations do not adjust to the particular whims or notions of thousands of investors. Rather do investors adjust to the policies and practices that they find in host countries and demand only that the principles governing their investment be consistent, clear, and equitable.

To the extent that foreign investment is a threat to Canadian independence—and the only evidence is the clumsy effort of Washington to impose guidelines on Canadian (subsidiaries) citizens—it is a political not an economic threat and, therefore, should be solved by intervention at the political and federal level. Economic countermeasures such as capital levies, discriminatory taxes, forced equity sales, etc. cannot solve the problem; they can only serve to confirm two normally intelligent peoples in unhealthy and destructive ways.

The American guidelines were imposed by a government beset by the incalculable problems of world military and economic leadership in the space age. With some bitterness, the United States must envy her allies the luxury of such grand pronouncements as the bomb must be banned, down with discrimination, and Vietnam for the Vietnamese. To the leaders are left the daily, tedious, and irksome decisions involved in simply carrying on, in living out the present, in enduring the consequences of past decisions and policies both good and bad. One can easily visualize the Washington bureaucracy, the Treasury, State, the Department of Commerce, bending grimly to the task of organizing for victory, victory in Vietnam, space research, aid to underdeveloped countries, the war against poverty. Total mobilization of the economy, not simply the United States economy, but the whole sphere of American economic influence. This sphere is worldwide as Calvin Coolidge observed in 1928: "Our investments and trade relations are such that it is almost impossible to conceive of any conflict anywhere on earth that would not affect us injuriously." Mr. Fowler, Secretary of the Treasury, was only bringing the position up to date when he stated in an address before the U.S. Council of the International Chamber of Commerce on December 8th, 1965, that multi-national corporations "have not only a commercial importance, but a highly significant role in U.S. foreign policy".

One of the great unresolved questions! Is an American subsidiary a Canadian citizen? Indonesian? German? French? No matter; it must be prepared, according to Mr. Fowler, to contribute to the U.S. war effort and so return a greater flow of dividends to the American parent, to purchase more from the United States, to reinvest less of its earnings abroad.

This has nothing to do with economics. This is politics, and the challenge must be met on the political level. The argument is quite simple and straightforward. Since the subsidiary is a Canadian citizen, incorporated under our laws and enjoying special concessions in the form of licenses to exploit our forest and mineral resources, it should have the right to buy in the best market, to declare dividends and to reinvest earnings in the fashion deemed to be in the shareholders' best interest. If any nation's economic or national objectives are to be considered, they should be our interests and objectives. Otherwise the rules and guidelines imposed by other nations on Canadian citizens become an infringment of our political sovereignty.

The fault, however, lies not with the thousands of American corporations that have invested in Canada, developed our resources and employed our people. It lies with the American government, which has sought to organize their activities so as to achieve an equilibrium in the U.S. balance of payments. Discrimination practised against the corporations which have invested here, or hostility towards foreign investment itself, misses the point entirely. Our quarrel is not with the American investor, the international corporation that sees opportunities which Canadians do not to develop our resources, and in the process earns a profit and pays taxes. It is not their purpose to interfere in our politics, for they would not last a minute if they did and they know it.

Presidents of parent and subsidiary alike resent the Washington guidelines and fear the consequences of a rising tide of suspicion and hostility towards their operations. Our quarrel is with a mistaken U.S. Treasury and Department of Commerce policy, which seeks to control the operations of thousands of competing corporations making their independent ways, and to direct their activities to the attainment of specific American objectives. Employing discriminatory tax policy or introducing restrictions on direct investment penalizes the bystander, the subsidiary or parent corporation, but does not go to the root of the problem. We meet the problem head-on when we make a polite but firm rejection of any attempt by foreign governments to assert their authority over Canadian firms or citizens. Our economy cannot be guided from abroad.

Our position is a valid one. If any nation's interests or economic objectives are to be considered, they should be the national interests of the country in which the subsidiaries are located, as laid down by the political authority of that country. Canada has permitted a degree of economic penetration that other nations would not tolerate. This is not necessarily grievous, but can become so if corporations are asked to serve not only the economic interests of their shareholders but also the political objectives of other nations. In the process the international corporation, a magnificent means of increasing output and incomes, raising standards of living, and spreading technology and modern management methods throughout the world, loses much of its effectiveness.

The independence of Canada does not depend on the American or on what the Americans do. It depends on ourselves, for while others may weaken us, only we can make ourselves strong. If we have become unsure and uncertain of ourselves, turning towards policies of economic nationalism will confirm us forever as a second-class nation lacking quality, imagination and courage.

Let us be clear about ourselves. We are not too different from the Americans. Our national aims include increasing consumption, a higher standard of living, and full employment. We import huge quantities of American consumer goods, theatre, and art, and spend heavily on their tourist services because we value them. To approach the American scale of living, we adopt their production techniques, build miniature replicas of their factories, and try for increasing productivity. We copy their management techniques and patterns of organization, and model our business schools on American lines, because we correctly consider them to be the most efficient and productive people in the world.

We have voted ourselves in Canada a comprehensive program of social security, improved health care, and more education for our children. We are putting more quality into our lives, a sound and necessary objective but also a costly one. We shall never be able to afford quality on the consumption side if we do not demand quality on the production side, quality of economic performance.

The economic nationalists seem to be at odds with themselves. On the one hand, they are proponents of extended programs of social services, and on the other, advocates of restrictive measures against the foreign capital which alone could ensure an economy sufficiently productive to support these costs. (The socialist-minded separatist of Québec faces the same contradiction in his advocacy of a welfare state and of independence at one and the same time.) In repudiating foreign capital we also deprive ourselves of the latest managerial techniques, research and development that accompany such capital.

I am not denying that some foreign investment has had harmful effects on specific Canadian industries and the Canadian economy. Take the case of a subsidiary which consistently loses money—and there are many in this category. They have been established for reasons of prestige (other major international competitors being located here) and against the day when a Canadian population of 25 to 30 millions would make them viable. Such corporations do not disappear but charge back their losses to an indulgent parent which uses the losses to reduce its own tax liabilities. Such foreign investment is bad for the home country (Uncle Sam loses tax revenues) and the host country (Canada has an industry in which there is overinvestment and uneconomic splitting of the market). New entrepreneurs, of course, cannot compete against firms which can indefinitely charge losses to a parent with profitable operations elsewhere.

Several years of experience as head of two Canadian stock exchanges have proven to me that this is a real problem. Corporate behaviour is "justified" by the desire to establish footholds in countries where economic development looks promising and shareholders are rarely aware of the use of the funds or the alternative opportunities for profitable investment in new products and other areas that are foregone.

The solution is not to discriminate against all foreign investment, but to bring to light the investment decisions that are unprofitable and in the interests of no one, neither shareholder nor home nor host country. The solution is a rather simple one— full disclosure of the operations of all subsidiaries. At the present time the vast majority of subsidiaries do not publicly disclose information relating to their activities in this country. Companies with less than 50 shareholders are exempted from publishing their financial statements. Subsidiaries with only the parent company as shareholder are able to take advantage of a privilege clearly reserved for family of closely held enterprises. This is a ridiculous situation for a subsidiary; for example, Canadian International Paper, owned by a public company, International Paper Company, with tens of thousands of shareholders cannot be considered a private company in the normal meaning of the term. An amendment along the lines of British Company law would resolve their status, for in Great Britain a private company does not qualify as an exempt private company if some of its shares or debentures are held by a corporation. Such companies must file with the registrar copies of their financial statements which are available to anyone.

It is important that shareholders of a parent company know that many of their foreign operations lose money and cannot be justified by normal investment criteria. If this were so, managements would be reluctant to continue many commitments that now escape the searching gaze of shareholders, and the resulting withdrawal of much uneconomic investmennt would improve the performance of Canadian industry. In short, it is not the well-run, profitable subsidiary that we want to discourage, for such a company is an asset to the Canadian economy by making profits, paying taxes, employing Canadians and Canadian resources. It is the loss company which is a burden by contributing to excess capacity in an industry, high costs of operations, etc. In addition, this type of company is, of course, a charge upon the treasury department of its base country. The simple requirement of more disclosure, without discrimination against anyone, would alert shareholders and policymakers in both countries to investment decisions that are damaging to all our interests. It is a simple measure and long overdue.

Our rate of saving is among the highest in the world, but so is our rate of investment. Unfortunately for Canadians, social services cost more in Canada, and for all the usual reasons: a large land, scattered population, smaller markets. Furthermore, our wants came before we were able to build up the huge pools of investment capital necessary to finance them or to develop the managerial and entrepreneurial skills needed to secure and maintain a major position in world trade. We have largely overcome the latter handicap and no longer have to borrow management, but the need to borrow capital will persist for many years. It is a gross exaggeration to suggest that this dependence on foreign capital means a return to colonial status. We have political control over our own affairs; let us use it. If we move from colony to nation to colony, it will be our own fault.

Our difficulties are compounded by our size and by our late start in the race for technological excellence. Our position in time (a late start) and space (a big land) have increased the costs of pulling the nation together into a political entity, and if it were not for the unparalleled magnitude of our natural resources we would never be able to attract the huge pools of capital necessary to finance our highways, bridges, schools, hospitals, and the overhead costs of keeping Canada going. Social capital absorbs approximately half of all our investment funds.

The only manner in which we can possibly finance all that we want to do in Canada is by putting our productive system to the test. Although we depend much more on state intervention and initiative than the United States, and are less capitalist in content, the driving force of the Canadian economy depends largely on private enterprise. Our businessmen, therefore, must be challenged to prove their quality. We cannot achieve better living for Canadians if we protect our businessmen from competition. Similarly, we cannot excuse our government from the responsibility of mastering the difficulties which may accompany vast injections of foreign investment by permitting it to refuse the capital and so avoid the problem.

There is a perfectly legitimate set of economic policies which will help to ensure our independence and freedom of action and, at the same time, secure for us a greater control over our monetary, fiscal, and trade policies. Foremost among these policies must be the firm, positive decision to work harder for the removal of restrictions to the free flow of goods, services, and capital. Tariff policy may be a legitimate policy for developing nations to follow. It is not appropriate for modern Canada, however, for we are too well-endowed with natural resources, access to capital markets, and entrepreneurial and managerial talent. We need the will to put our economy, and our businessmen, to the test.

We have used the infant industry argument for too long and risk, as John Dales has pointed out, the sobriquet of infant nation. With too many firms dividing up relatively small markets, the Canadian consumer bears the cost of misallocation of talent and capital and high costs. With the excess direct investment flows of the last two decades, approximately 30% of firms in our manufacturing sector lose money. This industry is not only established, it is too well-established. The challenge is to make manufacturing efficient in world markets by exposing it to the pressures of increasing competition, reducing the number and increasing the size of firms, and forcing the peace of specialization. Imported ideas and technology do not create new comparative advantages or a distinct national identity, and Canada must achieve a better distribution of its resources by investing more heavily in capital—intensive techniques and research—employing goods and services. A developing nation must rely on the production and export of primary resources. Canada is not an underdeveloped country, says Secretary Fowler rightly, and as it becomes more industrialized and as its economy becomes more complex it must move into the production of more specialized goods, new products, new ideas and new services, leaving room for the nations developing more slowly to depend on basic resources. Progress and new challenges are the constant goods of nations and individuals. This is quality of economic performance.

With freer trade the rate of penetration of our markets by American direct investment would gradually diminish, thus creating a vacuum for Canadian enterprise to fill. There is the rub. No one can make our economy strong except ourselves. If our businessmen are weak, uncompetitive and unenterprising, then Canada cannot be strong, competitive and independent. If our present massive investments in the education of our human resources create a class of entrepreneurs and imaginative self-starters, then the problem of direct investment flows will become less acute. Entrepreneurs borrow money for their own account; managers handle the ideas and capital of others. The reversal of capital flows from equity to debt forms depends on the supply of entrepreneurial skills and investment opportunities available in Canada, and not on the application of restrictive and discriminatory laws. These latter policies solve the problem by extinguishing investment interest in Canada and by condemning us to reduced rates of growth.

If Canadian entrepreneurship exists, it will have ample opportunity to adjust to the opportunities offered by expanding domestic and foreign markets as we bargain our entry into them. Clearly, there will have to be a rationalization and regroupment of firms into larger, more powerful units capable of inventing, directing and controlling change. This is the new orientation that Canadian economic policy must take. It is the trend in many spheres of economic and social living. When farmers are urged to merge with their neighbors to become economically viable, when municipalities are asked to regroup to provide better services for their communities, when school commissions amalgamate in regional boards to attain uniform standards and higher quality of education across the land, is there any reason why businessmen should consider themselves exempt from changes in trade policy?

Contrary to what the economic nationalists tell us, there is no country in the world that should work harder for the removal of restrictions to the free flow of goods, services and capital than Canada. Per capita trade is three times more important to us than to our neighbours to the south, and relatively much more important to us than to the Germans, Italians, French or British. We are a highly industrialized nation without the larger domestic markets necessary to sustain large scale firms. Without access to large markets we will be unable to take advantage of the new and costly technology, and the age of specialization may easily pass us by. We should not recommend or introduce measures which impede the flow of capital and goods and should resist, even if we cannot prevent, the introduction of such policies by other nations.

If Canada pursues an aggressive free trade policy it is obvious that our fixed exchange rate policy will not work. We will have to go through so many fundamental changes in industrial organization that only a freely moving rate will be able to adjust to the productive process and measure our success or failure in achieving our aims. As J. E. Meade has written, there is no choice for free traders. "Free trade and fixed exchange rates are incompatible in the modern world." This is particularly true for a Canada which depends on trade, has a heavily protected manufacturing industry, and is much affected by the slightest changes in the economic policy of its neighbor. Freer trade will bring a more efficient use of our resources and expand our possibilities of growth, but these changes cannot possibly work their way through the economy within the constraints of a fixed rate.

The basic argument for fixed exchange rates is to protect the Canadian businessman from fluctuations in the value of the dollar. With a fixed rate he can plan; he knows what the costs of imported tools and machinery will be; he can measure precisely the net receipts from his exports. But why should the businessman be protected from risk and change? Is it not precisely the function of entrepreneurs and innovators to take advantage of economic change to control and direct the forces of change? By protecting the Canadian businessman from change, whether by tariffs or fixed exchange rates, we content ourselves with less than optimum performance and should not be surprised if our control over our economy lessens. Fixed exchange rates mean that we shape the Canadian economy to maintain an external equilibrium. For example, we are presently committed not only to maintain a fixed rate of exchange for the Canadian dollar but also a fixed ceiling to the amount of our exchange reserves. Our efforts, then, to employ more fully our human and material resources, including the 300,000 new jobs that we must find each year, must be circumscribed by these commitments. Exchange rates, which should adjust to the productive process, control and order our affairs. The whole weight of our economic policy is brought to bear on marginal problems, the problems of stabilizing a rate of exchange or maintaining rates of interest to control capital flows. We are forced to ignore the fundamental problems of growth and employment. Our balance on current account is approximately 2% of our Gross National Product, and one would normally consider that economic policy directed to the composition and growth of G.N.P. would yield more satisfactory results than policies which have the effect of containing G.N.P. for the sake of maintaining a given balance in international payments.

CONCLUSION

Sir Wilfrid Laurier must surely qualify as one of the most optimistic of Canadian Prime Ministers. Predicting that this half of the twentieth century would see Canada front and centre on the world stage, he showed his confidence in Canadians and Canadian businessmen by advocating reciprocity with the United States. Unfortunately, Canadian manufacturers have had less confidence in themselves and we remain a protected and costly economy. Laurier was right. By 1967 we should have had greater economic achievements to our credit and a greater measure of economic independence.

Canada will not survive if it continues to turn inward. Concentration upon ourselves can only serve to magnify our differences and to create the economic islands that will weaken and destroy us. The lesson of the first century is that Canadians can do better, much better. The single most important political decision that Ottawa can take is to demand more and better performance from all Canadians everywhere during the next hundred years.

John
Robarts

PROVINCIAL POWERS AND NATIONAL GOALS

John Robarts
  John Robarts Q.C. was born in Banff, Alberta, in 1917. He
received much of his early education in London, Ontario, and
graduated from the University of Western Ontario and from
Osgoode Hall. Mr. Robarts was first elected to the Ontario
Legislature in 1951. In 1958 he entered the Cabinet as Minister
without Portfolio and one year later was named Minister of
Education. Since 1961 he has served as leader of the Ontario
Progressive Conservative Party and Premier of the Province.

Canada is moving towards a fundamental reshaping of the economic framework of Confederation. The stature and economic importance of the provinces are inexorably changing. This resurgence
of the provinces within our federal union will have far-reaching influence upon the course and character of our nation-building
in the years ahead. It also has immediate significance for the
progress of our nation in economic affairs. This chapter is a discussion of the effects of this changing degree of economic influ-

ence and the increasing interdependence of the federal and provincial governments in the sphere of economic policies.

To begin, the present situation in Canada in regard to economic policies is examined. Such an examination reveals a high
degree of overlapping in the responsibilities and powers of the
federal and provincial governments, both in respect of particular
economic programs and in matters that impinge on the economy
at large. This leads to a view of the appropriate economic role for
the provinces and for the federal government. In many instances,
however, it is evident that there can be no clear separation of
interest or division of federal and provincial responsibility. This
interdependence of the two levels of government in the economic
sphere points up the need for improved machinery for intergovernmental consultation and co-operation if federalism is to work
in Canada.

The second part of this article looks to the future and dis-
cusses some of the emerging economic and social problems in
Canada which will require important action by both the provinces
and the federal government. As our society becomes increasingly
urbanized and industrialized, governments will face immense new
responsibilities in fields related to the working and living environment of our citizens. These new and expanded responsibilities of
government may be expected to involve substantial expenditures.
Hence joint federal-provincial action in many fields seems desirable, perhaps inevitable.

FEDERAL AND PROVINCIAL ECONOMIC POLICIES

In Canada's varied economy governments intrude into economic
and business life in many ways—by maintaining an overall climate conducive to growth and impetus in the private sector, by
stabilizing business fluctuations, by redistributing income and
wealth among people and regions, by regulatory activities, and by
direct participation in various enterprises and functions. Both
levels of government participate within this broad spectrum,
though the policies of the federal government are generally geared
for a national impact while provincial programs are designed to
influence commerce and economic activity within their own borders.

Inevitably, however, the policies and programs pursued by each province have a substantial impact on other provinces and on the national economy; conversely, federal policies filter down and work themselves out at the provincial level. This interdependence and overlapping of the provincial and federal governments in the economic sphere is an inescapable reality. It is a reality which challenges all eleven governments to consult and strive for agreement on policies and to co-operate in implementing economic programs.

A vital prerequisite for greater consistency and co-ordination among our governments in economic matters is agreement on general priorities and goals for Canada. All provinces and the federal government must be prepared to put forward their own objectives and proposals for common examination and discussion so that a cohesive plan for national development can be hammered out. The establishment of the Economic Council of Canada was an important first step in this direction. In its first two reports the Council clearly set out basic economic targets for Canada and focussed attention on the areas where government initiative and action are required if we are to meet these objectives. The province of Ontario, and we hope the other provinces as well, agrees with these national goals and expects to participate fully in seeking their achievement.

Agreement on principles and goals is, however, but the beginning of the task. In addition there must be a thorough review of the whole catalogue of economic policies and programs presently in force at the provincial and federal level. Our governments must strive to clarify matters of jurisdictional dispute, to resolve which spheres of action properly belong to each level of government, and to agree on a co-operative and complementary approach in the many instances in which the provincial and the federal interests are entwined.

1. *The Provincial Role*

Any efforts to rationalize and harmonize federal and provincial economic policies and programs must recognize at the outset the growing importance of the provinces in the national economy. Today provincial-municipal expenditures on goods and services loom twice as large as those of the federal government. Thus, by the sheer weight of their budgets the provinces, particularly the large provinces of Ontario and Quebec, have assumed a strategic role in expenditure policies. Similarly, on the investment side, capital outlays at the provincial-municipal level are four times as large as at the federal level. Moreover, the recently enacted Canada Pension Plan and Quebec Pension Plan have broadened the horizon for provincial investment decisions by ensuring to the provinces access to very substantial long term capital funds. With respect to fiscal powers, the provinces have gained back from Ottawa substantial occupancy in the major tax fields over the last decade. These comparisons indicate the large and accumulating economic powers now in the hands of provincial governments. In addition, because the responsibilities of the provinces are centered in fields such as education, social welfare and health, which are particularly affected by industrialization and the shift to urban living, the initiative for change over a broad range of socio-economic policies rests with the provinces.

This expanding influence of the provinces in the national economy requires of them a greater responsibility in the exercise of their powers. In general this means that the provinces must take into account what effects their budgets and economic policies have upon neighbouring jurisdictions and on the Canadian economy at large. For example, in respect of stabilization and policies designed to balance out the business cycle, which are the overriding responsibility of the central government, the provincial-municipal governments can largely offset or accentuate federal action. The provinces should consciously adapt their budgets so as to complement federal measures to combat unemployment or inflation. In particular this would require that the provinces co-operate in the timing and direction of their capital outlays, both because of their size relative to total public investment and their sensitivity to cyclical variation. Greater sophistication is also required of the provinces in their fiscal policies. As more tax room is made available to the provinces by Ottawa, the possiblity of anomalies and perversities in the overall tax system is greatly increased. If we are to avoid competitive tax measures and fiscal policies operating at cross purposes, co-ordinated action by the provinces and in concert with Ottawa is imperative.

In the last few years several important steps have been taken to improve the machinery and procedures necessary for concerted budgeting and fiscal measures in Canada. There have been numerous federal-provincial conferences under the aegis of the Tax Structure Committee. These have provided a basis upon which better interchange and understanding among our eleven governments can be developed. The Tax Structure Committee has also set in motion a study by the Institute for Intergovernment Relations, at Queen's University, on ways and means of improving intergovernmental liaison in fiscal and economic matters. Another innovation of great potential value has been the convening of a annual meeting of ministers of finance devoted to pre-budget discussions. If all participants come to such meetings prepared to discuss their problems and proposals, we shall not only improve our appraisal of the state of the economy but also, perhaps, agree on what actions are required by each level of government to bring about desired changes. These developments in intergovernmental relations are of very recent origin, but they do give promise that the provinces and the central government can find procedures and methods of working together on broad economic matters.

Turning to the narrower scale of particular policy areas and specific programs, the role of the provinces is at once both more distinct and more consequential. Broadly speaking, the provinces are concerneed with policies:

(1) to improve the quality and mobility of the labour force through education, retraining, health and welfare programs;

(2) to foster improvements and remove impediments in the manufacturing, construction, agricultural, resource, and service sectors of the economy;

(3) to provide the essential capital investment in roads, housing, power, water, and waste disposal and other public facilities necessary for development; and

(4) to assist in urban and regional planning.

In today's world these are areas of public action which are vital to the improvement of productivity and economic growth. They also are the fields in which provincial expenditure has risen most rapidly. Federal government policies are also operative in these fields and Ottawa shares in the financing of many of the programs operated by the provinces. That there is a legitimate degree of participation by the senior government in these matters primarily under provincial jurisdiction must be recognized, but federal initiative and actions should not upset or undermine provincial policies and priorities concerning internal economic development.

In the field of education, for example, Ontario reserves the right to determine its own policies and priorities and expects to carry out its own programs without duplication, competition or collision with Ottawa. Federal participation in this field and in other areas under provincial jurisdiction should be mainly of a financial nature rather than direct involvement. In this way Ottawa can play a positive role without interfering or conflicting with the aims and implementation of overall provincial programs.

Another policy area in which federal programs have not adequately meshed with provincial plans is in the important field of regional development. In our view the provinces have the paramount responsibility for reducing economic disparities among their communities and fostering efficient development in all regions. It may well be doubted that the federal government has the appropriate means for adequately assessing regional interests or for determining regional policies within the provinces. The present 'designated area program', for instance, does not encourage the optimal geographical and industrial allocation of human and capital resources in Ontario or, we believe, in the nation at large. This federal program is the type of self-defeating restrictive measure which the Economic Council warned against in its second annual review. Rather, as the Economic Council of Canada advised, regional development should be attacked by methods which do not retard the development of faster growing regions and do not interfere with the free flow of goods, capital and labour between all provinces.

Problems of regional development in Ontario and in other provinces require a package of consistent, coherent, long-run policies worked out by both levels of government. In such an approach the central role of assessing needs, designing policies and operating programs should remain the function of each province; for its part, the federal government would act as a focal point for co-ordination and research and provide much of the essential financing. The existing Canada Assistance Plan and Agricultural Rehabilitation and Development Act programs are of this nature and we believe they are sound models on which to build.

Other important provincial policy areas which affect the business and economic environment include labour relations, energy and resources development, securities legislation, licensing and incorporation of companies, and agricultural marketing. In these fields, as in the others we have discussed, the federal government also is involved, often because of its responsibility for interprovincial trade and commerce. In the main, provincial and federal responsibility in these areas is reasonably distinct and unambiguous and policies and programs are complementary. There are areas, however, in which neither level of government has clear authority, hence jurisdictional uncertainties have appeared. Such a situation has recently developed in respect to subsidies to milk producers and in the dispute over off-shore mineral rights. In the former case the problem suggests that both levels of government confer and work out a national dairy policy or even a national farm policy. In the latter case the conflict must be resolved in favour of one government or the other, either through the political or the judicial process.

To sum up the role of the provinces in economic and business policy, one may say that it is manifold, growing, and interdependent in many fields with that of the federal government. The problem for each province is to try to strike a balance between what is sound practice for the province and what is in the national interest. I submit that the national interest will be best served if the provinces are allocated the financial resources and left the responsibility to carry out their own functions, while consulting and co-operating as closely as possible with other provinces and with the federal government in matters of mutual responsibility and concern.

2. *The Federal Role*

The preceding section has referred to some activities of the federal government in economic fields that fall principally under provincial jurisdiction. Let us now look at the other side of the coin and discuss the overall economic policies for which responsibility rests chiefly with Ottawa.

The federal government must be concerned with national requirements and policies for:

(1) maintaining stability and promoting long term growth in the Canadian economy as a whole;

(2) balancing the effects of uneven levels of prosperity and rates of growth among different provinces; and
(3) preserving a sound external financial position and international stature.

The following paragraphs elaborate upon these three axes of federal economic policy with particular reference to those aspects that have important bearing upon provincial economies.

The stabilization and growth objectives of federal policy require the creation and maintenance of an overall economic environment in Canada such that the private sector can operate boldly and efficiently. This entails a high and rising level of output, new job opportunities for the burgeoning labour force, steadily rising productivity and industrial efficiency, as well as stability of costs and prices. For these purposes the federal government must have broad control and direction of monetary, fiscal and debt policies. As previously noted, however, the provinces have sufficient fiscal and spending powers to significantly inhibit or supplement federal contracyclical policies. Surely there is an obligation upon the provinces to recognize their very considerable weight in these respects and consciously to strive to complement national policies and actions. The provinces can also contribute significantly towards achievement of national growth and productivity targets by pursuing manpower and development policies which are neither restrictive nor parochial.

The balancing function of the central government is necessary in a country like Canada because of the gross disparities in levels of income and wealth in different parts of the country. It is an important task of our senior government to even out the effects of these differences so that Canadians in every province can enjoy at least a minimum level of welfare and public services. As a large and well-endowed province, Ontario has for many years been the paymaster for a considerable part of these federal transfers to the "poorer" provinces. We accept this situation and support the principle of federal equalizing measures as the basis for developing a truly national economy in Canada. Such redistribution, however, must be accomplished without retarding growth and development in the "richer" provinces. Similarly, there should be caution expressed against policies that merely create temporary activity or prop up declining industries and low productivity sectors. Canada cannot afford to sustain uneconomic ventures or sacrifice its overall economic growth potential for the sake of short run regional balance. Rather, federal policies should encourage growth sectors within the lagging provinces and concentrate on building up industries which can be viable and competitive. In dealing with the problems created by regional imbalance the federal government must take into account its whole range of policies and activities that have differential regional impacts—i.e., tariffs, transportation policies, monetary policy, manpower policies, direct grants, subsidies, cost-sharing programs and equalization payments. Moreover, the rapid pace of technical change and industrial innovation which is the cause of much of the regional imbalance demands an approach to provincial and regional problems that is readily adaptable to changing conditions. To resolve these complex and sometimes conflicting regional elements in the Canadian economy will require wise decisions and strong leadership from Ottawa.

The international aspects of federal economic policy require only brief comment. It is generally recognized that the federal government has ultimate responsibility for the solvency of the nation, the strength of our dollar and the soundness of our balance of payments position. Because of Canada's open economy federal government measures designed to deal with balance of payments problems may run counter to national and provincial growth objectives. The provinces must accept the fact that these external considerations can give rise to sudden changes and emergency actions by the federal government which inhibit provincial policies and programs. While learning to live with such short run disturbances, the provinces and the federal government should be seeking all possible means of improving the competitive position of the Canadian economy. This can best be achieved by provincial and national policies that encourage the free flow of labour, capital, goods and enterprise within and among provinces.

In concluding this discussion of the role of the federal government in economic matters, I would stress the essentially national scope of federal policies. Additionally, it bears repeating that there is no necessary connection between national programs and similar provincial projects for economic growth and development. In fact, provincial policies in such matters as taxation, borrowing, or industrial development can conflict with the economic objectives of the central government. For this reason there must be a maximum of consultation, co-operation and collaboration between the two levels of government to produce the best mix of policies to serve the national interest.

3. *Interprovincial Co-operation*

So far this discussion of economic policies has been in terms of provincial governments or the federal government, or some combination of both. Now I wish to add a few thoughts about the scope for joint action among the ten provinces themselves. It seems to me that the provinces by consulting and co-operating among themselves can make significant advances in many areas. For example, greater conformity in respect to company law, provincial charters, securities legislation, labour legislation and interprovincial licensing, would be of great benefit to the Canadian business community. Similarly, the ten provinces should work towards uniform standards in various aspects of education, pension regulation and consumer protection. There is also a great need for more co-operation and co-ordination among provinces in highway planning, energy and resources development, conservation programs, agricultural marketing and tourism promotion. Up until very recently there have been only sporadic examples of fruitful interprovincial co-operation in these and other fields. In the last few years, however, there has been increased formal liaison and communication among provincial officials and ministers. To yield practical solutions and real improvements in many areas of common concern to the provinces, this trend must continue and accelerate.

FUTURE AREAS OF PROVINCIAL-FEDERAL INTERACTION

In the years ahead a whole new array of social and economic needs will come to the fore in Canada. As this nation continues its transition towards a modern, urban and industrial society, governments will have thrust upon them new and expanded responsibilities in such fields as urban redevelopment, public transportation and housing, pollution control, provision of recreational and leisure facilities, and scientific research. In these and many other emerging areas of public concern, jurisdiction is largely provincial, though the federal government also has an important role to play by way of establishing and financing national objectives. To tackle these problems effectively, therefore, our governments must extend the range of their consultation and co-operation and must work together as partners in progress.

In the following paragraphs let us look briefly at some of these newer fields of public action and discuss the problems and possibilities they raise for governments in Canada.

In the future, governments in Canada must be prepared to intensify their support and provide new resources in the field of scientific and industrial research. Already important steps have been taken in this direction. In Ontario we have established a major research and development centre in Sheridan Park. This large and growing complex combines the resources of personnel, industry and government to further our research effort. At the national level the Science Council of Canada has recently been formed to provide expert advice to the federal government on problems of science and technology. These government efforts must be continued and expanded and further efforts made to stimulate greater scientific research and development in Canadian industry if our economy is to keep abreast of technological advances elsewhere.

The physical circumstances of Canada's large cities and the urban well-being of the millions of people who live in them merit increasing attention and action by governments. In Ontario particularly, because of the advanced degree of urbanization, we are acutely conscious of the need to improve the housing conditions and living environment of our city dwellers. The types of programs involved include slum clearance, urban renewal, provision of more and better housing, provision of more parks and public facilities for social and recreational purposes, as well as general beautification of the urban landscape. All these programs to upgrade the quality of our society require large amounts of social capital, capital which also will be required for schools, roads, and other public services. Thus the problem for the provincial-municipal sector which has primary responsibility in these matters is one of financing. With present tax resources the provinces and their municipalities cannot hope to undertake these programs on the scale required. This means that in one form or another the federal government will have to ensure that massive financing is made available to the provinces for these urban needs.

Industrialization and urbanization have also brought the problems of air and water pollution. These are evils which require collective action at the provincial and national levels. To varying degrees, the solution of these problems is being advanced. The ten provinces and the federal government have established a Canadian Council of Resource Ministers as a forum where our governments may exchange information and discuss future plans. In 1966 the Council sponsored a national conference on water, soil and air pollution to assist governments, communities and industry in establishing co-ordinated programs of pollution abatement and control throughout the country. As well, comprehensive studies of pollution in the Great Lakes are being undertaken by the Ontario Water Resources Commission, in collaboration with the federal government. These examples of a common approach and joint action by the provinces and the federal government provide a hopeful sign for the future. Such co-operation can and must be extended to a broad range of programs if Canada is to cope effectively with the problems brought on by rapid economic and social change.

SUMMING UP

Since the character of Canada's federal structure is constantly evolving, it would be premature to end this chapter with conclusions. Rather, I must content myself with a reiteration of some pertinent points already considered and a summary of my views on federal-provincial interaction in economic matters.

At present there is extensive overlapping and interdependence between the provincial and national levels of government in Canada in respect to economic policies. This situation has developed as the result of the steadily widening role of the public sector in economic life and the increase in provincial powers and responsibilities relative to those of Ottawa over the last two decades. These trends may be expected to continue in future as industrialization and the shift to urban living create new demands on governments, particularly the provincial governments.

The joint jurisdiction and shared responsibility of Ottawa and the provinces in a whole range of economic programs creates problems of compatibility and co-ordination and opens the possibility of governments operating at cross purposes. It is essential that these matters be clarified and resolved if Canada is to make maximum progress toward achieving its broad national goals. There is an appropriate economic role for each level of government and the present division of constitutional responsibilities generally defines these roles. In my view the national interest will be best served if the provinces are allocated the financial resources and left the task of devising their own solutions and meeting their own responsibilities. On the other hand, the overriding responsibility of the federal government to pursue national policies must be recognized and the fact that at times the national interest must take precedence over provincial interests must be accepted. Moreover, in many areas of economic policy there can be no clear separation of provincial and federal responsibility. This makes it imperative that both levels of government strive to work out integrated and coherent policies and that they consult and co-operate to the fullest extent. In looking to the future it is apparent that an active federal-provincial partnership will be the most effective means of achieving our economic goals.

Mitchell Sharp

DOMESTIC SURVIVAL THROUGH FOREIGN TRADE

Mitchell Sharp

Mitchell Sharp was born in Winnipeg, Manitoba, in 1911. He studied economics at the University of Manitoba and the London School of Economics, London, England. Following a career in the Finance and Commerce Departments of the federal government and in private business, Mr. Sharp was elected to the House of Commons in 1963 and appointed Minister of Trade and Commerce. In 1965 he was named Minister of Finance and Receiver General of Canada.

Foreign trade has always been essential to the development of Canada and the incomes of Canadians. First it was fish from the waters off Newfoundland, and furs from Hudson's Bay and from the "upper country" beyond the lakes. Then it was square timber and, by the turn of the century, western wheat. In the 'twenties and 'thirties new products became important—pulp and paper, non-ferrous metals, aluminum, and asbestos. More recently, with the opening up of the great iron ore deposits in Quebec and the development of oil, natural gas, and sulphur and of the potash deposits of Saskatchewan, we have become major world suppliers of an even longer list of basic materials. We have also begun to make our mark as a supplier of synthetic rubber and as a source of a variety of highly-manufactured goods.

Although our domestic market has grown considerably, 50 per cent of the output of our goods-producing industries goes to world markets, and exports of goods and services represent about 21.5 per cent of the Gross National Product.

For as far ahead as we can see, our survival as an independent political entity may well turn on our success in maintaining—if not increasing—our share of world markets.

PATTERNS OF WORLD TRADE

World trade has virtually doubled in the last decade, and the range of products exchanged between nations has expanded significantly. New suppliers of existing products have come into the market, and changing needs have prompted demands for new products and led to the appearance of new customers. For more than ten consecutive years international trade has been increasing more rapidly than the volume of world production.

Two features have marked this expansion—both of considerable importance to Canada. First, the most dynamic area of growth has been in trade between the industrialized countries. Second, trade in manufactured goods has increased much more rapidly than trade in other products.

These developments, in turn, reflect the changing distribution of the types of goods being traded on world markets. Trade in industrial materials and in primary or lightly processed products has increased, but at much less than the rate of increase in the trade in more fully manufactured goods. The main benefit of the upsurge in world trade has thus gone to the countries producing the more sophisticated types of capital equipment and consumer products.

Price developments have also tended to favour the industrialized countries. The prices of many primary commodities declined through most of the past decade, partly due to the uneconomic expansion of production during the Korean War. As a result, the terms of trade have tended to go against the exporters of primary products and in favour of those nations that traditionally are sellers of manufactured goods. It is true that prices of some primary commodities have risen sharply in the last two years, e.g. metals and certain industrial materials, which have particularly benefited from the growing demand generated by the accelerating economic growth in the industrial nations during the 'sixties as well as by defence purchases.

On the other hand, prices of most agricultural products have tended to remain at low levels, and countries depending on commodities such as cocoa, coffee, and sugar for the major part of their exchange earnings have not had any easy time. This is, in part, because the elasticity of demand for most basic foodstuffs is not great, particularly at higher income levels. Prosperity in the industrial countries has thus not generated a substantially larger demand for those tropical products which traditionally provide such foreign exchange earnings for producing countries. There is, however, an immense potential need for certain basic foodstuffs such as wheat and rice simply because of increasing world population. The problem is how to find the finance to pay for the food required.

There are a number of reasons why the growth in international trade in the last ten years has been particularly significant for manufactured goods. Consumer incomes have been rising rapidly in the developed nations, and higher living standards have created mass demands for products once considered luxuries. There has been an exceptionally rapid rate of technological change, and this has often led to the development of new production facilities and to increasing international specialization of production. There have also been significant reductions in tariffs affecting trade in manufactured products. These developments can be expected to continue and will undoubtedly have a pronounced affect on future patterns of world trade.

It may be that we are, in fact, in the middle of a technological revolution, and that some of the most significant changes are only beginning to make their impact. The greater use of electronics, the development of atomic energy, the application of new techniques of automation and data processing—involving the creation of an "information industry"—and the emergence of new types of synthetic products—all these have already changed the economics of production in many industries, and their impact can be expected to be even more pervasive and important in the future.

Many of the new techniques have given rise to considerable economies in the use of materials. This factor, when combined with the use of new materials, often synthetic, has limited the growth of demand for many traditional materials. In recent years the consumption of synthetics, such as man-made textile fibres, plastics, and synthetic rubber, has grown four times as rapidly as consumption of natural materials. Moreover, there has been a tendency for the use of raw materials, both of natural origin and of synthetic manufacture, to decline, in relative terms, for a number of reasons. Many modern products are highly engineered and require a large degree of manufacture. They tend, therefore, to involve the use of more capital and labour for their transformation into final products. Moreover, manufacturers have had considerable success in finding new ways of making use of hitherto "waste" by-products or of salvaged or scrap materials. All tend to reduce the need for materials per unit of output, and to retard the growth of world trade in these products.

Important developments are also occurring in transport and communications. The development of new and improved methods have reduced costs of transportation, thereby encouraging a greater flow of goods. And the relative importance of transportation costs in total costs has declined as foreign trade had become increasingly focussed on more sophisticated, higher-value manufactured goods.

Better communications have helped to make producers aware of new export possibilities and have enabled exporters to service overseas customers more readily. Consumers have also become better informed, so that they are more discriminating in their choice of products. Today's market demands a greater variety of goods, many of which can only be supplied by imports.

These trends have undoubtedly affected Canada's performance in world trade. They help to explain why our share of total international trade has declined from 6.2 per cent in 1952 to about 4 per cent today. This has occurred despite an increase in our exports from $4.3 billion in 1952 to $8.5 billion in 1965. The fact is that in recent years our exports have been rising less rapidly than the world average.

THE ROLE OF EXPORTS

Canada's export package is heavily weighted with primary products and industrial materials; both categories, as we have seen, are of declining importance on world markets. Since 1960 our exports of highly-manufactured goods have been increasing rapidly, partly because of technological advances in Canadian industry, partly as a result of our defence production-sharing arrangements with the United States, and partly as a result of the competitive advantage that devaluation gave to Canadian manufacturers. Expressed in U.S. dollars, the export price index of Canadian manufactured goods actually declined by about 4 per cent between 1960 and 1963. The rate of increase in Canada's manufactured exports during this period was more than 20 per cent per annum, almost ten times as high as the rate of increase in exports of agricultural products and four to five times as high as that of other non-manufactured goods. While this was a heartening development, the fact is that manufactured goods still account for only about 15 per cent of our exports, a much smaller proportion than that of any other industrialized country.

Substantial increases in exports are essential if the domestic economy is to operate at full potential. The Economic Council, in its projections for the economy to 1970, has said that a sharp increase in exports is essential if we are to contain the growth in the current account deficit and at the same time provide for a rate of growth in the economy sufficient to absorb the anticipated expansion in the labour force. Canada's labour force is expected to increase at a rate of 2.6 per cent per annum during this period. Between 1965 and 1970 jobs have to be found for an additional million workers. New job opportunities will also be needed to provide for re-employment of workers affected by shifts within the economy brought about by changing market conditions at home and abroad, and by new technological development. Many of these jobs will have to be found in export industries, particularly in manufacturing.

The Council's export target for 1970 will require an average annual increase in exports of 5.3 per cent per annum. It presumes a continued rapid increase in exports of highly manufactured goods—possibly of the order of 10 per cent per annum—and a generally higher order of increase for non-agricultural as opposed to agricultural exports. The alternative, in the Council's view, is either acceptance of higher payments deficits and thus increased dependence on capital imports to finance them, or a cutback in the growth rate of the economy—which would mean a loss of output, unemployment, and a drain of skilled workers and professionally trained people through emigration.

POLICY IMPLICATIONS

Our success in achieving these export targets will depend on a number of factors, some of which are more within our own control than are others. Our ability to maintain our relative cost and price position in the production of traditional export products, our success in increasing the efficiency of our manufacturing industries —so that we become more competitive in world markets—and the willingness of Canadian businessmen to seek out and develop new export markets will all be factors of great importance.

These clearly impose certain limitations on domestic economic policy. First, our fiscal and monetary policy must be such as to maintain a realistic and stable exchange rate for the dollar and reasonably stable prices in Canada. Second, consequently we may have to set limits on the rate at which governments at all three levels can undertake new commitments, however desirable these may otherwise be. Third, wage and salary increases and other returns must be geared to increases in our national productivity. Fourth, as a nation, we cannot afford to perpetuate high-cost industries which make use of manpower and resources that could be more usefully employed elsewhere. Fifth, Canadian businessmen must be encouraged to seek out export markets and, where necessary, to invest in overseas undertakings in order to ensure their continued presence in such markets. Sixth, foreign-controlled firms must participate more fully in the development of export business and in the exploitation of efficient Canadian sources of raw materials, components, and capital equipment.

Equally important, although obviously much less subject to our own control, are the rates of growth in foreign markets and the reduction of barriers to our goods seeking to enter these markets. These two factors are not unrelated. Attempts to lower tariffs and other barriers to trade are more likely to command support, both in Canada and abroad, when the economies of the industrial nations are expanding and are providing full or near-full employment. But the actual rate of growth in foreign economies is also a key consideration. One reason why our exports failed to grow as rapidly as might have been expected in the late 'fifties and early 'sixties was the relatively slower rate of economic growth during these years in two of our principal markets, Britain and the United States. The expansion in other industrial countries was much more vigorous.

In recent years the United States economy has been moving forward with much greater momentum, and this has undoubtedly helped the growth of our exports. The United Kingdom, when it emerges from its present economic difficulties, is bound to achieve higher rates of growth than in the recent past. And it seems likely that Japan, another important customer, is entering a new phase of expansion. Thus the outlook for our exports, judging by the level of activity in our principal markets, is promising.

ACCESS TO FOREIGN MARKETS

The question of access to these markets is complex. Compared to the experience of the 'twenties, the progress made in the period since the end of World War II towards the objective of freeing world trade and facilitating its development on a multilateral and liberalized basis has been impressive. Successive rounds of tariff negotiations under the auspices of the General Agreement on Tariffs and Trade have resulted in a significant reduction of tariffs. Other barriers to trade, such as quantitative restrictions, have also been tackled in the GATT with considerable success. On the other hand, there has been less success in freeing trade in agricultural products. Moreover, the activities of the GATT have, in the past, failed to meet the expectations of its newer members, the less-developed countries.

A new round of tariff negotiations—the Kennedy Round—is now entering its final stages in Geneva. It is still too early to know the extent to which these negotiations will succeed in improving the terms of access for our goods in world markets. Clearly, the negotiations will not achieve everything that was originally hoped of them when President Kennedy signed the United States Trade Expansion Act. But it is probable that many important reductions in tariffs will be made. There is some reason to hope, too, that arrangements for a measure of liberalization in agricultural trade can be agreed and that some progress can be made in reducing so-called "non-tariff" barriers to trade.

Canada has been a member and firm supporter of the GATT

since its foundation; our concern that world trade be conducted on as wide and as free a basis as possible follows directly from our dependence upon trade for our economic growth. It is easy enough to state this general orientation. The real problem is how to move in this direction in a realistic manner. I believe it is important that in the Kennedy Round, and in future trade negotiations, we ensure that the particular problems of the Canadian economy are adequately taken into account. This requires a sure grasp of our history—and of our geography, too. Unlike most Western European countries, for example, whose economic and commercial relations are largely oriented towards neighbours of more or less equal strength, we exist alongside a country whose resources and competitive ability in most fields vastly exceed our own. This is an inescapable geographic and economic fact. We all know that the inevitable closeness of our relations with the United States has enabled us to achieve in a remarkably short time one of the highest standards of living in the world. But it has also shaped our economy and our policies in particular ways.

It is too easy to forget that Canada's commercial policies have evolved essentially as a response to the policies of our two main trading partners, Britain and the United States. That our policies should be responsive to their policies is inevitable; relatively we are a small country.

Thus the protective tariff policy, which was launched as the National Policy of Macdonald, and which in an exaggerated form culminated in the Ottawa Agreements of 1932, embodying high tariffs and high margins of preference, was largely designed to counter the highly protectionist policies of our neighbour. This sixty- or seventy-year period in which we protected our infant industries, essentially because the United States was also doing so, has left us with a manufacturing economy too diversified for our present home and export markets. It has left us with a legacy of small manufacturing firms scattered over the industrial sector. These firms were set up to serve only the Canadian market and the markets of the Empire which accorded tariff preferences to Canada. For many types of manufacturing this market has proved to be too small for adequate economies of scale.

The proliferation of small-scale manufacturing in Canada has been further encouraged by the hallowed policy of reducing tariffs on raw materials and components to assist the production in Canada of more advanced products. This has resulted in a level of effective or real protection on the value added in Canada in certain sectors of manufacturing which is often significantly higher than the ad valorem rates would suggest, involving some misallocation of our scarce resources of capital and skills.

Given that our economic survival depends on our ability to increase our exports in the face of increasing competition, and given that the best prospects for further increases in world trade lie in the manufacturing field, our present industrial pattern clearly has limitations. Obviously we must diversify our exports. This means more specialization and more rationalization in the manufacturing sector of our economy. To put it another way, we will increase the range of our exports, not by trying to make everything in Canada, but by concentrating on making fewer products better and cheaper. This means, too, that our neighbours and trading partners must be willing to accept our manufactured exports without imposing excessively high tariffs.

I have always strongly supported the efforts of successive United States Administrations to lead the way to freer trade, but the fact remains that many of Canada's exports and potential exports still face protective barriers in many markets. Thus the United States and Japan, two of our major markets, still impose sharply higher tariffs on manufactured goods than on raw materials and semi-processed goods. This so-called "progressive" tariff structure discriminates against the import of more fully manufactured goods. Even some of our raw materials have been denied easy entry into certain markets. For example, for many years the United States imposed quotas on Canadian lead and zinc and maintained them, in my view, for much longer than was justified, if they were ever justified. In Japan a wide range of Canadian raw materials (pig iron, copper, lead, zinc, and nickel, for example) have, it is true, been freed of quota, but they now face sharply higher tariffs. Canadian aluminum faces a substantial tariff in the EEC (and also in Japan) and a not unimportant tariff in the United States. Many Canadian forest products face effective tariff barriers in world markets. These examples should make clear that we have a long way to go in getting reasonable freedom of access to world markets for our exports. It remains just as true now as it did a hundred years ago that our ability to build up a competitive economy in Canada is determined to a very great extent by the willingness of our trading partners to accept our goods on reasonable terms.

Needless to say a policy of seeking to pull down the barriers to our exports involves some adjustments in our own tariffs. In making such necessary and consequent tariff reductions we must take account not only of the need to rationalize our industrial structure, but also of the time and the resources which may be required to make the necessary changes in the operations of many firms and in the jobs of so many individuals. The lives and fortunes of individual Canadians, and sometimes of whole countries, are involved in the process of adjustment.

We must also bear in mind when we face these issues at the bargaining table—in Geneva, in Washington, in Brussels, London, or Tokyo, and in Ottawa—that while our exports of manufactured goods represent only a small proportion of our total exports, our imports of such goods run at very high levels. In these circumstances we cannot hope to receive equivalent trading benefits if we cut our tariffs on these products in precisely the same proportion as our more powerful trading partners. It is for this reason that in devising our approach to tariff negotiations we have always shied away from simple mathematical formulae.

While multilateral negotiations are being pursued in Geneva, there are other economic developments which cannot be disregarded. One is the emergence of powerful regional blocs. Another is the growing pressure from less-developed countries for special treatment, particularly for new tariff preferences. In their own way both of these developments are threats to the principle of non-discrimination on which the post-war multilateral trading system was founded.

If the trend towards regional economic groups should proceed much further, there would be a danger of the whole world economy splitting up into a number of large and potentially hostile economic entities. In these circumstances the interests of Canada, and of other nations that remain outside such groupings, might well be lost sight of by our partners and become increasingly difficult to defend.

THE DEVELOPING COUNTRIES

The ending of colonial rule and the emergence of new nations in the less-developed parts of the world also raises problems for the continuance of the postwar world trading system. In the GATT and in the United Nations Conference on Trade and Development the developing countries have asked for special tariff preferences. They believe preferences help them sell their manufactured products to the markets of the industrial powers. They have also pressed for international agreements to increase and to stabilize their earnings from primary products, and for expanded aid from the developed nations to permit them to finance more economic development.

In my view, it is by no means clear that preferential tariffs would be of great assistance to developing countries. But, clearly, if these countries are to develop they must obtain foreign exchange to pay for their imports, and in the long term a large share of these funds will have to come from their export earnings. No matter how the demands of the developing countries are met, adjustments will be required of the richer countries. In the longer view, the development of these countries' economies and the raising of standards of living in the less-developed parts of the world will ultimately provide great scope for the expansion of trade, not only for manufactured goods, particularly capital goods, but also for foodstuffs and primary materials.

There is a danger that the failure to find satisfactory solutions to these problems on a multilateral basis may result in a series of new and increasingly anarchic preferential arrangements between the metropolitan powers and their former colonial territories, and the establishment within the world of more clearly defined and antagonistic spheres of economic influence. There have been suggestions of special trading arrangements between the Latin American and North American countries. Any such rigid structure of world trading arrangements would, I believe, inhibit the growth of world trade. They would be likely to work to the particular detriment of countries like Canada which do not fit easily within any defined geographical or political groupings.

STATE-TRADING COUNTRIES

In seeking to work out a new trade strategy, and in seeking to understand the new world economy that is developing, one should not overlook the importance for world trade of the state trading economies of the Far East and of Eastern Europe. Mainland

China, the USSR and the socialist countries of Eastern Europe are becoming increasingly significant in world trade; certainly they are important customers for Canada. So far, the trade on the export side has been heavily in wheat—but from time to time we have also sold substantial amounts of other primary products, such as sulphur and tobacco. There have been some sales of specialized machinery, for example, asbestos mining equipment, and undoubtedly other possibilities will develop.

The market in the state-trading countries is a difficult one to cultivate. Often the willingness to buy is limited by the preoccupation of the governments of these countries with achieving bilateral balances with their individual trading partners in the West, as well as by their shortage of foreign exchange. In Eastern Europe competition from traditional suppliers in the West—from Britain, France and Germany—is a powerful factor. These countries have been trading with Eastern Europe for many years. They know these markets; they are in a position to give effective after-sales service, and they are not hesitant about extending fairly generous credit facilities in order to gain sales.

So long as the state-trading countries buy large amounts of wheat from us their willingness to buy other Canadian goods will be limited. However, as their sales in the Canadian market increase, we can look for some expansion in our other exports to them. Much will depend on the initiative and imagination of our businessmen and financial institutions in developing trade with these countries. Recently there have been increasing indications of a breaking up of the former "monolithic structure" of these countries—and there are signs of a greater readiness to pursue independent trading policies and to restore or create, at least to some degree, the essential features of the market economy.

In negotiations with the governments of these countries, the Government of Canada seeks to remove obstacles to freer trade. We do not offer to trade commodities against commodities or quotas against quotas. Ours is essentially a multilateral approach in which we trade the opportunity to sell in Canada on equal terms with other countries against access on non-discriminatory terms for Canadian exports. This means that on both sides ultimate results depend upon the ability to compete, the willingness to allow competition, and the spirit of enterprise.

In summary, then, we in Canada have always depended for

our national existence on foreign trade, and we shall continue to do so.

Because the main growth in world trade will be, as it has been since the war, in manufactured goods, clearly it is here that our main efforts must be made. The cost of failure would be either a higher current deficit in our balance of payments—and therefore increased dependence on other countries—or a slowing down in our economic growth, and among other consequences, a dangerous drain of skills from this country.

In order to succeed in this task we must exercise restraint in our public and private spending. Wages, salaries, dividends, and other income must not rise faster than our productivity. We must be constantly seeking to improve the efficiency of our industries by research, by ready adoption of the latest production techniques, and by specialization and rationalization. We must not only refrain from shackling the spirit of enterprise but must actively cultivate that spirit, so that our businessmen are encouraged to seek out and establish new markets for our products throughout the world. Companies earning their profits in Canada but controlled from abroad must, as good corporate citizens of this country, assume their rightful share in this adventure.

We must continue, through the GATT and in all our trade negotiations, to secure lower barriers to our goods, so that they have reasonable access to the markets of the world. We in turn must be prepared to make adjustments to our own tariffs and allow products that can be made more cheaply in other countries to enter the Canadian market more easily. Our energies and skills must be concentrated on producing those goods in which we enjoy a comparative advantage.

At the same time we must work actively with our trading partners to find solutions to the trade problems of the developing countries, and be ready to encourage the participation of the state-trading regimes in the multilateral trading system. We must do this not only as responsible members of the world community, but also in our own enlightened self-interest. But again, these tasks may well require us to make adjustments to our own tariffs.

I see few reasons for pessimism. The prospects for our sharing fully in the growth of world trade are favourable. Certainly, great and continuous efforts will be required. With multilateral trade as our main objective fixed firmly in mind and aware of the undoubted difficulties—but even more mindful of the penalties of failure—Canada, as a great trading nation, can face the future with confidence. But this means that we must be determined and skilful in defining our ends and formulating the means to reach those ends.

W. I. M.
Turner

A BLUEPRINT FOR INVESTMENT IN CANADA

W. I. M. Turner, Jr.

*W. I. M. Turner graduated from the University of Toronto in
1951 with a B.A.Sc. degree in mechanical engineering, and from
Harvard Business School in 1953 with a Master's degree in
business administration. In 1963 he was appointed Vice-President
of Power Corporation of Canada Limited, and in 1964 was named
Executive Vice-President. Since 1966 he has been President of
Power Corporation of Canada Limited.*

It is only natural that, conceived in defiance of the alleged laws of
geography and economics, Canada should periodically be con-
fronted by the Berkelian* spectres of retribution and destitution.
The truly unfortunate aspect of this cyclical occurrence is that it
tends to perpetuate our national economic inferiority complex—a
complex which is without substance but which nonetheless appears
to have had serious repercussions on our investment policies.

---

*George Berkeley (1685-1753), English Churchman and philosopher, one of the
most important thinkers of the philosophical school of idealism. He maintained that
the objects of sense perception are only ideas in our minds, with no independent
existence outside of the perceiving mind.

Conversely, this article is premised upon the writer's confidence in both Canada and her future. Its concern is to reflect Canadian needs for (1) investment here and (2) international access in a trade or business sense. The combination of these might be entitled *A Blueprint for Investment in Canada*.

The importance of a continuous inflow of foreign capital and the proper handling of our domestic capital should be obvious. It stems in part from the need for rising productivity to: increase our living standards, meet our national aspirations, compete with our neighbour to the south, keep pace with a geometrically expanding technology, and deal with ever-shortening obsolescence cycles. We must strengthen our international trading position in order to hurdle the world's tariff barriers to supplement our own small markets. The demand is such that our domestic capital can go but a short way towards satisfying it.

This dependence on investment underlines the problem of its ownership. There is no question but that ownership represents power, as, for example, in the deployment of assets, labour, and utilization of markets. While it is true that the development of the modern corporation has witnessed an increasing separation by management from the bulk of ownership of this power this is pertinent only in relation to immediate corporate operations and ends. Ownership of the units of economic power in relation to a country is a barometer of national feeling and represents susceptibility or lack thereof to government. As such, its control is a legitimate aspiration for a nation.

To the owners accrue the profits, the principal catalyst of business and an indispensable source of new capital generation. This factor which operates to the benefit of established business has some interesting ramifications when translated into the context of our present discussion. For example, the November 1965 issue of the *Survey of Current Business,* United States Department of Commerce, reports that investment in new plants and equipment by United States affiliated companies in the Canadian mining, petroleum, and manufacturing industries rose to a peak of 1.37 billion in 1964, an increase of $260 million over 1963. At the same time, it reported that the amount of funds actually drawn from the United States to finance this increased outlay was reduced to $126 million from $192 million in the latter year. This means that the increase in U.S. investment was accomplished with an actual withdrawal of funds from the United States of only 9% of the total amount of new capital invested. The remaining 91% came from the retained earnings of U.S. affiliaties in Canada, depreciation and depletion allowances, and money borrowed primarily from Canadian sources.

It is proper that foreign capital invested here should harvest its rewards and that the profits should continue to be reinvested in Canada. Indeed were the last not the case we would insist on it. Any reversal of this trend would seriously impair our present economic advance, and were it to occur precipitously under external pressures, the private sector might be unable to cope with the reversal without massive government initiative.

Paradoxically, there is no doubt that the untoward effects of this self-perpetuation from within do contribute to the compromise of our financial and political integrity. However, this interdependence is a fact of life that every nation must endure and its negative aspects become absolute only in a Hobbsian sense. Recognizing this last, Canada has remained one of the freest countries in the world in its attitude toward foreign investment. Unfortunately, we feel the effects in like proportion. The continental pull, the need for capital have made us so dependent on outside capital markets that virtually 100% of our automobile, 75% of our chemical, 70% of our petroleum and natural gas, 60% of our mining and mineral processing, and roughly half of all our manufacturing is foreign, primarily American, owned. These figures become even more alarming in light of our geographical proximity to the dominant investor and our similarity in backgrounds, institutions, and goals. In other words, in a setting completely foreign to the outside investor, the need for an accommodation to, and perception of, national aspirations is easily recognizable. Not so when the two branches spring from the same tree.

Foreign capital has not come in as part of any a priori scheme seeking to take away from Canadians control over their economic destiny. It is the consequence of innumerable individual decisions by private corporations, individuals, and financial institutions, who have seen the opportunities for investment here, and who have shown more faith in our future than we. We are among the world's largest per capita buyers of life insurance. Our caution has developed banks and life insurance companies which rank among the world's largest. However they, the trust companies, and other financial institutions of which we can be proud are governed essentially by a lender-trustee philosophy. This influence cannot be said to have encouraged an entrepreneurial spirit amongst Canadian investors and businessmen.

Furthermore, our economic growth is taking place at a time when conditions are not as conducive to the accumulation of large concentrations of private entrepreneurial capital as they were in the United States prior to the introduction of strict combines legislation and large income and corporation taxes, although the present wide diffusion of prosperity is infinitely preferable to an era of laissez faire. Nor have we had the centuries given Europe and Great Britain to accumulate their great sources of individual wealth.

In addition to this, we live next to a nation which has accumulated this wealth and the skills to go with it and which possessed the foresight, accentuated no doubt by rising world demands for our natural resources, to see the profitable advantages of participating in our development.

Putting the problem in perspective, therefore, we are faced on the one hand by the deliberating effects of absentee ownership caused by massive foreign investment, and on the other by the demand for a full employment economy. In other words a reduction in foreign investment would necessarily entail a corresponding slowdown in growth.

The solution, therefore, becomes one not of impeding foreign investment, but of formulating our "blueprint" so that we minimize the disadvantages while maximizing the advantages to be gained therefrom. This could be accomplished by channelling it into those areas where in addition to providing investment capital it could serve our self interest further, by providing access to those benefits of a more highly developed economy that would otherwise be unavailable to us, e.g. research, markets. Our own equity could then be directed into fields compatible with our socio-economic and political goals.

The great threat to foreign capital is not domestic direction or control but uncertainty .We must establish rules for foreign investors which they can understand and evaluate before taking their decision to come, rather than giving them an open invitation and then complaining because they take us up on it. We must be more concerned with what we can do for ourselves, not what we can prevent others from doing. We must establish policies that are positive, not negative; forward-looking, not reactionary.

Therefore, it is submitted that a determination be made by a body analogous to the Economic Council of Canada, or indeed by the Council, of those areas of the economy where the optimum benefits of Canadian and foreign capital may be obtained. These findings should constantly be reviewed. It is further suggested that the conclusions drawn should reflect the benefits of concentration rather than dissipation of Canadian investment capital, and of liberal trade policies rather than protectionism.

For discussion purposes it may be said that Canadian capital should be encouraged to be preeminent:

1) *in those areas vital to our national integrity*, e.g. our major financial institutions, the energy and transportation fields, communications media.

2) *in new enterprises or ventures.* The presence here of large numbers of wholly-owned subsidiaries limits the scope of the purely domestic Canadian investor in comparison with his counterpart to the south for whom the parents are potential investments. Canadian capital should, therefore, largely find its way into those new ventures that do not rely too exclusively on foreign technology, markets, and seemingly inexhaustible supplies of start-up capital. Change plays such a determining role in the life of a corporation that the inability of many seemingly well-established companies to adapt thereto often paves the way for newer enterprises better attuned to altered conditions, perhaps even born of them. The creation of new ventures by marrying native entrepreneurial skill with equity capital will enable Canada to avoid in part at least the crutch of constantly following an external lead. One key is to create a climate favourable to research and development. Another is to create organizations that are alert to exploitation domestically of advances and new technology developed here and elsewhere. It is often said of the United States that their strongest efforts are made in this latter regard. In point of fact our major equity institutions are showing some encouraging signs of acknowledging this responsibility with a small portion of their capital by fostering speculative new undertakings.

3) *in those industries where foreign capital brings no inherent advantages and simply replaces Canadian ownership.* An example here might be the many subsidiaries that service other foreign

subsidiaries simply because of similar arrangements between the parents. In other words, when foreign-controlled companies are no more competitive than their Canadian counterparts, they should not be permitted lightly to use the superior placing power of their capital to obtain advantages that would otherwise be unavailable to them.

4) *in those industries where our geographical location, natural resources, or other natural advantages point without question to the benefits of repatriation and/or give us a solid base upon which to establish companies of international stature and leadership.*

The sixteen years between 1948 and 1964 witnessed an increase in the volume of international commerce from $50 billion to $170 billion in round figures. This explains in part why large international companies with sophisticated and centrally directed physical, technical, and marketing skills are becoming less the exception than the rule.

Although they are often not wholly beholden to any one government or series of guidelines, a nation without a number of these "head offices" lacks the optimum means of achieving its economic aims. It becomes unable to provide its own citizens with the horizons required for individual economic creativity. In a world largely wthout barriers to human mobility the best management talent will often be drawn to the centers of power, rejecting in the process the countries of their birth. The frustration of feeling incapable of making a dent in, or changing the course of, one's corporate employer because the big decisions are made elsewhere is symptomatic of the "branch plant mentality". Horatio Alger becomes a myth.

The history of most large corporations and their rise and fall continually attests to the influence of men over events as well as to the excitement of the undertaking near the helm. The modern corporation calls for the development of a new cadre of management, possessing the skills, knowledge, and experience, which are the outgrowths of involvement in the highly competitive process of international commerce. While foreign-controlled companies often are the major sources of such management through exposure to the parent or sister company activities, it is also apparent that a significant number of these companies confine their Canadian subsidiaries to domestic operations, with the obvious results on the individual employees and through them on the national makeup.

The even greater importance of indigenous international corporations to the development of the Canadian economy becomes manifest when our export figures are compared with those of the United States, i.e. 20% of our G.N.P. as compared to 5%. Our merchandise exports reached $8.75 billion in 1965, double the level of ten years ago, and yet our deficit on current international transactions in 1965 was $1.1 billion

The creation of companies of international stature operating from a Canadian base can be brought about in a number of ways, for instance repatriation, building from the beginning here, capturing control of offshore but related corporations or working in conjunction with them. The repatriation of control of major companies that have a strong Canadian component might necessitate a consortium approach for the purchase of controlling blocks of equity. Often changing international conditions or fluctuating monetary policies create such opportunities. The need for corporate mergers to secure substantial, even dominant, positions in the Canadian market, if not recognized as an essential requirement for expansion into world markets, cannot in any event be dismissed out of hand. Co-operation at least between companies in research and in areas such as marketing and utilization of resources often frowned on by present combines legislation will clearly be required. Although we do not advocate monopolies, it becomes apparent that under certain circumstances co-operation between companies in industry is more in the national interest than is competition.

This opting for majority equity participation in these companies operating in fields out of which world dominance is possible is the antithesis of the argument that calls for across the board minority participation in foreign-controlled subsidiaries. One does not have to point to our lack of capital nor to the inadequacy of our markets to refute this latter point of view. Its basic premise is untenable. It is not upon these that survival of our national integrity will depend, but on the existence of a number of international giants making the Canadian presence felt in the councils of world trade. From an investment point of view, considerable doubt might be raised at the suggestion that Canadians should invest in foreign-controlled subsidiaries. Needless to say, this entails greater downslide risk, as the subsidiary will lack the parent markets, probable diversification, longevity, and earnings record. Nor can a partially owned subsidiary always command the same amount of the parent's time due to the lesser return when compared to a wholly owned subsidiary. Furthermore, the present state of American anti-trust jurisprudence as it would apply to a parent with a subsidiary having Canadian shareholders, while not clear, would seem to encourage total parental control or total parental abdication. Neither of these is beneficial; the first often checks development by suffocation, the second by withholding the advantages of a more advanced technology.

Therefore, rather than seeking minority subsidiary participation, we should encourage Canadian investment in foreign parent companies which have extensive operations in Canada or which control substantial Canadian markets. Often the capital that would otherwise represent a substantial investment in a Canadian subsidiary if placed in the foreign parent could permit Canadian representation on the parent board. Thus many times 4% or 5% of the shares of the parent could give Canadians a far greater influence in its affairs than would a considerably greater percentage in the subsidiary. This would be facilitated if our government gave consideration to extending to foreign companies which have a certain Canadian content in the parent the same tax advantages that can now be obtained by offering 25% of the voting shares of the subsidiary to Canadians. This content could be defined as an amount equivalent to a 25% equity investment in the Canadian subsidiary. Further requirements could be Canadian representation on the company's board and a listing of the shares of the parent company on a Canadian stock exchange.

Generally, for investment by the private sector to be effective, in accordance with national objectives, it should be invested in long-term, large equity positions in companies where the investor is prepared to take an active interest in the company's affairs. The corollary of this is that one group of investors can afford only a few such situations. This fear of "all your eggs in one basket" and the distaste of many investors for involvement in management problems, or for situations that lack liquidity, largely leave the field to closed end investment trusts, international corporations, or large private pools of capital. Clearly, the Canadian representatives of these institutions are of insufficient number to meet the need. The dimensions of our present opportunities, the amount of capital required to finance them, and the corporations able to muster the combination of skills, capital, and markets for exploitation all bespeak great size. If Canadians are going to participate in the development of their own resoures, the required mechanisms for the mobilization of these opportunities must be increased and improved.

Most of the equity capital in Canada is in fact managed by large institutions in the life insurance, trust company, pension fund, and mutual fund fields. The equity holdings of pension funds and investment trusts in Canadian companies now exceeds $2 billion.

These institutions, dominated by the desire for short-term security and liquidity, openly shun involvement in management problems within their investments. Thus they usually operate widely diversified portfolios that do not normally have a large percentage of the shares of any one company. They become passive shareholders, selling their stock when the outlook becomes unfavourable rather than taking remedial action.

In a study that was done in the New York Stock Exchange in 1964, it was shown that the percentage of all common shares listed on the exchange owned by institutions rose from 12.7% in 1949 to 20% in 1963. The same survey extrapolated a figure of 24% by 1970 and 30% by 1980. It is believed that the situation is comparable in Canada.

Consider then the effect of this rising institutional disinterest. In the United States a company weakened from within by the perpetuation of weak management through the lack of effective shareholder intervention will sooner or later find itself the target of a takeover bid, probably rendered more successful by the acquiescence of the institutional investor. In Canada the disintegration is not merely corporate but national. For in such a situation the Canadian company becomes the target of a foreign interest seeking entrance to the Canadian scene and making its bid in a buyer' market. Alternatively, the Canadian gradually loses ground to a foreign-controlled competitor where no such lack of shareholder interest is evident.

Clearly, the situation could be improved if certain of these funds were permitted by legislation to pool their resources and interests in such a manner that they could collectively play the active role of the large equity holder that individually they are reluctant to assume. Needless to say, this presupposes a change of attitude not only on the part of the government but even more pointedly on the part of the institutions.

Those presently playing these cards must have their hands strengthened. Few major closed end funds have been started in Canada since 1945 because of the irrational yet prevailing discount from asset or breakup value at which their shares sell. In the United States and the U.K. some capably managed closed end funds have commanded premiums to their breakup value, while poorly managed or sluggish funds have sold at discounts.

If the creation of more of these pools is believed to be in Canada's national interest, it is suggested that legislation allowing these funds to maintain the price of their shares at a more reasonable level from breakup would be beneficial. Again more sophisticated methods of reporting earnings, which should include the residual earnings in the major holdings as well as a more informative treatment of capital gains and their effect on income, is required. Needless to say, the Carter Report provides interesting reading on this subject. If there were a general recognition of the unusual opportunity that the closed end fund concept gives Canada to control its enterprises, much greater use could be made of this vehicle. The suggestions for government-sponsored funds such as the Canada Development Corporation are indicative that this is gradually being realized. The criticisms levelled at the concept both in its private and public guise may have merit. However, it is important to note that apart from those levelled at the government concept because of its government sponsorship, they are of a remedial nature and do not strike at the core of the idea.

Briefly then, whatever the form used for control, the investor should:

1) make long-term equity investments in industries which have the potential for substantial growth and profitability.

2) concentrate his holdings in a limited number of companies which are or can become leaders in their respective industries.

3) develop and support competent, self-contained management in each company and assist that company to realize its full potential.

4) encourage the development of improved management techniques and new technology, products, and markets.

5) invest primarily in Canada and in situations outside Canada which are related to Canadian interests and experience.

There are, of course, in a resource-dominated country such as Canada, ventures of such size and speculative nature that render sole domestic participation unfeasible. For example, the iron ore development of Labrador required not only large sums of capital apparently not available here, but a guarantee of access to the foreign, in this case American, market provided by the eventual investors themselves.

A joint venture between a Canadian corporation and a foreign partner or partners in the development of a resource would mean that a proportionate share of the eventual cash flow would remain in Canadian hands. This money, if re-invested in similar projects on an escalating scale would result in greater and greater participation by Canadians in their country's riches. It may be that the initial Canadian participation would have to be in the form of convertible debt in order to allow an American partner to offset early losses against his U.S. taxable income. Again it should be noted that restrictive marketing of the product of the joint venture could run afoul of current United States anti-trust jurisprudence as a conspiracy in restraint of trade.

We have touched briefly on the government role. Government action will be decisive in the shaping of the private sector's investment initiative. Government involvement in the growth of the economy is hardly new. We have come a long way since Jeremy Bentham's statement in 1793, "The request which agriculture, manufacturers and commerce present to governments is as modest and reasonable as that which Diogenes gave to Alexander, 'stand out of my sunshine'." The present levels of government intervention began when governments adopted the Keynesian thesis of their responsibility for full employment. Since then, so concerned with the constituents of growth have governments become, that their value judgments put into effect by selective intervention through persuasion, or direct action, have become an accepted fact of life. The recent auto pact between Canada and the United States may be cited as an example. It is not unreasonable therefore to ask for the formulation of policies concerned with the employment of foreign and domestic capital, delineating those areas where each is desirable, and then structuring the rules and incentives to see that national objectives are met.

It is assumed that this analysis, which as mentioned earlier could be done by the Economic Council of Canada, will reflect our need for freer world trade. Indeed it must rest on that assumption if it is to have any validity. We have the human and material resources to be internationally competitive. We can no longer tolerate inefficient industry to suffer from insufficient markets. It is true if one rejects the specialization of industry based on natural advantages, pointing the way to the development of Canadian international giants, then a high tariff becomes attractive. This is because protection becomes necessary for a people restrained not by inferior capabilities but by inferior capacity. Very few Canadian businessmen with any experience on the international scene will accept the protectionist view as a realistic one.

Against the analysis mentioned above, the following specific suggestions might be made:

1) Combines legislation should be reviewed in the light of our competitive position, not within the country but on the world scene.

2) Inasmuch as foreign investment in our natural resources is often seeking only an assured supply of raw materials and has no need for Canadian management partners, it may be that legislation will have to be introduced requiring joint ventures as described earlier.

3) The granting of letters patent could be reviewed as a means of insuring that foreign- and domestic-controlled companies do not expand into different and, from a national point of view, less desirable areas than those for which they were originally intended.

4) A procedure for takeovers should be enunciated which, among other things, could stipulate that in certain circumstances voting rights thereon are to be restricted to Canadian shareholders. France's treatment of the Suez Canal company is an example of the latter technique in a broader sense. In any case, the government should be allowed to intervene to prevent any major transfer of control to foreign hands that is not in the national interest.

5) As mentioned earlier a careful study should be made of existing corporate methods available for pooling and channelling Canadian savings into long-term equity positions. The quasi government-controlled bodies should similarly be examined and, if necessary, new structures or vehicles created for this purpose. Once the best form of company is determined, however, (and in my opinion, it might well be a modified closed end investment

trust) existing tax legislation should be revised to encourage the formation and growth of such companies.

6) In respect to taxation, the government should:

a) grant tax benefits to Canadians who invest in priority areas, with similar benefits being given to foreign capital invested in those areas where it is deemed Canada can obtain from this capital non-monetary advantages unavailable otherwise.

b) review the foreign exchange control and tax possibilities of discouraging the raising of Canadian debt capital by foreigners seeking to supplement their equity investments here.

c) remove or further reduce the taxation of dividends received by Canadians in those companies in which a majority of the voting shares are held by Canadians where it is actuarily reasonable.

d) consider the removal of death duties on that proportionate amount of an individual's estate that is invested in Canadian companies or, alternatively, to completely remove death duties, thereby eliminating the pressure put on many family-owned businesses to deliver themselves into foreign hands.

7) give the necessary leadership in an effort to educate the Canadian people on the value of investing in equities as a means of obtaining a personal stake in the growth of Canada and impress upon them the financial attractiveness (and possible risks) of such investments.

Any paper that treats such an exhaustive topic in such a cursory manner will of necessity be incomplete. However, it is hoped that some thought and discussion may at least be stimulated thereby. We are dealing not only with dollars and cents, but with the shaping of our future.

What about the idea that Confederation
meant only that the new federal gov. was
only taking over the role of the British
government in the colonial structure?
∴ did the Commonwealth concept begin
in 1862, rather than 1926?